THE
MOTHER
OF THE
BRONTËS

For Christine and Roddy

THE
MOTHER
OF THE
BRONTËS

WHEN MARIA MET PATRICK

With very best wishes
to Michael,
Sharon Wright

SHARON WRIGHT

PEN & SWORD
HISTORY

AN IMPRINT OF PEN & SWORD BOOKS LTD.
YORKSHIRE – PHILADELPHIA

First published in Great Britain in 2019 by
PEN AND SWORD HISTORY
an imprint of
Pen and Sword Books Ltd
Yorkshire – Philadelphia

Hardback ISBN: 978 1 52673 848 6
Paperback ISBN: 978 1 52675 760 9

Typeset in Times New Roman 11/13.5 by
Aura Technology and Software Services, India
Printed and bound in the UK by TJ International

Pen & Sword Books Ltd incorporates the imprints of Pen & Sword
Archaeology, Atlas, Aviation, Battleground, Discovery,
Family History, History, Maritime, Military, Naval, Politics, Railways,
Select, Social History, Transport, True Crime, Claymore Press,
Frontline Books, Leo Cooper, Praetorian Press, Remember When,
Seaforth Publishing and Wharncliffe.

For a complete list of Pen & Sword titles please contact
PEN & SWORD BOOKS LIMITED
47 Church Street, Barnsley, South Yorkshire, S70 2AS, England
E-mail: enquiries@pen-and-sword.co.uk
Website: www.pen-and-sword.co.uk

Or
PEN AND SWORD BOOKS
1950 Lawrence Rd, Havertown, PA 19083, USA
E-mail: Uspen-and-sword@casematepublishers.com
Website: www.penandswordbooks.com

Contents

One day in the autumn or winter succeeding Mrs Brontë's death, Charlotte came to her nurse, wild and white with the excitement of having seen 'a fairy' standing by Baby Anne's cradle. When the two ran back to the nursery, Charlotte flying on ahead, treading softly not to frighten the beautiful visitant away, no one was there besides the baby sleeping sweetly in the depths of her forenoon nap. Charlotte stood transfixed; her eyes wandered incredulously around the room. 'But she *was* here, just now!' she insisted. 'I really and truly did see her!' – and no argument or coaxing could shake her from the belief.

From an interview with nursemaid Sarah Garrs in
Charlotte Brontë at Home by
Marion Harland, 1899

Acknowledgements

My most profound thanks must go to Dr Melissa Hardie-Budden MBE, founder of the Hypatia Trust and the pre-eminent expert on the Branwells and Carnes of Cornwall, maternal forebears of the Brontë siblings. She is an extraordinary woman who is unstintingly generous in sharing her scholarship and her friendship. I am indebted to Melissa for details of Maria's family tree, an understanding of her father's will and for drawing to my attention the nature of the Kingston scandal. Her detailed work on the scientific and literary networks of Cornish influence on the Brontë siblings is hers alone and I do not attempt it here. If I have made any errors in my account of Maria's life in Penzance or if our conclusions do not concur, any fault lies with me.

So to the peerless Ann Dinsdale, principal curator at the Brontë Parsonage Museum. Her knowledge of the Brontë canon and collection is without equal and she has helped me navigate both with her trademark patience and interest. I owe a great debt of gratitude to Ann and her team – curator Sarah Laycock, volunteer researcher Linda Pierson and former curatorial assistant Amy Rowbottom.

Sincere gratitude is extended to James Lockwood, Donna Shoesmith-Evans, Roger Howard, Sam Cadman and Hugh Knowles at Woodhouse Grove School, who were extraordinarily helpful throughout the writing of this book. It was also a privilege to work with Brontë dress historian Eleanor Houghton.

I was greatly aided in my research by the generosity of Dr Peter Forsaith of the Oxford Centre for Methodism and Church History, Ian Graham of the special collections team at the University of Manchester Library, along with Methodist heritage officer Owen Roberts and John Lenton, librarian of the Wesley Historical Society. Heroic services to history were given by Rowan Musser and David Thomas, archivists at the Cornwall Records Office who undertook emergency (to me) research the day before they closed to relocate four miles of archives from Truro to Redruth.

For an educated opinion on Maria's final illness I must thank Dr Emma Storr of the Leeds Institute of Health Sciences. Jackie Burnett of the Pram Society gave advice on how the baby Brontës travelled and pub historian Roger Protz explained stagecoach routes. Jan Moore kindly assisted with researching early Cornish Methodism.

My thanks to the Reverend Peter Mullins, Mr Brontë's successor in Haworth, for help with registers and reflections on Maria's faith. The people of St Peter's Church in Hartshead and Dewsbury Minster were also most helpful. Steve Stanworth of the Old Bell Chapel Action Group went out of his way to give practical assistance. Thanks also to Michael Smith and Christine Tidswell of Thornton Antiquarian Society for their time and expertise. A special thank you goes to another society member, Maureen Leonard, with whom I enjoyed an interesting afternoon at Ashtree House in Thornton. Her late husband Frank was a dedicated local historian and I was privileged to see his work.

Sara Hodson, manager of Ilfracombe Museum, helped me to piece together the untold story of the Brontë shipwreck, not least with evocative images, for which I am grateful. Thanks must go to Lisa di Tommaso at the Morrab Library in Penzance, Miki Ashton and Maggi Livingstone at the Hypatia Library, the staff of the British Library reading rooms and Nicola Tobias and Jon Moore at Dittons Library in Surrey.

I was welcomed into Maria's former homes by the artistic Emily and Ian Barker in Chapel Street, marvellous Mary Crowther and Sally Cooper at Clough House and the delightful De Luca family at *Emily's* in Thornton. Thank you to all, and also to Sarah Dixon of Kipping House for tea and cake in the drawing room like Maria and her Regency friends.

Jennifer Jones, retired chartered librarian and all-round bookish genius, once again gave invaluable help with my research, not least with the complexities of public and family records, searching the Morrab archives and deciphering centuries-old handwriting. Thank you Julie, Steve, Kizzy and Noah for inspiring conversations in front of the Aga at beloved Ponden Hall, plus help with the Heatons. And to my dear, saucy David, thanks for all the practical support entailed with being married to a writer who lives in her head.

Thank you to terrific Carol Trow, excellent editor who lets me leave in lots of alliteration. Especially heartfelt thanks to Laura Hirst, production editor at Pen and Sword, for her trust, endless good grace and professionalism.

And finally… thank you most of all to those newspaper reporters and magazine journalists from two centuries ago, my comrades across time.

ACKNOWLEDGEMENTS

I certainly put more store by the accuracy of their work than that of Mrs Gaskell. From the *Leeds Mercury* and *Leeds Intelligencer* that carried Patrick Brontë's work and reported from the front line of the Luddite riots, to *The Lady's Magazine* that gave a platform to women writers and female opinion, to journalists who diligently sought out and recorded facts and memories from those who knew the Brontës. Once living memory is gone, it's really gone.

Sneering at 'traditional media' is in the ascendency, maybe forever. With a good local press comes a diversity of voices, the various, unvarnished goings-on of a huge range of real people, oversight of the powerful, court reporting where justice is seen to be done, a sharing of the stories of ordinary people caught up in extraordinary events. To all the excellent journalists who have gone before, I salute you. Without them, we have no papers of record. This is not the place to lament the slow death of the regional press, except to say, we know not what we have lost. They may not have got everything right, but at least they were *there*.

Foreword

How did I grow up in Bradford without anyone introducing me to the Brontës?

The closest I ever came to the famous family as a child was a *Rita, Sue and Bob Too* style school trip to the Parsonage in Haworth. I studied English literature to A Level without a Brontë book in sight (being forced instead to read Jane Austen). Haworth is part of Bradford and the Parsonage just eleven miles from my childhood home. Yet while I enjoyed Victoria Wood's *Brontëburgers* sketch ('...the famous Brontë sisters, now, alas, no longer with us – but they have left us their novels, which I've not read, being more of a Dick Francis nut.') and recognized Larry Olivier as Heathcliff on a film poster, I felt no real connection.

My real introduction to the Brontës was through my first job, as a cub reporter in the 1990s on the local paper that covered Haworth. When the Brontë Society made the news – which has always been often – I was there with my 100wpm shorthand to take notes on the latest source of twisted knickers in Brontëland. Planning applications that had locals up in arms, Machiavellian goings-on in committee rooms, scholarly high dudgeon over some affront to the sacred memory, that sort of thing. The Brontës themselves were often invoked but to me, remained entirely invisible.

I reported on these things as a trained observer, the role that was to become mine for life. If there was a slight 'town and gown' feeling back then about the folk who lived in Haworth and the literary shrine on the hill, I definitely felt like a townie.

Then I left Yorkshire. My career as a journalist took me around Britain before, inevitably, to London and the national press. I put the likes of the *Guardian*, *BBC*, *New York Post*, *Mail on Sunday* and *Red* on my author blurb and website but it's the years on the *Keighley News*, *Bridgwater Mercury* and *Evening Herald* in Plymouth that I remember most fondly. Nothing on a national newspaper or best-selling magazine ever compared to being out and about with a notebook and pen in the West Riding or the West Country, finding local stories. Finding out what really happened.

People always think journalists make things up – 'fake news' accusations are nothing new – but the best retort is, we don't have to. Real life is always infinitely more interesting than anything I could concoct. People are surprising, aren't they? They think and act in unexpected ways. We all weave our life stories from the materials we are given and the ones we find along the way. Or more often, trip over or have flung at us.

Of course, I never really left Yorkshire. My deep family roots, my lifelong friendships and my profound connection to the landscape are sustained when I return, which is often. And it was only then, coming home as a writer, a wife and a mother that I truly crossed paths with the Brontës. I went on a Brontë walking tour of Haworth accompanied by the cousin and close friend I grew up with and was genuinely outraged. We all were. How, *how* had we not known all this? This absolutely extraordinary human saga on our doorstep?

Suddenly all the misconceptions I had about the clever but worthy (boring) Victorians vanished. They were flesh and blood Bradfordians and I found their life stories as gripping as their novels. I joined the Brontë Society, nowadays a broad church. Better late than never, as they say. The more I discovered, the more I wanted to know and I became preoccupied by Maria, the mysterious Mrs Brontë. For two hundred years, she has been an absence. The dead wife of the famous reverend, the dead mother of world-famous authors. A life eclipsed by the genius of her children.

So I do not approach the family with an air of reverence but of fascination. My Brontës are not the famous ones. The ones people know intimately. Mine are the 'before they were famous' ones, Miss Branwell and Pat Prunty and their young family. The Brontë backstory, I suppose. The prequel.

When I first wondered aloud why no-one has ever written a biography of Maria the answer came swiftly: 'There isn't enough on her.'

I bet there is, I thought. If you grab your pen and your notebook and go looking properly.

Sharon Wright, July 2019

Chapter 1

Daughter of Penzance

To the little girl gazing from the windows of her cosy attic nursery, the whole world seemed arranged for her entertainment. Six-year-old Maria Branwell's vantage points above Penzance's busiest street afforded uninterrupted views of a most interesting place. Out front was the sea, with mysterious St Michael's Mount in the distance, sometimes crystal clear in the bright sunshine against a blue sky, sometimes wreathed in sea mists, the waters of the bay slate grey and restless. Not far from her door the small boats and tall ships arriving, or departing to trade or to fight or to fish. All the mercantile and military hullabaloo of a busy port in a seafaring nation. Directly below her window, merchants and redcoats stopped to discuss the French Revolution just over the horizon in one direction, American Independence an ocean away in another.

If Maria padded to the rear of the house, she could watch the comings and goings in the graveyard of St Mary's Chapel, a short cut for locals and sailors that ran almost up to the back door. She fell asleep to waves slapping the harbour and if she awoke in the night, it was to the muffled clatter from smugglers' tunnels below the old tavern nearby. The life swirling around 25 Chapel Street in the late eighteenth century was full of trade and science, myths and legends, war and peace. Maria was born into one of the most important families in town. She was a Branwell and in Georgian Penzance, that meant something.

As Maria drew her first breath on 15 April 1783, her parents Thomas and Anne (sometimes spelled Ann) could only have felt both hope and fear. Five Branwell babies had already died before their fifth birthday. Their first child was born in April 1769 and named Anne for her mother. Fifteen months later came Margaret and the following summer, 1771, a son named Thomas after his father. September 1772 brought Elizabeth, with Jane born in November 1773, followed by Benjamin in March 1775.

Then in early 1776, three-year-old Elizabeth and four-year-old Thomas fell ill, maybe from that winter's influenza outbreak in west Cornwall.

1

Thomas died on 22 February, followed next day by his little sister. Anne and Thomas stood in the chapel graveyard huddled together beneath the winter sky as their tiny children were placed in the family tomb. At 33, one third of her children were lost but within a month of the pitiful double funeral, Anne was pregnant again.

The baby was born in December and given the name of her dead sister, so the Elizabeth that Anne nursed at the close of that painful year was not the one she had held at its start. This second Elizabeth Branwell was strong and would again bring comfort after bereavement, to her Brontë nieces and nephew.

The terrible proximity of birth and death in the late 1700s meant the Branwell story of infant mortality was not unusual and the couple's suffering far from over – their next three babies died one after another. A second Thomas was born in March 1778 and was dead by the following January. Four months later came baby Alice, who may have lived only a short time as there is no record of her baptism. The second baby Alice arrived in December 1780 but survived only ten months and the defeated parents never used a name three times. Causes of death went unrecorded but at the time, parts of the country suffered epidemics of smallpox and a particularly virulent scarlet fever.

After this string of bereavements, Anne was shattered and took – or was allowed – a break from childbearing to recover. Three and a half years had passed in a whirlwind of short-lived joy and consuming grief as she and Thomas welcomed three children and buried them one by one before they outgrew the cradle. It was a bleak time and difficult to navigate as a family, the older children growing towards adulthood as the little ones perished. Anne carrying one baby in her belly as she held another in her arms, already slipping away. It was a common story for a woman of her day, though no less painful for that.

By the time she fell pregnant with Maria in the summer of 1782, she was pushing 40 and her youngest, Elizabeth, was almost seven. With five children safe in their beds and five in their graves, Anne took Maria to her breast in the spring of 1783 with no way of knowing where this newborn girl would end up.

Though petite like Elizabeth, Maria was healthy and for the next six years the baby of the family. For a long time, it seemed she would remain the youngest of the Branwell brood, then in November 1789 the attic nursery had a new addition. At the age of 46, Anne had her twelfth and final baby, a little sister for Maria called Charlotte.

Maria arrived into a comfortable clan, when the family was newly established as a prosperous and important part of Penzance society. The journey to Chapel Street, however, was a long one. 'For the whole of the 1800s the name of Branwell was one of distinction in Penzance,' writes Richard G. Grylls in *Branwell and Bramble: a brief history of a West Cornwall Clan*. Once they settled on the spelling in the 1700s, that is. Grylls has done an admirable job of untangling a devil-may-care attitude to spelling that obscures Maria's family tree. Branwells and Brambles, were they related? Almost certainly, as were Bremells, Brembels, Bremhalls, Brymmells, Brembles, Bromewells and Brummoles.

Some forebears juggled names over a single lifetime, so in 1719 the will was read of Maria's great-grandfather Martyn Bramwell who had been baptized Bromwell but was Bremble on both his wedding day and at his funeral. Recording names came down to the best guess of the official holding the pen. Though Thomas appears in earlier records as Bramwell, when Maria was baptised on 29 June 1783 her name was fixed as Branwell. When Westcountry worthies could spell their own name, they fared better at keeping it. It was a final permutation that would later echo through the Brontë branch of the family better than, say, Brummole might have done. Maria's only son would suffer many torments, but that was not among them.

The eighteenth century had been a slog. The family began the march towards wealth and influence as butchers in Market Jew Street, with Maria's great-grandfather – he of the three surnames – leaving money and property in his will. It was a town of opportunities, as *Robinson Crusoe* author Daniel Defoe, also a merchant, noted in 1724:

> 'This town of Penzance is a place of good business, well built and populous, has a good trade, and a great many ships belonging to it, notwithstanding it is so remote. Here are also a great many good families of gentlemen...'

The Branwells were soon among them. Maria's granddad Richard was a mason. It was his eldest sons Richard and Thomas, also masons, who really ramped up the family fortunes, branching out into imports, exports, brewing and property. Where there was money to be made, there was a Branwell. The town was a good place for entrepreneurs, according to someone writing to the *London Magazine* in 1749 as 'Penzantiensis.' Not only was it 'one of the richest, most flourishing' maritime towns it was not a case of 'a few overgrown mushrooms' lording it over 'inhabitants almost vassals' like elsewhere, 'but its wealth is in a great many hands, which constitutes no small part of its happiness.'

Maria also had relatives to be reckoned with on her mother's side. The Carnes, too, were pillars of the west Cornish community, possibly doing even better than the Branwells in the 1760s when ambitious young Thomas was courting eligible Anne Carne. They too were masons, carpenters, craftsmen and merchants. Anne's father John was a silversmith and clockmaker. Both families took a close interest in the scientific advances of the eighteenth century. Several Carnes backed the local engineer Jonathan Hornblower, an early pioneer of steam power, appearing on the 'List of Adventurers concerned in Hornblower's Engines' in the 1790s.

When 22-year-old (probably, no baptism can be found) Thomas set his cap at 24-year-old Anne, it was a very suitable match. The families had professional links and lived close to one another. But first things first, could they produce children? It was not unknown for lovers to find out sooner rather than later and tie the knot only when the family line was assured. When Anne arrived at her wedding at Madron Parish Church in November 1768, she was at least four months pregnant with Anne junior. Ambitious and with a finger in every pie, Branwells and Carnes branched through all areas of Cornish life.

Maria may have been born over the family's large grocery shop known as Branwell's Corner, between the marketplace and Causewayhead. While so much of eighteenth-century Cornwall struggled with poverty, Penzance thrived thanks in part to its lucrative royal charters. These dated back to one woman whose devotion to putting her town on the map in 1332 paid dividends for centuries. Powerful Alice de Lisle, determined lady (technically, lord) of the manor of Alverton, persuaded Edward III to grant the right to hold markets and fairs in Penzance. Market town status was bolstered by Henry VIII granting permission to charge harbour dues to shipping, on condition the quay was kept in good repair. The status of Penzance Borough was awarded by James I in May 1614. This made the town a corporation that ran its own affairs with a mayor, eight aldermen and twelve councillors known as assistants. Despite Alice de Lisle's shining example of civic savvy, women were locked out of any such role.

Ringing the commercial hub of the Jacobean market house were dotted the properties and businesses that comprised the wider Branwell empire. Thomas owned pilchard warehouses and properties across town and beyond, including the Golden Lion inn run by his brother Richard. By the late 1700s, Penzance had a population of around 3,000 and a constant flow of visitors. Commerce was queen, with lively markets and fairs bringing people to town to trade their crops, catches and goods. The port brought the fishing fleet, travellers, traders and the military.

Jewel in the commercial crown was the status of Coinage Town for the whole of Penwith, awarded in 1663 by a grateful Charles II for its royalist sympathies during the English Civil War. Miners from across western Cornwall were obliged to take their tin to the Coinage Hall off the marketplace in Penzance to be coined. This was the method of paying dues to the Duke of Cornwall. Officials removed a corner (*coin* in French) from each big block of tin, stamping it with the duke's coat of arms if it was considered pure. Blocks were then turned into bars for Mediterranean markets, ingots for the East Indies and the tin trade powered much of the borough's wealth.

Though often seen as remote and isolated by the rest of eighteenth-century Britain, Maria's prosperous home town was in reality a hub of regional and international trade. At the heart of it all, Branwells regularly raised their glasses for the Penzance Corporation toast: 'May the market and pier bring a thousand a year!'

When people were done with the ships and the shops, they went in search of entertainment. Showbiz arrived in Chapel Street with the opening of the first Penzance Theatre in 1787, when Maria was four. Impresario Richard Hughes was known as the father of provincial drama and created the theatre over the stables behind the Ship and Castle (renamed Union Hotel to mark the union of Great Britain and Ireland in 1801). It could accommodate 500 people around a raked stage complete with trapdoors. The only drawback was the pungent odour from the horses below.

Maria was born when Branwell business was booming and it was high time they had a better address than over the shop. Thomas was a gentleman and could afford a home that reflected his success. He chose a new build in a sought-after location, Rotterdam Buildings at the coastal end of Chapel Street. The three-house terrace with a red brick frontage adorned with fashionable green woodwork had a majestic view out to sea and was built for merchant families of note.

There are two versions of where the handsome Dutch brick came from. Brick houses were rare and either it came ashore thanks to a privateer who acquired it by force at sea or it was salvage, ballast on a Dutch ship bound for America that came to grief on the rocks during a storm in Mount's Bay. Either way, it gave the smart terrace its local name of Rotterdam Buildings.

As was common in Georgian architecture, more attention was paid to the front of the house than the rear. So the smart red brick was used for the frontage, while parts of the sides and rear were built of local granite. However they found their materials, one of the builders was Thomas' brother, Richard, and the other Edward Hambleton, related by marriage. They kept it in the family, employing relatives as masons and carpenters.

According to the late house historian Lilian Oldham, who lived there from 1968, these fine Georgian abodes were built for gentleman merchant Thomas Love, who moved into one. The second was taken by Captain Richard Hosking of the merchant navy and the last house by Thomas Branwell between 1783 and 1784. Thomas and Anne probably moved their family from over the grocers when Maria was still a babe-in-arms. Though just a few hundred yards away, the family went up in the world. Tiny Miss Branwell would know only an upmarket and comfortable home at the heart of Penzance society.

Maria shared the nursery under the eaves with Elizabeth and later, with Charlotte. As the adults oversaw the move, Elizabeth joined her older siblings Anne, Margaret, Jane and Benjamin in exploring their new home. The front door had fine granite steps onto the busy street with its endless traffic to and from the harbour. To the rear was a kitchen overlooking a garden leading into St Mary's churchyard. South-facing, it was sunny and warm in summer but caught the force of the gale when a winter sou'westerly blew in from the Atlantic. Nearby stood a carpenter's shed and it seems likely that this was where coffins were made for funerals at the chapel.

Rough steps from the kitchen led to a cave-like cellar dug from the rock, not unlike the smuggler tunnels on the other side of the street. A Cornish range with a slate surround had brass rails overhead for drying laundry. There were also two carved wooden racks for holding Thomas' pistols, always oiled and ready during the intermittent wars with the French.

The toilet was an earth closet at the end of the garden. Unfortunately for children who needed the privy, this was a stone's throw from the graves. Fortunately, the graveyard was rarely deserted, serving as a sheltered spot for retired sailors sunning themselves on the flat tombstones and a playground for the town children. It served day and night as a shortcut to town.

Inside the new house window seats were perfect for sewing, reading or people watching. Some beams across doorways and windows were made from reclaimed ship timber. Climbing the central staircase, the first floor had bedrooms for the parents and eldest children along with a small dressing room. All rooms had a fireplace, some with integral surfaces known as hob cheeks for resting items to warm.

The youngest children, including Maria, probably slept in the two third floor attic rooms at the top of the house and almost certainly with a servant.

One was an L-shaped room with a window looking out onto the length of Chapel Street leading up into town. The other was square, with a bigger window revealing the slender tower of St Mary's, a whitewashed landmark for sailors, the graveyard and coast beyond. From the chapel every May Day, the sexton would emerge, waking Maria along with the rest of the town by blowing a traditional tin horn at dawn.

The rooms for entertaining and family use were either side of the front door, off the half wood-panelled hallway. The room to the right had an alcove with wooden bookshelves for the family library between the fireplace and window. Both front parlours had a view across the bay to St Michael's Mount and a constant parade of anyone who was anyone passing their door. The fine new house had all the trappings to be expected of such an address.

The Branwells had arrived.

Though well to do, Maria did not grow up on a country estate or in some rural backwater. Chapel Street linked the sea to the land, fish to the market, cargo to ships, fighting men to Nelson's navy, adventurers to the next tide. The Branwells were intimately connected with this gateway to the world and in 1785, Maria's father and uncle Richard were awarded the £1,050 contract to build a new town quay in partnership with another relative, Solomon Cock.

Once a day, the melee in Maria's street briefly abated for an invasion by at least seventy mules. Gentry, servants and sailors alike stood aside to allow beasts from the mines at St Just to plod down to the ships loaded with copper ore or tin, then plod back bearing coal. This daily parade was the reason Branwell ladies were obliged to wear protective wooden pattens over their shoes. Hundreds of hooves churned Chapel Street into a muddy mess, to say nothing of the dung and the red slime dripping from sacks of ore.

Elizabeth took a pair of pattens to Haworth in 1821 and for the Brontë children the clink-clink on flags was a warning of Aunt Branwell's approach. As girls in Penzance, however, Maria and Elizabeth were not alone in their practical footwear. A kind of elevated wooden clog, resting on a metal hoop, with leather straps, they were indispensable for any lady stepping out into the town's main road, no matter what their social position. Maria slipped her small feet into shoes, then strapped on pattens like her mama, sisters and maidservant. Some pattens were ten inches high to guarantee clearing the mud and dung. Thus protected from the mucky streets, they could sally forth to the market.

The most westerly market town in England, Penzance was the place everyone met to buy and sell everything – from an array of seafood (especially abundant pilchards) to livestock, housewares and shoes. A democratic affair, middle class matrons such as Maria's mother mixed with matelots, miners and farmers, all brought to town to trade goods and gossip from miles around. Every kind of staple and delicacy could be bought, including the clotted cream still unknown outside of Cornwall.

Among the most striking characters Maria encountered on market days were the fishwives who walked the beach road from neighbouring Newlyn clad in blue skirts, red jackets and buckled shoes. They carried huge cowels (baskets) of fish on their backs. They were held in place by a strap across the front of the head over a large bonnet. Penzance doctor and author John Ayreton Paris, who was almost the same age as Maria Branwell, was certainly impressed:

> 'Every description of fish in season … may be purchased from the Newlyn fish-women, who are in daily attendance at their stalls, and whose fine symmetry, delicate complexions, curling ringlets, and the brilliancy of those jet black eyes, as they dart their rays from beneath the shade of large gypsey hats of beaver, fill the traveller with admiration.'

One theory for their good looks was the Spanish raid on Mount's Bay in 1595, another that they were descended from a lost tribe of Israel.

The Branwells were followers of John Wesley, the Evangelical Anglican minister who galloped around Cornwall urging Christians to get back to bible basics. Wesley preached at open air revivals, to the thousands fed up of conventional religion. The mainstream Church of England was seen as remote and uninterested, more concerned with the upper classes than the problems of parishioners. Wesley encouraged social action, such as prison reform and education for the poor. He also advocated a simple and orderly routine of study and devotion, earning his followers the epithet Methodists.

His down-to-earth outdoor preaching and rousing singsongs of brother Charles' hymns were a hit with Cornish miners and peasants. They also struck a chord with merchants from the new middle class. Wesley harnessed the widespread hunger for change among the poor and directed it away from revolutionary thinking – such as that in America and France culminating in the 1780s – and towards a reward in heaven rather than on earth. Maria was six years old when she met this spiritual superstar. In August 1789, the aging Evangelist was in town for the final time and he was staying with the Carnes.

William Carne, her mother's cousin, was known as the father of Cornish Methodism. A wealthy merchant and banker, he too lived in style in Chapel Street. Maria may have encountered the famous preacher when he lodged with the family that summer. When the crowds poured into town to hear him preach, Maria had no inkling that the small, charismatic old man was placing an invisible seal on her destiny. His influence on her family would lead her to Yorkshire, to Patrick Brontë, to a place in history that would bring strangers to stare at her home 200 years in the future.

Unusually for the time, Methodists were keen to let women in on the act. Families such as the Branwells educated their daughters as well as their sons. In February 1789, Thomas Branwell sold a plot of land at the end of his garden to the Corporation to build a Penny School. So called because it was affordable for the poor, Maria and her siblings also attended when they were young. Later, the girls were taught at home and Benjamin went to Penzance Grammar School.

Sunday school teachers were known as class leaders and included females. John Wesley was a great advocate of Christian education and his drive to instil biblical teaching hung on his followers being able to read. Maria and her sisters would almost certainly have assisted with bible classes at the early Methodist chapel in Queen Street. It had a schoolroom where the poorest worshippers could learn to read and write. Wesley sanctioned women preachers after being convinced by Mary Bosanquet – later Fletcher – a rich and powerful Evangelist who would also have a profound impact on the life of Maria Branwell. It was only after his death that Wesleyans began to backtrack on women leaders.

Piety was a theme of Maria's childhood, witnessed by the sampler she completed on 15 April 1791, her eighth birthday and the month after John Wesley died. Girls of all classes were taught to sew and the Branwell sisters learned from their mother, showcasing their skill with samplers traditionally completed on their birthday. Maria's was no soothing homily about lilies of the field or lambs, however. She spent the day she turned eight completing in thread: 'Flee from sin as from a serpent, for if thou comest too near to it, it will bite thee, the teeth thereof are as the teeth of a Lion to slay the souls of Men.'

Though Wesley's al fresco methods among the working classes irritated conservative high church Anglicans, he remained within the Church of England and so did Maria's parents. It was, as they say, complicated, and Maria's family was nothing if not ecumenical. In 1807 they helped build a new Jewish synagogue, before chipping in for a bigger Methodist chapel.

The Carnes had Quaker connections and Branwells were Freemasons, that not without a mystical dimension. Thomas was also a practical man, renting out one of his houses for Wesley's itinerant Evangelists.

Meanwhile, the family's secular status grew apace as in the spring of 1790, Maria's very important papa was elected as one of the twelve assistants to the Corporation. They ran the town and it was a lifetime appointment. Thomas Branwell, gentleman merchant, was officially a Penzance bigwig.

He was also in business with smugglers.

In order to fund wars with France and America, the government raised import duties on goods arriving from abroad and excise on those made in Britain. It made life expensive and all classes were united in resenting the revenue men tasked with collecting taxes. There were several kinds of civilian shipping complicit with the well-organised and armed smuggling rings that flourished in Mount's Bay, across from the French coast and with coves to hide in. Merchant ships were often co-owned by importers such as Thomas Branwell. Meanwhile, privateers were essentially mercenaries. They had letters of marque – authorization to be armed – that gave them carte blanche to capture and sell any ship from an enemy nation. Pirate ships did not have an official licence to loot, so they robbed any and all at sea.

Maria Branwell's papa was not a pirate. He was, I contend, a smuggler. There are two startling facts on record and each a smoking gun. The first is that on 10 December 1778, according to Custom House records: 'Thomas Bramwell was indited [sic] for obstructing the Customs Officers in searching his dwelling.' The second is to be found in the Penzance shipping registers.

First, the charge for obstruction. Why a tea importer and owner of a nearby inn would refuse customs men access to his home seems to point to only one conclusion. Especially if his home was over the biggest grocers in town and the inn was run by his brother. It seems there was something in Thomas' dwelling he did not want them to find and he used a legal loophole to buy time. This is revealed in the customs records for 12 December 1778, referring to Penzance customs officer Edward Hosking asking London for clarification and an official warrant known as a writ of assistance or assistants. These are still used today by Her Majesty's Revenue and Customs to search suspect premises. Headed 'Customhouse London' it begins:

> 'Gentlemen, Having read the affidavit of Edward Hosking Deputy Comptroller and several other Officers of your Port against Thomas Bramwell for an Obstruction in the

Execution of their duty, We acquaint you that, although the said Affidavit takes Notice that in the Presence of the said Constable, the Officer searched the Dwelling House etc, it does not appear to Us that any Constable was present. An Officer of the Customs having a Writ of Assistants and a Peace officer is in the daytime authorised by law to enter any House in search of Prohibited or Uncustomed Goods; And if in the Execution of such his duty, he is therein obstructed the Persons by whome he is obstructed, may be Prosecuted, but it should appear, upon Oath, that he had such Writ of Assistants and Peace Officer, if that the Search was founded upon a well warranted Information for which Purpose we return you the Aforesaid Affidavit in Order to be resworn, & when that is done you are to transmit it to us for our further consideration and Directions.'

It is signed on behalf of four commissioners of customs, Sir William Musgrave, Edward Hooper, Sir John Frederick and James Jeffreys. While the legal paperwork was being sorted out by head office, suspect Thomas Bramwell had plenty of time to rid his dwelling of any prohibited or uncustomed goods and the matter falls from the record.

Maria's father was clearly on the Custom House watch list and was far from alone in having the confidence to defy the revenue men. Avoiding import taxes was widely considered as 'free trade' and much of Cornish society played its part in the late eighteenth and early nineteenth centuries. The problem is spelled out in a helpless letter to London written in January 1775 by his majesty's men in Penzance:

We beg to represent to your Honble Board that smuggling was never carried on at so great a Height on this Coast as at the present time and never in so audacious a manner. One striking instance we presume to mention, on Tuesday last … an Irish wherry came to anchor in this Port within half a mile of the Shore and continued there in Open defiance till this morning. She is mounted with 4 large Carriage guns, 10 Swivels [small cannons], full of Men and Small Arms by Night. We imagine she was employed in running her cargoes of Tea, Brandy, etc on shore, we had no force that dare attack her.'

It is interesting to note that tea was among the goods the Branwells traded. The general population was no more inclined to listen to the Penzance customs men, as noted less than a year earlier:

> 'When the *Triton* from Bordeaux went aground near Helston laden with wine, the Master and Agent agreed with the assembly of Country People that they should have half the Cargo in order to save the other half for the Proprietors. Customs officials on arrival were asked to concur but refused, however, ipso facto that was what happened.'

Even the mayor was in on the act. When soldiers billeted in Penzance proved a deterrent to smugglers for a while in 1769, not everyone was happy according to one report:

> 'The Mayor of Penzance has always paid for fire and candles for the guardroom, but the present Mayor refuses to. At this I do not wonder as he is at present bound over in a considerable sum not to be again guilty of smuggling.'

Mayor John Pender was also the chief magistrate. In 1783, the year Maria was born, things were getting worse for collector John Scobell. In October, he recorded 'that Smuggling is very rife in this Port' and 'it is carried on with far greater audacity' by larger and more heavily armed smuggling ships. He freely admits that one, appropriately named *Wellard*, was crewed by 'most insolent fellows' and 'no officer of the Revenue dare go near her'. Custom House records showed every kind of illicit cargo being run into Mount's Bay. From French, Spanish and Portuguese rum, brandy and wine, to salt, fruit, tea, coffee and sugar. From Turkish raisins to 'a box of undressed Ostrich feathers', though quality control was a case of buyer beware. In 1786, 200 tons of liquor smuggled in during the previous 12 months was of inferior quality, remarked the Custom House, to that of the 'Fair Traders'.

Maria was eight years old and completing her sampler about fleeing from sin when we find her family's second remarkable link to smuggling. Ten years after being charged with refusing the revenue men entry, her father was in business with two of the town's busiest tax dodgers, James and John Dunkin. The Dunkin shop was just four doors away from Branwell's Corner. The brothers described themselves as merchants of Penzance, while the *Reading Mercury* described them as 'the most notorious smugglers in that part of the kingdom'.

They were, of course, both. Merchants often had shares in ships that carried their goods and the line between businessman and smuggler was fairly elastic. The Dunkins, however, were ruthless. In 1791, their ship, *Liberty,* had a deadly encounter with custom men off the Scilly island of Tresco, reported in the *Mercury* on 12 September:

> 'Last night the brig Friendship, the property of Messrs. John and James Dunkin, of Penzance, the most notorious smugglers in that part of the kingdom, came into Old Grimsby, a harbour belonging to this part, where James Dunkin, in a sloop called the Liberty, long accustomed to the same infamous traffick, had been waiting near a fortnight, in daily expectation of her arrival. About the hour of eleven, the custom-boat, with Mr. Hall the Surveyor, five boatmen, and one assistant, rowed within the length of the boat along side, which was no sooner discovered than the said James Dunkin, and those on board, fired into the boat repeatedly, without the least provocation; by which inhuman proceeding, John Oliver and William Millet ... fell, and expired; the former by shot received in the chest, the latter by two or more balls through the head and chest. John Jane is also desperately wounded in the face, his right cheek being nearly carried away; and little hopes are entertained of his recovery. The assistant, a son of one of the officers, was also wounded. An inquest has been held on both bodies; and the Jury have determined it – *Wilful Murder, by James Dunkin, and others on board, acting as servants under his immediate influence.'*

But the Dunkins were long gone, slipping out to sea with both ships before first light. A reward was offered for their capture, but they laid low for a while and were never arrested.

At exactly this time, all three merchants in Rotterdam Buildings had stakes in the Dunkin traders. Thomas Branwell and his neighbours Thomas Love and Richard Hosking all co-owned different Dunkin ships. If the newspapers and authorities knew the Dunkin sloop was known to be 'long accustomed to the same infamous traffick' it was clearly common knowledge. Yet the Penzance shipping register for 1786 to 1791 shows Thomas Branwell was in business with James Dunkin when he was wanted for murder.

Before, during and after the Tresco shoot-out, Thomas Branwell appears as the co-owner of another ship called *Penzance* with John Quick, Richard Oxnam and John and James Dunkin. Four years after the murders of John Oliver and William Millet, Thomas Branwell appears once more in the shipping register, this time with Thomas Love and another grocer, Barnaby Lloyd.

In June 1795 they own the *Liberty*.

It is little surprise that Branwells were among the well-organised free traders trying to keep prices down and profits up. Involvement in running goods in from the Continent was common from the aristocracy down and did not dent most reputations. Custom House records attest to the rearguard action being fought by the hopelessly outnumbered officers charged with policing Penzance when merchants such as the Bramwell-cum-Branwells were making their mark. Barnaby Lloyd, for example, is remembered in the memoirs of John Sampson Courtney, *Half a Century of Penzance*, only for how he, 'used gallantly to escort his lady customers across the place'.

When Maria was growing up in Chapel Street, she was never far from free traders. Like the little girl in Kipling's *A Smuggler's Song*, she would have known not to ask questions and to 'Watch the wall my darling while the Gentlemen go by'. Across the road and 60 yards to the left was the Admiral Benbow tavern and further on, 150 yards from her front door, was the Custom House. The labyrinthine tavern was the base for the Benbow Brandy Men, a gang of smugglers who made use of a network of secret tunnels running from the harbour to the tavern and up to Causewayhead and Market Jew Street. Though in use when Maria lived in Chapel Street, they were not rediscovered until 2008. Believed to have been dug by moonlighting tin miners, they operated under the very noses – or rather, feet – of the revenue men.

Contemporary accounts of smuggling activity in Penzance at the time leave questions that may never be answered about the grandfather of the Brontës. The circumstantial evidence is difficult to dispute. Thomas Branwell had a conviction for obstructing the revenue men and a business partnership with notorious smugglers who ran infamous operations. Even after their cat-and-mouse games with the law turned deadly.

One apposite fact is that being a devout Wesleyan was no bar to illicit trading. At the time Thomas worked with the Dunkins, Mount's Bay was also the base for John Carter, the self-styled King of Prussia, and his brothers Charles and Henry. They ran a huge smuggling operation out of hidden Porthleah (or Prussia) Cove from 1770 to 1807. Then Harry became a Methodist preacher and in 1809 wrote *The Autobiography of a Cornish Smuggler* about 'afishing and smuggling'.

The definitions of smuggler and pirate have become muddied over the centuries and were even more blurred in Maria's lifetime. Forever evoked by the Gilbert and Sullivan comic opera decades later in 1879, the pirates of Penzance were no laughing matter when Maria was growing up. *Treasure Island*, the story of Long John Silver by Robert Louis Stevenson, opens in an inn named the Admiral Benbow, like the one a few paces from Maria's front door. Stevenson visited Penzance in 1877 and was inspired to make the pub his setting, though transported to Devon. Jim Hawkins and his parents may have been upstanding fictional proprietors but the real Benbow landlord was a lynchpin for illegal operations when Maria lived nearby.

Years later, her 15-year-old son Branwell Brontë became preoccupied by the double lives of seaside gentlemen. In his story *The Pirate*, fictional antihero Alexander Rogue lives in a fine house with '…a gorgeous view of the vast Glasstown harbour, with its endless shipping, crowded quays and mighty expanse of blue water stretching away…' Not unlike the one his mother and aunt will have told him about at their childhood home. It seems likely that Branwell's imagination was fired at least in part by dark tales of Cornwall.

As the eighteenth century progressed to its end, Maria's family attended to both wealth and respectability and whatever their association with duty-free 'traffick', it was carefully managed. One very respectable marriage took place in 1790 when Maria's favourite aunt wed a minor local celebrity. Jane Branwell had been courted by a driven young schoolmaster and lay preacher from Shropshire called John Fennell, who arrived in Penzance the year Maria was born. His godfather and mentor was the famous Swiss clergyman John Fletcher, who married Mary Bosanquet and was John Wesley's best friend. This gave Fennell instant entrée to the Branwell circle. He lived and breathed religious education and found romance amid the Cornish revival.

Jane was an early member of the Penzance Methodist Society just as the widowed Mary Fletcher had her own standing as a leading Wesleyan in Shropshire. There was almost a decade difference in their ages but John, 28, and Jane, 37, were a match made in Methodism. They shared an equal fervour for the Evangelical way of life and on 13 December, St Lucy's Day, they were married at Madron Parish Church. The couple made their home in Chapel Street and in October 1791, Aunt Jane gave birth to a girl and followed family tradition by calling her Jane too. Little Jane grew up with the cousins who were closest in age and location, Maria and Charlotte Branwell down the road. It was a close-knit family in a close-knit town, with most influential families connected by marriage.

Young Maria's contemporaries included a singular boy called Humphry Davy. He would become Sir Humphry, Britain's most famous scientist, inventing the miner's safety lamp and discovering chlorine and iodine. As a boy in Penzance, however, he was simply everyone's friend. Humphry was a charismatic presence in young Maria's life. He was four years older, loosely related by marriage and went to the grammar school with her brother Benjamin. He was the eldest of five, with three sisters called Kitty, Grace and Betsy and a little brother called John. His water poodle Chloe, who he rescued from being drowned, followed him everywhere, with floppy dark curls not unlike his own. When not roping in Kitty as his first lab assistant for a stab at making fireworks, he was walking the fields and writing poems by moonlight.

Life was never boring with handsome Humph around and he certainly had the makings of a schoolgirl crush. Who knows whom he sent valentines to but he was in demand at school from less poetic pals. His brother John Davy reports that '...in writing valentines and love-letters he shone so pre-eminently ... that he is said to have been generally resorted to on all emergencies of boyish loves'. You always knew where the young scientist and poet was, either from the explosions at his home with guardian Dr John Tonkin in the Marketplace, or the crowd gathering under the balcony of the Star Inn. There he told ghostly tales of 'wonder and terror' from the back of a cart. The Cornish loved a storyteller and Humphry liked to oblige, holding forth not far from Branwell's Corner.

Maria's life cannot be seen in isolation from these formative influences of her Celtic heritage. Ellen Nussey remarked later that Maria had the 'inestimable blessing of a well-balanced mind, yet she was imbued with a degree of superstition...' While her family had been ardent Wesleyans for two generations at most, they had always been great storytellers, steeped in the folklore of centuries. Humphry Davy was not the only one to relish a good gothic tale. Maria learned the old stories from her own elders and the female servants who cared for the children. This sense of the other – very real and very present – was part of the sensibility of Maria's era in general and her home town in particular, according to John Davy:

> 'All classes were very superstitious; even the belief in witches
> maintained its ground, and there was an almost unbounded

credulity respecting the supernatural and monstrous. There was scarcely a parish in the Mount's Bay that was without a haunted house, or a spot to which some story of supernatural horror was not attached.'

Maria knew that only too well. Just a few doors away in Chapel Street, a Mrs Baines was reputed to haunt the orchard at the back of number 20. The unlucky old lady was mistaken for a fruit thief by a servant and shot in the bottom with a blunderbuss. Understandably furious, she was believed to have stayed on to haunt the place. Young Branwells and little Jane Fennell knew to hurry on by, as John Davy recalls:

> 'Even when I was a boy, I remember a house in the best street in Penzance, which was uninhabited, because it was believed to be haunted, and which young people walked by at night at a quickened pace, and with a beating heart.'

For Wesleyans, ghost stories were not simply a fireside entertainment. When Maria was only a year old, John Wesley published his 1784 book, *The Haunting of Epworth Rectory: An Account of the Disturbances in My Father's House.* Unexplained groaning, knocking, footsteps, rattling chains, quaking crockery, the sound of horns and, most alarming of all, levitating beds, plagued his family's home for eight weeks beginning in late 1716. The exasperated Wesleys even gave the poltergeist a name, Old Jeffrey, and it remains one of the most famous hauntings in British history.

Though witch trials were (largely) a thing of the past, the Branwells might easily have shared 'the belief in witches' John Davy disdained. Certainly John Wesley did. Paranormal experience was generally categorized as demonic, bringing hauntings within the Christian lexicon. The existence of demons merely underlined the existence of God, according to Wesley:

> 'With my last breath I will bear testimony against giving up to infidels one great proof of the invisible world; I mean that of witchcraft and apparitions, confirmed by the testimony of all ages.'

From church to hearth, West Penwith was awash with apparitions and other weird tales. Maria was both a child of the Enlightenment and of keeping the candlelight on. The dramas of the past collided with those of the present to make Maria and her sisters Cornishwomen to the core. Their imaginations were fuelled by wild and mysterious surroundings. The landscape they grew up with was peculiarly loaded with strange tales, not least St Michael's Mount seen from Maria's window. Dr Paris described its allure in *Guide to the Mount's Bay and The Land's End,* first published in 1816:

> 'The western shores are sprinkled with picturesque villages, churches, cottages, and villas; and near the eastern margin of the bay, a pile of rocks, supporting a venerable chapel on its summit, starts abruptly from the waves, and presents an appearance of a most singular and beautiful description – this is *Saint Michael's Mount*, an eminence equally celebrated in the works of the poet, the naturalist, the antiquary, and the historian.'

To Maria and everyone else, the gothic island dominating the bay (reached by a stone causeway from Marazion at low tide) was an endless source of fabulous yarns. It always had been. First recorded as an Iron Age trading post, it later became a Benedictine priory. Both holy and strategically handy, the imposing rock doubled as a fortress in numerous battles from the Wars of the Roses to the English Civil War. By the 1780s, the priory had evolved into a castle, occupied by the St Aubyn family.

For the people of Penzance, its fame rested less on hard facts and more on a series of myths and miracles stretching back to the fifth century. The Mount could mean death or glory for sailors, depending on what kind of unearthly being they happened to encounter. By 495 it was widely held that some seafaring souls had been lured by mermaids to perish on the rocks, while others had been guided to safe waters by the archangel Michael. Belief in the angelic appearance drew pilgrims for centuries, with no less than four miracles believed to have occurred in the 1260s. After which it seemed sensible to build a church.

More pagan appeal lay in the best story of all, that it was originally the lair of the Cornish giant Cormoran. He met his match with a lad from Marazion, Jack the giant killer. Legend has it that the giant built the Mount and regularly waded over to the mainland to swipe livestock and terrorise locals. Jack rowed over one night and dug a giant-sized well, then tricked the 18-foot ogre into toppling in. Hence the memorial ditty, 'Here's the valiant Cornishman, who slew the Giant Cormoran.'

The waves crashing against both the Mount and the shore near Maria's door concealed yet more mysteries and she heard of freak waves and doomed ancestors. On 11 November 1099, St Martin's day, a violent storm hit the Mount and caused flooding around the bay. First recorded in the *Anglo-Saxon Chronicle*, folk memory of the mediaeval tsunami fed the Cornish legend of the lost land of Lyonesse. The Scilly Isles were believed to be all that remained above the waves of the civilisation swallowed by the Atlantic. Equally enthralling to Maria and her playmates was the drowned forest in Mount's Bay. Unlike Lyonesse, this was known to exist. Her cousin Joseph Branwell was particularly fascinated, going on to publish a paper as an adult about the remains of beech and oak trees submerged 4,000 years earlier.

It was the age of wonder and scientific enquiry reached down the generations. Young Branwells and Davys could play on the sand dunes or search for fossils while concocting stories with equal dollops of myth and science. A lively Celtic imagination made good use of both. Bronze age surges and murderous mediaeval tides were part of Maria's coastal psyche, along with the strange tales that came with them.

When it was certain that ancient trees lay beneath the sea – the gnarled evidence glimpsed at exceptionally low tides – it was not hard to imagine mythical creatures darting around them. Mermaids and sea spirits keeping company with Cornish kelpies (waterhorses). On dry land giants supposedly fashioned the wild cliffs and at the other extreme, little people such as buccas and piskies caused trouble on the moors and in the mines. These were the folk tales Maria imbibed from babyhood and would carry with her to Yorkshire to tell her half-Cornish children.

Ghosts and smugglers, legends and liturgy, tea parties and revivals, all the weave and weft that made Maria Branwell. As to a more tangible inheritance, in faraway Yorkshire, Maria and Elizabeth would never stop feeling homesick for Cornish weather. In the second edition of his guide to Mount's bay in 1824, Dr Paris adds advice to patients looking for somewhere to recuperate:

'The climate of Mount's Bay ... renders its shores so beneficial to invalids. Its seasons have been aptly compared to the neap [when there is least difference between high and low] tides, which neither ebb nor flow with energy; for, notwithstanding its southern latitude, the summer is never sultry, while the rigour of winter is so ameliorated, that thick ice is rarely seen; frost, if it occurs, is but of a few hours duration; and the snow storms which, coming from the north and east, bury the fields of every other part of England, are generally exhausted before they reach this favoured spot, or their last sprinkling is dissolved by the warm breezes which play around its shores.'

The rare exception was when the marsh at nearby Marazion froze over thickly enough for people to go skating. This happened twice when Maria was a child, once in 1788 when she was five and again in 1794 when she was eleven. Such events were not unknown in Georgian England, giving rise to frost fairs on affected rivers and inlets. Under the mellow skies of Maria's home lay 'the undulating curves, and luxuriant herbage of the southern shores' where Dr Paris says, 'myrtles and geraniums, even of the tenderest kind, and many other exotics, are here constantly exposed during the winter, and yet they flower most luxuriantly in the summer.'

This, then, was the colourful, sub-tropical world of Maria's youth. By the closing decade of the eighteenth century, however, life in Rotterdam Buildings was changing. When she was nine, the family was again convulsed by tragedy, though the year of 1792 began happily enough. The list of notable marriages in the *Bath Chronicle and Weekly Gazette* of 19 January includes: 'Mr. Fisher, bookbinder, of Penzance, to Miss Branwell, daughter of Mr. Thomas Branwell, merchant.'

Mr Fisher was called Charles and Miss Branwell was Margaret, 21 on her wedding day and the first of Maria's siblings to leave home. Though services, baptisms and burials took place at St Mary's chapel-of-ease, weddings had to happen at Madron Parish Church two miles inland.

Then spring 1792 brought not life, but death. Maria's eldest sister Anne sickened and died suddenly at just 23. She may have suffered from typhus, influenza, smallpox or any of the diseases that frequently proved fatal. Thomas and Anne's firstborn, the bump on their wedding day, was taken away when they least expected it. Maria was forced to kiss a second sister goodbye, this one laid out in her coffin at their home. Jane was so distraught that she took on Anne's name informally in memory, and that was how she was known for the rest of her days.

As Maria's family dealt with their grief behind brick walls, Penzance had bigger problems. The French Republic was fighting monarchies across Europe and as 1792 progressed it seemed that Britain was next. Town leaders were convinced a French invasion could happen at any moment. Mayor Thomas Giddy called an emergency meeting of leading citizens such as Maria's father and brother, to discuss town defences. It was decided to buy a new pair of colours (flags) for the battery to show the French they were ready to defend themselves, plus new drums for sounding the alarm during an invasion. If townsfolk heard the drumbeat they should head for the Guildhall, prepared to take up arms and follow orders.

Like many of the landmark years throughout Maria's life, twelve short months brought a tumble of seismic events between the strokes of midnight at one New Year and the next. At the close of 1792 her two eldest sisters were gone, one dead and the other to start a new life with her husband. Meanwhile, her whole community was tensing for invasion. As the Branwells struggled to restore a sense of domestic normality at the beginning of 1793, world events intruded again. On 1 February, just before Maria's tenth birthday, France declared war on Britain.

Branwells were expected to do their bit and Maria's brother Benjamin joined the Georgian equivalent of the Home Guard, the Penzance Volunteers. As it turned out, they were called on to deal with domestic trouble, though inspired by the French. A report in the *Ipswich Journal* gives a glimpse of the homegrown unrest outside the prosperous Penzance bubble. Hunger and, for people like the Branwells, a crowd's worrying empathy with post-revolutionary France was reported on Saturday, 4 April 1795:

> 'Part of the Worcester militia was ordered to Penzance in Cornwall on Thursday last to quell a very formidable party of tinners. The present cry of these men is for 'Liberty and Equality, as the French have.' They undergo a regular drill. The occasion of their rising is the price of corn. About a week ago they entered Penzance, and fixed a maximum on provision, which the inhabitants, aided by the volunteers in some measure resisted; but as they threatened to return with a force of 10,000 men, it was thought necessary to strengthen them by a body of the Worcester militia.'

Militant miners marching on Penzance rattled the gentry and galvanized the town Volunteers. Benjamin's promotion was reported in the *Kentish Gazette* in February 1797 as: 'Benj Branwell, Gent, to be Ensign'. He was promoted again, to lieutenant. Meanwhile Maria's father kept his guns ready on the wooden rack, in case the French quite literally arrived at the door.

Penzance was more aware of the threat after the official declaration of war, but it did not mean an appreciable shift in the town psyche. They were accustomed to keeping a wary eye on the horizon. In 1595, the Spanish raided West Cornwall, setting fire to Mousehole, Newlyn and Penzance before escaping out to sea. The early 1600s brought raids on coastal villages by North African pirates known as Barbary corsairs. They attacked shipping and targeted coastal villages, carrying off thousands of men and women to work as slaves. In more recent memory, there was the alarming sight of a French and Spanish armada crossing Mounts Bay in the summer of 1779 before being driven back by a storm at sea. Maria's family helped with preparations to repel the French but on the whole, Penzance kept calm and carried on.

Alongside his military duties, Benjamin followed in his father's footsteps to become a merchant and brewer and when he was 22 in 1797, a member of the Penzance Corporation. Council roles were closed to women and it was his wealth and career that were protected by both law and tradition. In January 1799, Benjamin left home to marry the girl almost next door, Mary Batten, from a prominent family of Chapel Street bankers.

Romance was also in the air for Maria's eldest sister Jane, now calling herself Anne. Another of Wesley's converts arrived in Penzance in 1799 and like her namesake aunt, Jane Branwell fell for a preacher. John Kingston, from Northamptonshire, arrived after seven years as a Methodist missionary in the West Indies and America. His adventures had been serialized in the *Methodist Magazine* throughout the year, ending in August. At sixteen, he told his parents he had 'forsaken the mad and frantic ways of an evil world' and a few years later went to preach overseas.

Genuinely a man of the world, when he arrived in Penzance, he soon became friends with the influential Branwells and met Jane. He was an itinerant preacher on the Methodist Circuit in Cornwall and she was an educated and dedicated Wesleyan woman. Like John Fennell before him, Kingston's Evangelical credentials made him a suitable match for a Miss Branwell.

During this time, though growing in wealth and prestige, Maria's family was also dogged by more tragedy. Her brother-in-law Charles Fisher died in 1798, after six years of marriage to Margaret and without surviving children. Then in 1799 Margaret died too, aged just 28. Maria was 16 when she attended the second funeral of a beloved older sister, her views over the graveyard behind the house more melancholy than before.

Tellingly, this was the year that the remaining Branwells at Rotterdam Buildings had their portraits painted by celebrated local artist James Tonkin, a relative who specialized in miniatures. These are the only surviving images of Maria and her sisters as young women. Did Thomas and Anne regret never having their eldest daughters painted? Anne and Margaret's faces had to remain in their memory but those of Jane, Elizabeth, Maria and Charlotte could not fade or be forgotten.

As the eighteenth century gave way to the nineteenth, the girl in the white dress with the wide brown eyes and aquiline nose was 16 years old. Maria faced the future with an understanding of the fragility of life. Only five of the dozen Branwell children had lived to greet the new century. Thomas and Anne were middle-aged pillars of the community and their only living son Benjamin was dutifully following suit. Their daughters were altogether more interesting and would draw the attention of the nineteenth-century world to the Branwells of Chapel Street.

Chapter 2

Perfectly Her Own Mistress

The nineteenth century dawned in Chapel Street with another high-profile wedding and a new generation of babies to extend the clan. Maria's eldest sister had fallen for the new Methody man in town, she became a beloved aunt and Branwell coffers continued to fill from the many and mysterious branches of the family business. Though the war with France rumbled on, becoming the Napoleonic Wars when Bonaparte seized control across the Channel, life in the thriving port carried on regardless. For the first decade of the 1800s, Maria Branwell enjoyed all the advantages fashionable Penzance offered a prosperous young woman of her class.

Number 25 was again buzzing with wedding preparations. Jane had said yes to her missionary man. Marrying Mr Kingston would mean a life on the move with an itinerant preacher, travelling far beyond her comfortable life in Penzance – but she was ready for it. Just before midsummer in June 1800 Jane Branwell, 27, and John Kingston, 31, became husband and wife. Maria waved off the newlyweds as they left to begin married life at St Austell, more than forty miles away. That left only 23-year-old Elizabeth, 17-year-old Maria and 10-year-old Charlotte at home with Mama and Papa.

The following year Maria became an auntie, with both Benjamin and Mary in Penzance and Jane and John in St Austell naming their firstborns Thomas after their grandfather. According to Elizabeth Gaskell, who consulted Cornish relatives in later years, Maria was popular with the nephews and nieces who arrived in quick succession. She was 'their favourite aunt, and one to whom they, as well as all the family, looked up, as a person of talent and great amiability of disposition.'

This talent may have included music. Maria was 'possessing more than the ordinary talents, which she inherited from her father...' while 'Mr Branwell, the father, according to his descendants' account, was a man of musical talent'. Lilian Oldham states that he played the violin in the parlour at home. This inheritance may explain Emily Brontë's ability as a pianist, playing with precision and brilliancy according to Ellen Nussey.

Music was all around in the spring of 1804 when Maria turned 21, coming of age in a cosmopolitan town with plenty to occupy a privileged young woman. Until the end of the eighteenth century, female social life had mainly revolved around visits to one another's houses. John Davy described the low-key leisure pursuits of their parents' generation. 'Visiting was almost entirely confined to tea parties, which assembled at three o'clock, broke up at nine,' he wrote in 1832, 'and the amusement of the evening was commonly some round game at cards, as Pope Joan, or Commerce.' Both games were popular in Cornish homes, the former an old Protestant joke referring to the rumour that Pope John VII was actually a woman. There was also a concert room behind the Turk's Head inn in Chapel Street.

Then along came the assembly rooms.

Assembly rooms were the fashionable places to be seen and are remembered chiefly for their role in the novels of Maria's contemporary, Jane Austen. However, the refined Westcountry gatherings Austen observed in Bath were also to be enjoyed by the ladies of Penzance. Assemblies were simply gatherings of the great and the good and ranged from winter balls and summer parties to card games and dance performances. Such assemblies were *the* place to be for every well-to-do Georgian.

The handsome Penzance rooms opened in 1791 with ornate ceilings, chandeliers and gallery for the musicians. They were paid for by subscription and built by Maria's uncle, Richard Branwell. Naturally they were placed in Chapel Street, adding to the entertainment hub at the Ship and Castle, renamed the Union Hotel. The large room could hold up to ten tables and never had less than sixteen dancing couples and three or four card tables, according to wealthy Catherine Tremenheere. She lived at the top of Chapel Street, virtually opposite the lively hotel. The chic venue was 'very prettily lighted' with three chandeliers on the ceiling and eight smaller ones called girandoles on the walls or tables.

Despite such sophistication, Penzance was still being caricatured in faraway London, much to its annoyance. An 1803 comedy at Covent Garden by George Colman the younger called *John Bull, or An Englishman's Fireside* was reviewed in the *Morning Post*. The hero escapes a shipwreck by swimming ashore and reaches 'a poor inn, upon Muckslush-heath, and there learns he is near Penzance…' It was a hit in London and 'the audience manifested, by repeated bursts of applause, their approbation of almost every scene'.

Cornish gentry were less impressed by the farcical focus on rough smugglers, wreckers and most uncivilized behaviour. Charles Valentine Le Grice, later curate of St Mary's behind Maria's house, saw the play and took exception in a letter to the *Gazette*:

> 'Penzance is a very different place from the commonly received opinion. We have cards for the sedentary, books for the lounger, balls for the light-heeled, clubs for the convivial, and picnics for the gay and thoughtless.'

Another vivid picture of monied life is doctor John Ayrton Paris's account of the entertainment following a day of sporting festivities in St Ives:

> 'The ladies and gentlemen of Penzance returned to an elegant dinner which they had ordered to be prepared at the Union Hotel; and a splendid ball concluded the entertainment of the evening. The jolly god presided, – but a reproving smile from Venus restrained him, if he ventured beyond the due bounds of decorum. Hilarity and beauty danced to the most delicious notes of harmony; till the rosy finger of Aurora pointed to the hour at which … festivities should close.'

The Branwell sisters enjoyed such elegant dining and decorous dancing. For this certainty we have the reminiscences of Ellen Nussey, the best friend of Charlotte Brontë, in the kind of ruthless assessment a young woman gives of a much older one:

> 'She probably had been pretty. She always dressed in silk. She talked a great deal of her younger days, the gaities [sic] of her native town, Penzance in Cornwall, the soft climate &c. She very probably had been a belle among her acquaintance, the social life of her younger days she appeared to recall with regret.'

Belles went to the balls and if the extrovert Elizabeth was something of a socialite, so was Maria, her best friend and sister. A fashionable habit among Georgian ladies was the taking of snuff, powdered tobacco kept in ornate little boxes and snorted frequently up the nostrils. In her later years,

Elizabeth enjoyed scandalizing disapproving Victorian visitors such as Ellen with evidence of gaieties gone by:

> 'She took snuff out of a very pretty little gold snuff box, which she sometimes presented with a little laugh as if she enjoyed the slight shock and astonishment visible in your countenance.'

If only someone had recorded the memories shared often and in detail by witty, educated and homesick Aunt Branwell, we would know more of her life with Maria amid the beau monde. Before Elizabeth was an old lady to be indulged by the Brontës and their friends, then politely dismissed from the business of the present. As a belle in her heyday, she was simply a dedicated follower of fashion. Blowing one's nose at a party was all the rage. The queen, wife of George III, was such a fan she was known as Snuffy Charlotte. A room was dedicated to the royal nostrils at every palace.

More evidence of fashionable gentility is the pair of matching smelling salts bottles now at the Brontë Parsonage Museum. Maria's china bottle is an elongated heart shape. On one side is a posy of flowers in blues, pinks and dark red, along with an orange sunflower and leaves of olive green, all on a white heart surrounded in gold. The initials M.B. are spelled out delicately in gold on the front, framed by golden sprigs. Elizabeth's bottle is a rounder shape, though similar in decoration and possibly Jane and Charlotte had other ones. The bottles held carbonate of ammonia. It was known as eau-de-luce if it contained white soap and oil of amber in a wine spirit base. Hartshorn was another popular ingredient, as was perfume.

All fashionable ladies carried them as a defence against a fit of the vapours brought on by unpleasant smells or the sheer excitement of the social whirl. Maria's fictional heroines were much given to fainting, as we shall see shortly. Wafting ammonia under the nose forced a sharp intake of reviving breath. An advertisement in the *Morning Post* in August 1801 extolled the virtues of 'the best Smelling Bottle for reviving the Spirits, and recovering Persons immediately from Fainting, or Hysteric Fits' that was also 'so great a Purifier of Air, that no person should go into Play-houses or any crouded Rooms without it.' When Maria went out with hers, possibly worn as a necklace, the bottle was more about fashion than first aid. Such ornate and expensive items were carried only by the wealthy as small but exquisite status symbols.

The 'Play-house' in the stable yard behind the Union Hotel made a smelling bottle a practical adornment. Just before Maria's 23rd birthday, the *Royal Cornwall Gazette* advertised a lively evening:

> 'PENZANCE THEATRE, The Ladies and Gentlemen of that town and neighbourhood are respectfully informed, WILL OPEN on WEDNESDAY April 3, 1805; With a new Comedy, called THE HONEY MOON. Between the Play and Farce, Singing and Dancing. To conclude with an Entertainment, called THE SPOIL'D CHILD.'

Maria was a tiny woman, a Cornish piskie like her daughter Charlotte Brontë, who was around four feet nine inches tall. Elizabeth Gaskell describes her thus: 'Miss Branwell was extremely small in person; not pretty, but very elegant, and always dressed with a quiet simplicity of taste, which accorded well with her general character...' A prettiness rating is so subjective and irrelevant as to mean little. Maria's elegance and good taste were what people remembered.

In a land of Celtic custom, not all entertainment involved quadrilles and candelabras. Maria's house was directly in the path of a more ancient and less mannered celebration. Much older than the assembly room diversions were the midsummer frolics that engulfed Penzance around the longest day. They were a highlight of the year, war or no war. They always had been, with Mazey (midsummer) eve a time for merrymaking since pre-Christian times. Penzance in June was a carnival town with the festivities merging with the feasts of St John and St Peter, the fisherman. An account in the *Gazette* in summer 1801 was written when Maria was a young person, while Charlotte and cousin Jane Fennell were children of an age to wear garlands:

> 'I observed the young people all alert in the preparations for their favourite festival. No sooner had the tardy sun withdrawn himself from the horizon, than the young men began to assemble in several parts of the town, drawing after them, trees and branches of wood and furze; all which had been accumulating week after week, from the beginning of May. Tar-barrels were presently erected on tall poles; some on the quay, others near the market, and one even on a rock in the midst of the sea; pretty female children tript up and down

in their best frocks, decorated with garlands; and hailing the
Midsummer-eve as the feast of St. John.'

The night gathered momentum as old Cornish customs were enacted
through Chapel Street and beyond:

> 'The joyful moment arrives! the torches make their appearance!
> the heaped-up wood is on fire, and the tar barrels send up their
> immense flame! the ladies and gentlemen parade the streets,
> or walk in the fields or on the terrace that commands the bay!'

The villages around Mount's Bay competed to have the best fiery displays,
all reflected on the sea to create a magical night. Rockets and crackers were
let off so that 'the screams of the ladies on their return from the shew, and
their precipitate flight into the best passage, shop, or house, that happens to
be open, heighten the coloring and diversion of the night.'

Then a riotous finale in the streets nearest the sea, all around Maria's house:

> 'No sooner are torches burnt out, than the inhabitants of the
> quay-quarter, (a great multitude,) male and female, young,
> middle-aged, and old; virtuous and vicious, sober and drunk,
> take hands, and forming a long string, run violently through
> every street, lane, and alley crying 'An eye! an eye! an eye!'
> At last they stop suddenly: and an eye to this enormous needle
> being opened by the last two in the string, (whose clasped
> hands are elevated and arched) the thread of populace run
> under, and through: and continue to repeat the same, till
> weariness dissolves their union, and sends them home to bed:-
> which is never til near the hour of midnight.'

Mazey day was a more sedate, possibly slightly hungover, affair:

> 'The custom is, for the country people to come to Penzance in
> their best clothes, about four or five o'clock in the afternoon;
> when they repair to the quay and take a short trip on the water.
> On this occasion numbers of boats are employed, most of
> which have music on board. After one cargo is dismissed,
> another is taken in; and til nine or ten o'clock at night, the
> bay exhibits a pleasant scene of sailing boats, towing-boats,

sloops, sea-sickness, laughter, quarreling, drum-beating, horn-blowing. ... On the shore there is a kind of wake or fair, in which fruit and confectionary are sold, and the public houses are thronged with drinkers and dancers.'

Every Christmas there was another carnival that involved both rich and poor. Though the midwinter entertainment had a stranger feel. Every evening until twelfth night people walked the streets in masks and costumes, enacting the ancient guise-dance.

Britain had been at war since Maria was a little girl. Feuding with France was a fact of life. She had cousins in the military and invasion panic flared up occasionally, but it did not affect the daily rounds. If anything, the hostilities were good news for a family of merchants and landlords when the town became an upmarket resort. Being a wartime alternative to continental watering holes pushed up prices. It was even dubbed the Montpellier of England. In his travels of the time, Daniel Carless Webb observed as much about 'Penzance, said to be the most beautiful place in Cornwall' in *Observations and Remarks during four Excursions made to various Parts of Great Britain*:

'Many opulent inhabitants reside here. The great influx of strangers, whom the war prevents making a tour to the South of France, for the benefit of their health, has contributed to raise the price of lodgings, as well as every necessary of life.'

The French Wars that began when Maria was ten became the Napoleonic Wars in 1803. It was impossible to ignore the war when her father kept his guns within reach and her brother was drilling with the Volunteers, but Penzance was still more resort than front line. Then tension did increase when Napoleon amassed soldiers on the coast across the Channel. Spain became an ally, adding her ships to the invasion force in 1804. The Cornish joined the entire nation in looking to the revered Admiral Lord Nelson to thwart Napoleon in his obsessive quest to conquer England.

The day of reckoning came off Cape Trafalgar on the Spanish coast of Cadiz. Nelson aboard HMS *Victory* led another 26 Royal Navy ships against 33 enemy vessels. On 21 October 1805 came the Battle of Trafalgar and with it, Penzance's boast to be the first to find out.

A Monday night ball at the assembly rooms to mark 200 years since Guy Fawkes' gunpowder plot was interrupted with astonishing news. Mayor Thomas Giddy stepped onto the little musicians' balcony in the assembly rooms at the Union Hotel and raised his hand for hush. Ladies and gentlemen assembled below fell quiet as they saw the look on his face. The splendid occasion was about to be remembered for more than the gossip and dancing. It was 4 November 1805 and Giddy had both joyous and devastating news to impart in one breath. Victory over Napoleon at Trafalgar at the dreadful cost of England's hero, Horatio Nelson.

Thus Penzance partygoers became the first people on English soil to learn of the death of Nelson, thanks to the chatty crews of a local fishing boat and HMS *Pickle,* fresh from the battle. Two Mount's Bay fishermen learned of both the victory and the tragedy when they encountered the *Pickle* heading to Falmouth with the news. The fishing boat headed full sail back to port to give Penzance the scoop of a lifetime.

The hastily-made banner in Madron Church does lend weight to the story. It is also a tangible link with Maria's family during those momentous few days in 1805. The banner was carried from Penzance to a memorial service at the parish church as soon as the news broke. It was at the head of a procession to Madron with the mayor and corporation, which included Thomas and Benjamin Branwell, up front. The words painted on the impromptu canvas banner have the hallmarks of William Tremenheere, the versifying vicar of Madron:

> 'Mourn for the Brave
> the immortal NELSON'S gone
> His last Sea fight is fought
> His work of Glory done.'

Given to expressing himself in rhyme, Maria's parish priest prompted an arch assessment in *The Monthly Review* of his less hasty but no better *Verses on the Victory of Trafalgar*: 'Mr. Tremenheere is perhaps intitled [sic] to our respect as a man and as a clergyman: but as a poet we cannot say to him – 'Well done'.' So mourning over for one and all, it was time to plan another ball... A celebration was advertised in the *Gazette*: 'In honor of the Glorious Victory off Trafalgar, THERE will be a BALL and SUPPER at the Assembly Rooms, Penzance, on Monday the 30th December.' Amid the momentous events, Maria cannot have felt even a flicker of personal interest in one of the hero's many impressive titles. Vice Admiral Lord Viscount Nelson, Commander in Chief of the Royal Navy, was also the Duke of Bronte.

Maria's milieu was exciting and varied, with every diversion of early nineteenth century life on her doorstep and a wealthy family to free her from drudgery. Still, we cannot pretend to know the precise details of her personal social calendar or her timetable of religious and family duties. What we *do* know for sure is that Maria Branwell, the mother of the Brontës, was an avid reader. Her love of the written word is the most tangible and enduring fact of her life as an individual woman and not only as a daughter, wife or mother. Maria read books of poetry and scripture to improve her mind, magazines full of fashion and fiction for fun.

The year she came of age she wrote, 'Maria Branwell, 1804, Penzance' in her copy of *The Seasons* by James Thomson, an eighteenth-century Scottish poet most famous for the lyrics of *Rule, Britannia!* In July 1807, when she was 24, she wrote her name and the date inside a one-shilling version of *The Christian's pattern: or, a treatise on the imitation of Christ* by Thomas à Kempis and translated from the Latin by John Wesley. Wesley was of the opinion that the mediaeval monk wrote the perfect guide to living a Christian life (before dying of the plague in 1471). It was part of the Christian canon he urged Methodists to read, churning out cheap editions from his own printing press in London.

As a 27–year-old in 1810, Maria bought *The Remains of Henry Kirke White,* the works of the consumptive Evangelical poet who died at 21. It was edited and introduced by Robert Southey, later poet laureate (who later still, advised her daughter Charlotte Brontë against writing as, 'Literature cannot be the business of a woman's life, and it ought not to be'.) Maria's book was simply a Methodist must-read at the time but would come to play an unexpectedly poignant role in her future.

The fun came from *The Lady's Magazine.* The 'Entertaining Companion for the Fair Sex, Appropriated Solely to Their Use and Amusement' was published monthly in London at sixpence an issue. The pioneering periodical offered everything from society news to embroidery patterns, history and travel articles to medical advice, sheet music to fashion plates. They also ran juicy fiction, often by female authors. Maria loved to curl up with a *Lady's* and we know this because Charlotte Brontë inherited them and did exactly the same. Until, that is, her father found out.

In a letter to Hartley Coleridge in 1840 she wrote:

'I read them as a treat on holiday afternoons or by stealth when I should have been minding my lessons – I shall never see anything which will interest me so much again – One black day my father burnt them because they contained foolish love stories.'

Charlotte wished 'with all my heart' she had been born in time to be a contributor: 'I am sorry, Sir, I did not exist forty or fifty years ago when the Lady's magazine was flourishing like a green bay tree.'

In other words, when her mother was glued to its pages as a young woman in Penzance. It was the heyday of gothic literature, begun by Horace Walpole in 1764 with *The Castle of Otranto* but made mainstream by Ann Radcliffe's 1794 blockbuster, *The Mysteries of Udolpho*. From adolescence, Maria enjoyed the thrills of these wildly popular suspense stories as much as the spellbinding folktales of her childhood. Supernatural shivers, vulnerable virgins and wicked seducers were everywhere until well into the 1800s. Cheap and cheerless thrills were widely available in the form of gothic bluebooks, pamphlets also dubbed shilling shockers. The magazines were a more genteel vehicle for the Branwell sisters and were bound into volumes. Charlotte reports, 'they were old books belonging to my mother or my Aunt [Elizabeth], they had crossed the Sea...' and refers in passing to three stories in particular, '...of Derwent Priory – of the Abbey and of Ethelinda.'

Athelwold and Ethelinda; A Tale has a handsome hero who 'excelled in every manly exercise' while the heroine was the 'beauteous daughter' of King Ethelbert. Unfortunately, jealous courtiers plot against Athelwold and he ends up in a cave in the woods. One day, Ethelinda runs by, chased by a wolf. She is rescued and faints whereupon: 'He folded her in his arms, – he wept over her, – he called on her name...' and so on. Seeing his face, she faints again. She finally revives to reveal she has been banished for defending her manly man. The cry goes up that the king is being ambushed and Athelwold goes to the rescue, again, resulting in a patriarchal happy ever after where the king 'gave him his daughter'.

Derwent Priory, or memoirs of an orphan appeared as a serialized novel. Part of the gothic game was to present works as rediscovered mediaeval manuscripts or lost letters, leaving the real author anonymous. It was a classic example of the terrified inhabitants of a creepy old building beset by strange goings-on and plenty of fleeing down corridors. Then there was *Grasville Abbey: A Romance* supposedly related by an old hermit. Two sisters are dumped in a convent by their scheming father in seventeenth-century France. This does not go well. One dies and the other, Clementina, attempts to flee:

> 'She was already half-way up; but terrified at the thoughts
> of her situation she rested for a few moments against the old
> iron railing, when a light step seemed to move on the same
> stair. Almost convulsed with horror, she shrunk back, and

was fortunately unable to call out, when at the same moment a strong flash of lightning darted from the window above, and showed her the figure of a man; the sight of it was but momentary, and all again was silent and dark...'

No wonder Maria and Charlotte were agog. It was all a long way from Sunday school.

Gothic fiction was also popular in Maria's other source of good reads, the Penzance Ladies Book Club. Founded in 1770, the rules stated that no gentleman was to be admitted as a subscriber and club numbers were limited to 22. It cost six shillings to subscribe, there were strict rules for looking after books plus fines for late returns and lending to someone else. Members were expected to read quickly, a loan lasted four days, and fifty new books, periodicals and pamphlets did the rounds every year.

Several of Maria's relatives served as president of the club. By the time she was old enough to join, the reading lists reveal an eclectic mix, including the gothic novel *Castle of Wolfenbach* by prolific Plymouth-born writer Eliza Parsons. German heiress Matilda is fleeing from her lecherous uncle as the book opens, with an obligatory old castle, thunderstorm and straight away, the fainting:

'The clock from the old castle had just gone eight when the peaceful inhabitants of a neighbouring cottage, on the skirts of the wood, were about to seek that repose which labour had rendered necessary ... The evening was cold and tempestuous, the rain poured in torrents, and the distant thunders rolled with tremendous noise round the adjacent mountains, whilst the pale lightning added horrors to the scene. Pierre was already in bed, and Jaqueline preparing to follow, when the trampling of horses was heard ... He opened the door, and discovered a man supporting a lady who appeared almost fainting.'

Lightheaded Matilda is not happy with sleeping on the floor in the kindly couple's hovel and asks about the neighbours. Well there is the old Count at the castle, says Jaqueline, but does not recommend a visit: 'O! dear madam, why it is haunted; there are bloody floors, prison rooms, and scriptions, they say, on the windows, to make a body's hair stand on end.'

Matilda sets off immediately. Not unexpectedly, she ends up embroiled in a story of incest, kidnap and eventually, love, with a fair amount of running around castle corridors that echo with ghastly shrieks.

It is worth this sideways look at the gothic fiction that fed Maria's imagination as a young woman, in the context of her Celtic upbringing and all that was to follow in Yorkshire. The stories fed Charlotte Brontë's imagination too, to permanent effect. Ellen Nussey relates how Charlotte thrilled her friends as a girl at Roe Head School in Yorkshire with a terrifying tale of a sleepwalker. It has a familiar ring:

> 'She brought together all the horrors her imagination could create, from surging seas, raging breakers, towering castle walls, high precipices, invisible chasms and dangers. Having wrought these materials to the highest pitch effect, she brought out, in almost cloud-height, her somnambulist, walking on shaking turrets...'

From this imagination was to spring *Jane Eyre* and the madwoman in the attic.

Scary romances were not all Maria Branwell read. An unlikely-sounding source of sensational tales was the *Methodist Magazine*. John Kingston was not alone in writing about the highs and lows of preaching life. These tended to concentrate on dramatic conversions, wrestles with the devil and, especially, an exact record of the ecstatic words spoken by Evangelicals as they died. These were presented as regular proof of an eager exit from life and easy entry to Heaven.

Pamphlets and the press were a large a part of Maria's reading life and the new century brought a new newspaper. *The Royal Cornwall Gazette* was launched in 1801, a rival to the *Sherborne Mercury*, which had been the only one sold in town.

Well-heeled Maria, duly protected in pattens, crossed paths daily with an intriguing mix of people, from sailors to scientists, radical preachers to redcoats, émigrés to eminent landowners. She lived in the commercial and social heart of town, part of a family connected to it all. Her place in society was bolstered by good business, good marriages and good works. The Branwells were, above all, impeccably respectable. For gentleman, town councillor and churchman Thomas Branwell, then, the scandal that rocked his household in 1807 was almost unendurable.

Maria's sister Jane Kingston had lived an eventful life since leaving Penzance with her husband John. From St Austell they moved to Launceston, then left Cornwall for Nottingham and then on to Shrewsbury in Shropshire. Along the way she had four children, Thomas, Anne, John, and Maria. And while Jane was juggling house moves and childcare, John was living an even more eventful secret life that was about to shatter her world.

He was superintendent minister on the circuit so when he was caught stealing from the Book Fund, everyone soon found out. However, there was a far more serious accusation, improper behaviour towards two young men where his behaviour was 'very vile', coded language for homosexual encounters. He was kicked out of the movement at the July 1807 Methodist Conference in Liverpool. Conference minutes record only: 'Has any Preacher been expelled this year? A. John Kingston.' The unpublicized charges were embezzlement – and sodomy.

The following day, preacher George Lowe wrote to Wesleyan luminary Mary Fletcher in Shropshire with details of the less shocking crime: 'Mr Kingn. I believe has taken upwards of £100 of Book money with him.' Mary knew Kingston and elsewhere refers to him as a bad man. Strong words from Methodism's leading lady. Rules laid down by John Wesley himself stated that once Kingston was sacked it was 'as though he was naturally dead'. In 1807, sodomy was a hanging offence and Kingston had already hastily decamped across the Atlantic to America, dragging a miserable, pregnant Jane and the children with him. They moved to Baltimore, Maryland, where John had been a preacher. He set up in publishing while she gave birth to her last baby. Elizabeth, known as Eliza, was born in July 1808 when Jane was 34.

It is impossible to tell whether the stress of the Kingston affair affected Thomas' health, but it seems no coincidence that within a year of his daughter and grandchildren being forced abroad to escape ignominy, Thomas Branwell was dead. There is no record of his baptism and stranger still, no notices or obituaries marking his death. But he was buried in the family vault on 8 April 1808 and his will has survived the centuries. He died a rich man, leaving an estate worth £3,500 to his male heir Benjamin, with provision made for his wife and daughters.

Each woman received £50 a year from various property rents. By comparison, a female servant in Penzance earned £4 a year. Even these rents would revert to Benjamin when they died but Elizabeth at least saved enough of this annuity to play a significant role in the Brontë story. By the age of 24 Maria Branwell had inherited a comfortable private income for life.

For Jane in Baltimore with her bad man, her father's will threw her a lifeline. Thomas clearly understood that she was unhappy and equally clear that her annuity 'may not be at the disposal or subject or liable to the control or Engagements of her said Husband, but only at her own sole and separate disposal'. That man was not to get his hands on a single penny. It was her chance to get away and she took it. The money liberated Jane from her marriage to John Kingston, though leaving him came at a terrible price. She arrived home in Penzance in May 1809 with baby Eliza, leaving four children behind with their father.

On Thomas' death, 25 Chapel Street passed to his brother Richard Branwell, but Anne was bequeathed a similar sized house in Causewayhead, Penzance, in the part now known as St Clare Street. As a widow, she may have been allowed to remain living in Chapel Street or she may have moved with her daughters and granddaughter Eliza.

Benjamin's inheritance cemented his place as an influential gentleman and eighteen months after his father's death, he was elected as the mayor of Penzance. Too late for his father to bask in the family success, his mother and four sisters did see him take office on 7 October 1809. Benjamin Carne Branwell took the oath to 'faithfully and uprightly behave yourself' and received £100 in expenses to wine and dine on behalf of the town. He also became the chief magistrate.

Then out of the blue, ten weeks later, Anne, grandmother of Brontë children she would never meet, also died. The cause was not recorded but it came as a shock. A stark announcement in the deaths column of the *Royal Cornwall Gazette* of 23 December 1809 reveals: 'Suddenly, Mrs Branwell, widow of the late Mr. Thos. Branwell, of Penzance, aged 66'. Maria and her family attended Anne's funeral while the rest of Penzance prepared for Christmas feasts and guise-dancing. Anne joined Thomas in the Branwell vault by the sea.

For Maria, it was the end of an era. With their mother's death, she and her sisters faced domestic as well as emotional upheaval. Sons were favoured by inheritance law. Daughters were shunted sideways. Whether they were obliged to move house before or after Anne's death, it meant leaving the only home Maria had ever known. Causewayhead was the third main street of Penzance, after Chapel and Market Jew. Leading out of town to become the country road to Madron, it was the route to every wedding Maria had attended, along with landmark events such as the service to mark the death of Nelson. It did not have the view of the sea or the plum position in the very heart of town, but it was still a respectable address.

Though it must have been difficult to leave the Chapel Street house where she had lived all her life, there were ample compensations. The Branwell sisters were free to run their lives without having to defer to a man. Single mother Jane, outgoing and glamorous Elizabeth, witty and wise Maria, demure Charlotte and little Eliza were free to do as they chose.

Even before her mother's death, it was Maria who held sway in the all-female household. As she would reveal two years later, she was perfectly her own mistress, answering to no-one and consulted by her mother and sisters on all important decisions.

Maria remained pious but the zealous family elders were gone, either to their grave or to Shropshire like the fervent Fennells. Maria and her sisters had bid a fond farewell to cousin Jane Fennell, who left Penzance in 1806 with her parents when she was 15. Brother Benjamin was concerned with his own family and career and Jane was recovering from the traumas of her marriage to an immoral missionary. Though Elizabeth remained a Methodist as the movement moved inexorably towards a split with the Church of England, she also remained a snuff-snorting belle. The Branwell sisters shared a comfortable home and a pooled private income of £200 a year, free to enjoy a golden period of independence.

Meanwhile, 5 February 1811 brought in the Regency era, a decade that brought more unrest than romance. George III succumbed once again to recurring psychiatric illness and his playboy heir, a fourth George, was called upon to keep the throne warm. The profligate and wildly unpopular 49-year-old playboy became Prince Regent, stand-in king.

For the whole of Maria's life, the leader of taste and fashion in Penzance was the larger-than-life Mary Treweeke. She lived in a mansion off Chapel Street behind the Market House, was the first to have a carpet in her home and owned a horse-drawn carriage. She was the prime mover in the creation of the assembly rooms and would know Maria as one of the prominent Branwells, sister of the mayor. Maria's extended family had stakes in the banks and the corporation, so they moved in the same circles.

George Bown Millett shares the adventures of the wealthy widow in a lecture published in 1876 as *Penzance: Past and Present*, including how arriving by carriage, a rare sight, caused a sensation in north Cornwall:

> 'A concert had been announced to take place in that town; and
> some of the inhabitants at least must have known as much about
> concerts as they did about carriages, for when Mrs. Treweeke

was entering St. Ives, having driven from Penzance in her
vehicle of the period, she was followed by an admiring crowd,
shouting, 'The concert is come! the concert is come!!'"

She became a fashion victim for a second time when caught up in a
most undignified accident near Branwell's Corner, though she endured it
magnificently:

'One fine summer afternoon, in the days when ladies wore
skirts so closely fitting that they scarcely allowed of taking
moderately long steps, this same old lady, a portly dame, was
leisurely crossing the upper part of Market-place towards her
house. It happened to be market-day; and a lusty pig, having
broken the tether which bound him to the Market cross, was
hurrying towards Chapel street as fast as his wayward nature
would let him; but pigs are not famous for running in a straight
line, particularly when they are being chivvied by a fat old
farmer, and any number of small boys, so when near Mrs.
Treweeke he suddenly made a dive at her feet, and running
his head between her ankles fairly lifted her off the ground,
carrying her on his back into a china shop which was near;
the old lady keeping her balance however, and holding on
with might and main till she was safely landed on the floor
all among the crockery, much to the dismay of herself and
the proprietor, and to the amusement of the small boys giving
chase in particular.'

Millett adds, 'this somewhat extraordinary story is vouched for by a person
who was living at the time.' One of the amused onlookers presumably. It is
not fanciful to suppose Maria witnessed the commotion, considering the
lusty pig made its bid for freedom on market day.

When Maria was in her late twenties with her own money to spend,
Mrs Treweeke was president of the Ladies Book Club. While Maria was
perfectly her own mistress, the indefatigable doyenne noted her choices in the
ledger as 'Books sent for by Mrs Treweeke' between 1810 and 1812. Among
the magazines and reviews are the latest bestsellers hot off the press. The
gaieties up in Regency fashion HQ were described in comic verse as *The
Wonders of a Week at Bath*. Less frivolous but no less popular was *Self Control:
A Novel* by Mary Brunton. Among its readers was Jane Austen, whose own

first novel *Sense and Sensibility* was published in 1811 – and immediately bought by Mrs Treweeke for the Penzance ladies to read. Maria must have seen striking parallels with her own life. The Dashwood sisters are forced to move home when their father dies and leaves everything to their brother.

Meanwhile, upheavals in her family were beginning to change the direction of Maria Branwell's life. The career of her uncle, John Fennell, caused ripples long after he left Penzance for a headmaster's job in his native Shropshire. He had gone from strength to strength in the Evangelical movement since leaving with Jane his wife and Jane their daughter. Now they were heading north to where Methodism had another stronghold, the rapidly industrializing West Riding of Yorkshire. It was here that Wesleyans decided to open a school for the sons of itinerant preachers. On 21 September 1811 *The Royal Cornwall Gazette* reported:

> 'The Society of Methodists have, it is understood, purchased the superb mansion and grounds at Apperley Bridge in the west riding of Yorkshire ... for the purpose of a public school; to be founded on the model of the school at Kingswood near Bristol, and to be on a scale sufficiently large to accommodate 400 boys, principally the sons of the ministers of that community.'

Soon after came the exciting news that the Fennells had been appointed as the first governor and governess of the school called Woodhouse Grove, beginning in January.

Around this time, Charlotte Branwell became romantically attached to their first cousin, Joseph Branwell. Then came a death at sea. Joseph's brother Thomas drowned during a storm on Christmas Eve 1811. A Royal Navy officer on board the warship HMS *St George,* he was shipwrecked off the Danish coast. Was one of Charlotte's sisters – Maria or Elizabeth – in love with the 33-year-old lieutenant when he died? Elizabeth was closest in age and the only sister never to marry. There is no evidence to provide an answer, though a strange story about the tragedy appeared in the *Naval Chronicle* of early 1812 headed 'Supernatural Appearance':

> 'The father of Lieutenant Thomas Bramwell, late of H.M.S. St. George, now living at Penzance, has been confined to his bed for many years. On Christmas Day, so unfortunate to that ship, and nearly about the time when she perished, the old gentleman called for his daughters, and informed them that he

had seen his son Thomas, very wet, with his hair and clothes covered with sand, and he supposed that he had, in landing, fallen on the beach. He, therefore, desired them to get some refreshment, whilst their brother was shifting his clothes. The young ladies endeavoured, but in vain, to persuade their father that he had not yet returned, though the ship was expected home daily. This story is well known to all in Penzance.'

In March, the distraught old gentleman, Maria's uncle Richard, died. A month later was her 29th birthday, usually a time to take stock, though she had no idea that the twelve months before she turned thirty would bring a rollercoaster of events that would utterly change her life.

They began innocuously enough, with a letter from dear Aunt Jane in Yorkshire, who was feeling the strain in her new job. She was struggling to cope with the domestic needs of the boys pouring into the new Wesleyan boarding school and needed some help. Might her niece come to the rescue? Maria pondered the superb mansion and grounds and the chance to renew her friendship with cousin Jane, now 20. Part of the invitation was to be a companion to her childhood friend, who had no women of her own age at the boys' school. It was certainly tempting.

Without doubt, Aunt Fennell would have couched her S.O.S. in terms of God's will. Like Cornwall, God's own county was experiencing an Evangelical revival and it was all hands on deck. Wesley had been very big on the duty to be a useful Christian and her aunt needed help. Maria decided that a working holiday would be an adventure. With her parents dead and seemingly no romance to detain her, she made a fateful decision to visit Yorkshire. Possibly she had already been to Truro, Bath or Bristol. She knew well-travelled people and her sister Jane had been to America and back. Still, travelling 400 miles solo to Yorkshire was quite the undertaking and it took courage to answer the summons. Some time between April and June, Maria's trunk was packed and travel arrangements made. The school had just one holiday a year, a month beginning on 29 April. This may have been when Aunt Jane sent for reinforcements before the pupils returned.

All that was left were goodbyes. Walking was an intrinsic part of Maria's life. Her farewell wander over Cornish sand and soil with her sisters and little niece was maybe at sunset, like one described here by the lyrical Dr Paris:

'In the vicinity of the town are delightful walks through shady dingles, and over swelling hills, from whose summits we catch the most delicious sea and land prospects; and which are not a little heightened in beauty and effect by the glowing aerial tints so remarkably displayed in this climate at the rising and setting of the sun.'

As we shall learn from her own pen, Maria Branwell adored where she was born and raised, this place of delicious views of sea and land. Friends and family were all the world to her. Regency Penzance was busy and beautiful and she was plugged into life there as only an educated, well-connected gentlewoman with an independent income could be.

Yet one fine day in 1812, Maria Branwell embarked on a journey never to return.

Chapter 3

The Adventures of Pat Prunty

The 21-year-old caught kissing the landowner's daughter was a charismatic young man with ambition. He was also about to get the sack. The girl was 16 and Pat Prunty was her teacher. This became the least of his problems, though, as he was swept up in both the Evangelical revival and the Irish Rebellion of 1798, propelling him towards England and another educated woman of means, Maria Branwell of Penzance.

Before his career took a dive and Ireland was shredded by violence, life had been going well. Young Mr Prunty was born in Emdale in Drumballyroney, County Down, on St Patrick's Day 1777. He took his first breath on 17 March in a two-roomed hut with a thatched roof and mud floor. Hugh and Eleanor (known as Alice) Prunty named their firstborn after the saint who walked with a staff and drove snakes into the sea. The family moved to a bigger house up the road in Lisnacreevy, then to a farmhouse in Ballynaskeagh. Patrick was followed by four brothers – William, Hugh, James and Walsh – then five sisters, Jane, Mary, twins Rose and Sarah, then Alice.

Patrick grew up as the eldest son of a large family but had no intention of following his father into farming. In the years to come, he was in no hurry to reveal the whole story of why he left Ireland, either. His life there was boiled down to 'a few facts' to biographer Elizabeth Gaskell on 20 June 1855 as she prepared to pen *The Life of Charlotte Bronte*:

> 'My father's name, was Hugh Brontë – He was a native of the South of Ireland, and was left an orphan at an early age – It was said that he was of an Ancient Family. Whether this was, or was not so, I never gave myself the trouble to inquire, since his lot in life, as well as mine, depended, under providence, not on Family decent [sic], but our own exertions. He came to the North of Ireland, and made an early, but suitable marriage. His pecuniary means were small – but renting a few

acres of land, He and my mother, by dint of application, and industry, managed to bring up a family of ten Children, in a respectable manner.'

Patrick's childhood was as rich in Celtic myth, legend and storytelling as Maria's in Cornwall. Hugh had a reputation as a bard, a teller of old Irish tales, and the ancient family was that of famous poet, scribe and scholar Pádraig Ó Prontaigh. Patrick professes no interest in the claim but still puts it on record, albeit obliquely. He certainly was a scholar himself, developing a passion for reading and education at the village school in Glascar that would shape his life:

'I shew'd an early fondness for books, and continued at school for several years. – At the age of sixteen, knowing that my Father could afford me no pecuniary aid I began to think of doing something for myself – I therefore opened a public school – and in this line, I continued five or six years; I was then a Tutor in a Gentleman's Family – From which situation I removed to Cambridge, and enter'd St John's College.'

Thus Patrick dispatched the crucial years of his early manhood, though he was 25 when he crossed the Irish Sea. This was as much as he wished to discuss in public and with good reason. A little local scandal of his own making, dangerous politics in the family and the influence of a powerful patron had created a perfect storm that meant he must chase his ambitions in England.

Staying on at school without the bank of mum and dad was achieved by taking a part-time job as a boy with a local blacksmith. Even mending horseshoes, he was recognized as having a certain distinction. In old age, Patrick told a friend in Haworth that he never forgot what the blacksmith had said in conversation with a gentlemen customer. He had divided gentlemen up into those who were born to it, those who gained it through good fortune and those, nodding at young Pat, who are 'gentlemen by nature'.

By the age of 16 he was the master of his own small school and earning enough to buy books. Then Patrick fell in love. Edward Chitham identifies her as Jean McAlister. Almost the same age as Maria Branwell and of a similar standing, being the daughter of local squire Andrew McAlister, she was given the non de plume Helen by gallant William Wright, a contemporary of Patrick's from County Down and also a farmer's son.

He was taught classics by Reverend William McAllister who had known Pat as a boy. Wright investigated his past in their corner of Ulster for *The Brontes in Ireland* published in 1893.

He describes Pat's first love as 'a mature maiden' who had stayed on at school with her brothers longer than was usual:

> 'One afternoon, on approaching the farmer's house [hers], the master met his red-haired pupil among the corn-stacks and kissed her. The tender incident was observed by one of the brothers, who immediately reported the result of his observations at headquarters. War was instantly declared ... but the affair became complicated by the fiery-headed Helen ... rushing in and espousing Bronte's cause with great spirit and vigour. When the storm of battle had cleared away, it was discovered that teacher and pupil were desperately in love with each other, and that opposition had only fanned the flame. Helen's pockets and desk were found to be full of Patrick's amatory poetry, and both claimed the right to act as they pleased. It was understood that the first tender advances had been on the lady's part, and her lover felt bound to remain loyal to her so long as she held out.'

They were an influential family and it spelled the end of Patrick's days as a schoolteacher: 'Thus Patrick Bronte, by his own folly, found himself without employment or the prospect of employment in the memorable but miserable years of 1797 and 1798.' Luckily for him another influential man came to the rescue. This one had known him all his life and had been following the young rake's progress. The Reverend Thomas Tighe, landed gentleman and vicar of Drumballyroney, invited him to tutor his sons at the rectory. This is the inconvenient detail Pat skips over for Mrs Gaskell. Between the years as a schoolteacher and becoming a tutor to the gentry he was chased around town by his girlfriend's furious relatives.

Pat's personal problems may have been smoothed over but around him the world grew ever more complicated. While Penzance was united in being an enemy to the French, in Ireland it was a different matter. The downtrodden majority, ruled from England through a Protestant aristocracy, felt an affinity with the call for freedom and reform across the water. All Ireland was talking about the new American democracy when Pat was born and the French Revolution while he was growing up.

He was a schoolboy and blacksmith in 1791 when the Society of United Irishmen was formed. Conceived as bringing political and religious groups together to end the English control of Ireland, leaders looked to revolutionary France for support. When war with France was declared, the group was outlawed but continued as a secret organization, bolstered by the French who tried, and failed, to launch an invasion of England from Ireland in the winter of 1796.

In 1798 the United Irishmen staged a series of republican uprisings and in June the Irish Rebellion arrived on Pat's doorstep. County Down became an actual battleground and the Protestant Pruntys found themselves in the thick of it. At least one of Pat's brothers, William, joined the outlaws and took the secret oath. Soldiers interrogated blacksmiths about where the rebels were getting their metal pikes. At just 19, William fought in the battle of Ballynahinch. The rebels were decimated – their pikes no match for army pistols – and he fled, hiding from the vicious reprisals inflicted by government troops.

The rebellion to win self-rule was answered instead with the Act of Union, binding Britain and Ireland together. In 1801 Penzance it was marked merely with a change of name for the most popular pub in town. In County Down, it was a milestone in centuries of sectarian conflict. Pat came of age amid this violent political turmoil. The shocking events of the crushed rebellion and having a brother on the run made him a lifelong opponent of armed revolution. He saw the bloody consequences up close and would fear radical uprisings for the rest of his life. Bill Prunty might want to overthrow the establishment, but Pat Prunty did not.

He found the call to Christian reform more to his taste. Patrick's employer and patron Thomas Tighe was a Protestant with clout. A prominent Anglican clergyman, he had known the young Prunty since he was a child, witnessed his driven quest for an education and got to know him well in the four years he worked for the family.

Like Thomas Branwell of Penzance, Thomas Tighe of Drumballyroney was an Evangelical. And like Maria's family, the Tighes welcomed the tireless John Wesley as a friend whenever he was in town. He stayed with the Tighe family in 1789 just before he went to Penzance for the final time when Maria was six. The invisible ties that were to draw Patrick and Maria together were already being woven.

Patrick was impressed by both the loyalties and lifestyle of his mentor. Tighe instilled his protégé with an Evangelical mindset. He also taught him how to shoot a pistol. This combination of commitment to established order with the pursuit of social progress, notably education for the poor, hit home with Pat. A career in the church could offer everything he wanted and the vicar agreed, recommending his own university in England. A vocation was one thing but winning a place at St John's College, Cambridge, was another. Patrick could only go if he was accepted as a sizar, a charity place with reduced fees in exchange for basic accommodation and lower status. The college prided itself in offering a leg up to poor but clever male applicants. Tighe wrote letters attesting to Patrick's education and recommending him for the scholarship.

In 1802, the 25-year-old farmer's son, self-taught teacher and potential priest Pat Prunty set sail for England. Like Maria Branwell, he had embarked on a life-changing adventure and would never return to the land of his birth. He took his meagre life savings and a mindset for life. Education was the answer to everything, it paid to have influential friends and it was a good idea to carry a pistol.

Day one at university proved unintentionally momentous in the story of the Brontës. In common with Maria's family of Brummoles, Bramwells and Branwells, various recording clerks had called Patrick's family Brunty, Bruntee and Prunty. As he stepped up to register as an undergraduate, his northern Irish accent was an unfamiliar one. The registrar misheard Prunty and made a guess with Branty. It was rare for an Irishman to be standing in the college at all. Thus 'Patrick Branty' was written in the admissions book of the centuries old college and 'Ireland' was the scribe's only note for county of residence. He did not bother straining his English ears further by asking for the required details of the new sizar's parents, birthday or education.

The Branwells of Penzance were bigshots by 1802 and if someone misspelled Maria's name it would be corrected. Patrick, on the other hand, was a young nobody and fate had handed him a new identity. When he saw the misspelling two days later, he had his name changed – not to Prunty but to Bronte, the deity of thunder in Greek mythology. New century, new country, new name. Why not? Pat Prunty had already come a long way but Patrick Bronte had much further to go.

Patrick was already destined to stand out at university and not just for his working class brogue. He was almost a decade older than the other freshmen. Most teenage students had merely moved to Cambridge as the next step after an expensive public school, an automatic privilege. Above all, he was set apart by being a sizar. Being subsidized by the college meant being generally ignored or looked down on by largely aristocratic classmates.

One way to win friends and influence people was to join the local Volunteer corps bracing for a Napoleonic invasion, like Maria's brother in Penzance. The college corps was led by 19-year-old nobleman Henry John Temple, the future Prime Minister Lord Palmerston. Patrick had great faith in knowing how to handle a gun in a crisis and relished this call to arms. As Ellen Nussey later observed:

> 'From Mr Brontë's conversation it was evident he delighted in the perusal of Battle scenes and in the artifice of war, had he entered on Military instead of Ecclesiastical service he would probably have had a very distinguished career.'

Patrick powered through four years as an undergraduate, subsisting on self-belief and very little money. He even gave advice to a new sizar on the art of living frugally. Henry Kirke White was a butcher's son from Nottingham. He joined the Evangelical crowd at Cambridge and though feted as a brilliant young poet and scholar, he was also broke. Patrick explained the financial facts of life in October 1805, as Henry wrote to his mother:

> 'Mr. [Bronte] ... has been at college three years. He came over ... with 10*l* [£] in his pocket, and has no friends, or any income or emolument whatever, except what he receives for his sizarship; yet he does support himself and that, too, very genteelly.'

That £10 saved from his decade of teaching work was his admission fee and he had been surviving ever since on academic cash prizes. If they ate only milk-and-bread breakfasts plus free dinners and suppers, with wine on feast days, Pat told young Henry, they need not starve. However, by his final year Pat was casting around for that other necessity of impoverished scholars, a rich sponsor. He appealed to St John alumni, making it known he wanted to train for the ministry. Evangelical cousins Henry Thornton and William Wilberforce, the anti-slavery campaigner, stepped in with a grant.

The path to being a parson now more secure, Pat graduated in April 1806 as a Bachelor of Arts and with a useful clutch of Evangelical friends. He was then ordained as a deacon, stage one of holy orders, in the chapel of Fulham Palace. Here his name edged closer to immortality, acquiring an acute accent as Bronté, which would come and go in the following years. Sometimes he used it, sometimes not. Sometimes the accent faced one way, sometimes the other.

Ireland forever behind him, he headed to the quintessential English village of Wethersfield in Essex for his first job as a brand-new curate. Vicar Joseph Jowett spent most of his time in Cambridge where he was a law professor. Patrick was thrown in at the deep end, running the rural parish while Dr Jowett was away.

He arrived in the autumn of 1806 to lodge with the respectable and well-educated Mildred Davy, a seventy-year-old spinster. St George's House was close to St Mary Magdalene Church.

At 29 years old, Pat had a degree, a dog collar (or rather, cravat) and a job. Sadly, his impoverished chum Henry White did not fare so well. A week after Pat embarked on his new career in October 1806, Henry died of exhaustion and fever at 21 in his college rooms. His works were collected and published by Robert Southey as *The Remains of Henry Kirke White*, the book Maria later bought in Penzance.

Days before Christmas of the following year, 1807, Patrick travelled to the glitzy Chapel Royal of St James, Westminster, to be ordained priest by no less than the king's own chaplain, John Fisher, Bishop of Salisbury. The boy blacksmith was now the Reverend Patrick Brontë.

It had been a long time since the passionate young man had enjoyed any kind of love life. His college had a rule of celibacy. Even if it had not he could barely feed himself throughout his twenties, let alone a girlfriend. Perhaps that is why he fell so hard for the first girl he met in that chocolate-box town.

Mary Burder was almost 18 years old and lived three miles from Patrick's digs on her family's large farm. She was Miss Davy's niece and her father had died shortly before Patrick arrived. The story of their meeting was told to Liberal politician and author Augustine Birrell for his *Life of Charlotte Brontë* in 1887. He tracked down 'a daughter of the heroine of the tale of true love…' who 'I have to thank for her great kindness in putting upon paper the story as she heard it from her mother…'

The tale of true love started out well enough, with Mary being sent over with some game for her aunt. She went to the kitchen, rolled up her sleeves and began preparing the bird for her aunt's dinner. Which is how Patrick found the 'comely damsel, with her father's brown curls and her mother's blue eyes'. He was smitten and though 'subject to great tidal waves of passion' during their courtship, refused to talk about his background, sticking only to his reinvented self: 'He often showed her letters from titled friends and distinguished persons, but she would rather have seen the shortest, simplest home-letter.' Patrick was determined to disguise just how simple his home was.

Mary and Pat wanted to marry but until she was 21, she needed the permission of her uncle. Unfortunately, Mary's guardian was no more likely to give permission than Jean McAlister's family. Uncle Burder had no intention of Mary marrying the Irishman with the mysterious past. In late 1808, he ordered her over to stay at his home in Great Yeldham, eight miles away, while intercepting any letters between the sweethearts.

When Mary returned to Wethersfield in early 1809 Patrick had gone, to a new job in the Midlands. All that remained were her letters, left for her to find:

> 'When the poor girl opened the little bundle, thinking there might be some explanatory word, there was none; but she found a small card with her lover's face in profile, and under it the words, 'Mary, you have torn the heart; spare the face'.'

Patrick's attachment had come unstuck, though not for the reasons Birrell believed. For years, Mary thought he would come back for her. He never did and she came to realize it was not just her family's opposition to their marriage that had ended their engagement, it was that she would have held him back. As Birrell observed: 'She was not ... a member of Mr. Brontë's congregation, for she 'worshipped in the meeting-house'.'

Mary was a committed Nonconformist. As she pined away in Great Yeldham, Pat had time to develop cold feet. In November 1808, he became convinced God was keeping them apart. An Anglican man on the up could not marry a Dissenter and he revealed as much in a letter to his college friend John Campbell, now a curate near Leicester:

> 'The Lady I mentioned, is always in exile; her Guardians can scarcely believe me, that I have given the affair entirely up forever. All along, I violated both the dictates of my conscience and my judgment. "Be not unequally yoked", says the Apostle.'

The apostle was Paul writing to the Corinthians. Never a fan of marriage at the best of times, Paul was most assuredly against being yoked to a non-Christian, which as a Congregationalist, Mary seemingly sort of was to Patrick. He wanted a 'suitable marriage' like his parents but poor Mary was not suitable, she was a Dissenter. For an ambitious Anglican with only his wits and his will to propel him up the career ladder, Miss Burder would be a burden.

He wrote to his friends agonizing over his decision but seemingly never spelled out to Mary that she could consider herself unyoked. She spent years expecting him to return before it dawned on her he never would. No wonder she was bitter when, fourteen years later, Patrick wrote to her out of the blue as a widower. When he had the gall to try to rekindle the relationship her reply dripped with a decade and a half of pent-up sarcasm:

> 'Happily for me I have not been the ascribed cause of hindering your promotion, of preventing any brilliant alliance, nor have those great and affluent friends that you used to write and speak of withheld their patronage on my account, young, inexperienced, unsuspecting, and ignorant as I then was of what I had a right to look forward to.'

She may have been waiting to get that off her chest because it was only then that she married someone else. None of this stopped Patrick rewriting his romantic history, according to Ellen Nussey, when he 'boasted, as he did occasionally, of the conquests made in his earlier days...'

Patrick's new job in January 1809 was as curate of All Saints Church in Wellington, very different to the bucolic parish he left behind. Wellington was a place of coalmines and iron foundries, merchants and banks and the church was new. Here was growing wealth but also poverty. His new vicar was St John's graduate John Eyton. With poor health and another chapel in the parish, the vicar had employed Pat as a second curate for the clergy team. The other was William Morgan, a jolly Welshman who was as ambitious as Patrick and they hit it off immediately.

He was the son of a yeoman farmer in the South Wales village of Crickadarn and shared Pat's commitment to working class education. Through his new best friend, Patrick met the headmaster of the local school, one John Fennell, his wife Jane and their 18-year-old daughter. Maria's aunt, uncle and cousin were now Patrick's new friends.

What Wellington lacked in scenery, it made up for in career opportunities. Shropshire was the domain of that famous maven of Methodism, Mary Fletcher of Madeley. The widow of Uncle Fennell's saintly godfather, Mary still held court at the old vicarage and was a powerful fixer. She helped promising preachers and teachers by drawing them into her charmed Madeley circle. Patrick was introduced to the group by Morgan and while he was always church not chapel, he felt very at home among the Wesleyans.

This was the same year that Jane Kingston arrived home in Penzance, so it is not impossible that Maria's family came up in conversation. The Evangelical grapevine buzzed with constant written communication. Jane's return from her exile with the bad man John Kingston will have been known by the Fennells and noted by Fletcher.

However, more of the conversation turned on the demand for leaders to fuel the revival at home and abroad. Mary was an influential voice and she liked the look of this latest crop. John Fennell was practically family, while William Morgan and Patrick Bronté also had drive. The talk around the circle was all about Yorkshire, considered the Promised Land for promising young men because of its rising urban population of potential converts.

Pat desperately wanted to serve in this Evangelical northern powerhouse and after a word in the right ear from Mary, he was offered a curacy at another All Saints, the parish church of Dewsbury, West Yorkshire. She also helped engineer the Woodhouse Grove job for John Fennell and William Morgan was destined to join renowned minister John Crosse at Bradford Parish Church. Once again, Mrs Fletcher had a pivotal role in the life of Maria Branwell and ultimately, her daughters.

Considering the circuitous routes the parents of the Brontës were following, the most exceptional fork in the road was a letter Pat received while packing for the Promised Land. It was a letter from Cambridge and stopped him in his tracks. His old college tutor was offering an altogether more exotic posting as chaplain to the governor of Martinique. Fortunately, Pat was more drawn to West Yorkshire than the West Indies. He did not fancy the Caribbean and boarded a stagecoach to the Calder Valley instead.

Patrick Bronté arrived in Yorkshire in December 1809. His new vicar was John Buckworth, a star of the Church of England Evangelical wing. He was two years younger than Patrick and married to Rachel, of the wealthy manufacturing Halliley family. They gave him a room at the impressive fourteenth-century vicarage.

Patrick's new church (now Dewsbury Minster) came with a lot of history. Founded as a place of worship around 627 by St Paulinus when he baptized converts in the River Calder, it evolved over 1,000 years into an important mother church. Along with Saxon, Norman and Tudor features, medieval stained glass depicted a strange array of saints and monsters. Entombed beneath the floor lay Vikings but also a Yorkshireman called Henry Tilson. He was a protestant bishop in Ireland who fled home after the earlier Irish Rebellion of 1641.

Even Pat's lodgings were suffused with centuries of ecclesiastical mystery. A rambling, ivy-clad building from 1349, it was said to be haunted by the ghost of a woman in green. His rooms were a former butler's pantry, panelled with oak and near the garden where he liked to compose his sermons. It was all very comfortable and Patrick soon hit it off with his boss and his wife.

While the Buckworths were well off and the vicarage more of a manor house, out in the parish times were hard. The industrial revolution was disrupting established ways of earning a living and forcing more people into town to work in the woollen mills. Buckworth drove himself hard at the cost of his frail health and expected his curate to take up the slack. Pat played to his strengths, taking on the new Sunday School and teaching children to read and write, while visiting the flock in their cottages.

These visits would have involved a more demanding linguistic challenge than learning Latin as a scholar. The Ulsterman, often misheard himself as in Cambridge, had to master the broad West Riding dialect of his new congregation. Patrick is often remembered as slightly odd or withdrawn in company. Early struggles with very different regional accents must have played a part.

'Though somewhat austere, Mr Brontë was much liked by those swift and often correct readers of character, little children,' according to William Walsh Yates, editor of the *Dewsbury Reporter* and a founder member of the Brontë Society in 1893. In *The Father of the Brontës* four years later, Patrick is remembered as a complex character and described by one parishioner as 'a very earnest man, but a little peculiar in his manner'.

Yates was a journalist all his life and investigated Pat's life with the help of his readers. The *Reporter* reveals that Mr Brontë was a man of commanding appearance:

> 'He was tall and spare but his figure was good, and he was remarkable for agility and strength. In temper he was hot and impetuous, especially when he saw wrong doing, and it was only by the exercise of a resolute will that he at times prevented an outburst.'

Pat was quickly forgiven his eccentricities when he proved himself invaluable in a crisis. 'Though Mr. Brontë's stay in Dewsbury was not a long one, it was marked with stirring incidents,' reports Yates, who spent twenty years unearthing memories from elderly Dewsbury parishioners and their descendants. Stirring incident number one happened almost as soon as he got there, some time during the winter of 1809.

Taking a stroll from the vicarage along the Calder, which was swollen with rainwater, he saw a group of lads messing around near the water. They were tormenting 'an older boy of rather weak intellect'.

One bully gave the vulnerable boy a push, who 'to the horror of all, fell into the water and was instantly battling for life'. Patrick sprang into action:

> 'They screamed, and the gentleman, turning, ran back, and plunged into the flooded and swiftly-flowing river, and succeeded, though with evident difficulty, in reaching the drowning boy and bringing him to the bank.'

Pat revived the boy with learning difficulties and took him home to his widowed mother. Hatless, soaking wet and shivering, he stopped to remonstrate with the culprits then, 'he strode off, changed his walk to a run, and was soon out of sight'. Peculiar, but in a good way.

Patrick won more plaudits for standing up to a notorious thug and his cronies in front of the whole town. Whitsuntide, celebrated around the feast of Pentecost in June, was marked every year in Dewsbury with the Whit Tuesday walk. This was a procession of Sunday School children and teachers from Dewsbury to the village of Earlsheaton less than a mile away. There they would have The Sing on the town green, then walk back for a picnic with gallons of tea. Traditionally, the children would have items of new clothing or shoes for the occasion.

In the summer of 1810, Patrick took the lead. It was a gorgeous, sunny day and the whole parish was in holiday mood. Everyone, that is, apart from a 'notorious cockfighter and boxer' who was lying in wait, drunk and ready to rumble. He ran in front of the procession, spread his burly arms wide and swore at the children, telling them to go back to Dewsbury:

> 'As the scholars were marching up, a tall and lusty man seeing them approach, deliberately planted himself in their path, and would not move an inch. Mr. Brontë, seeing this, walked quickly up, and without a word, seized the fellow by the collar, and by one effort flung him across the road, and then walked by the side of the procession to the Town Green as if nothing unusual had happened, leaving the obstructionist agape with surprise.'

Though impressed with their hero, word during The Sing was that the thugs would be waiting for them on the way back and 'revenge would be taken':

> 'The procession re-formed, but many of the teachers and other scholars seemed afraid for their curate. Mr Brontë led the way, evidently expecting the man would again annoy the children, and prepared to do battle for his charges. The obstructionist was near the spot where he was so discomfited, along with several companions, but made no attempt to interfere with either parson or flock. The encounter, one our informant states, was the subject of conversation in and about Dewsbury for weeks.'

The curate was known as the man who did not miss a heartbeat before rescuing a drowning boy or defending all the town's children from an aggressive bully.

Pat had lived with John and Rachel Buckworth for several months when he had to move out. They needed the vicarage for a new project, training missionaries for India, so he decamped to the Ancient-Well House forty yards away, owned by a lawyer, Elliot Carrett. Carrett's daughter shared the landlord's opinion of the curate with Yates, which was that Pat was 'clever and good-hearted, but hot-tempered, and in fact, a little queer'.

Pat had shown his physical courage in the freezing Calder and during the Whitsuntide stand-off, but his moral courage was equally impressive. In Dewsbury, he decided the printed word was key to his calling. Buckworth wrote hymns and had his sermons printed. Patrick began preaching in print in early 1810 with *Winter-evening Thoughts*. It must have been a long evening. The twenty-page poem is a dire warning about the wages of sin, from prostitution to shipwrecks. An extension of his ministry, Pat was keen to be a literary Evangelical like his esteemed boss and friends back in Madeley.

Before 1810 was over, Patrick had once again rushed to defend a parishioner, this time by wielding his pen. William Nowell, described as an industrious and respectable young man of Dewsbury, was thrown into prison accused of deserting the army after enlisting at a local horse fair. In fact, Nowell had never been at the fair but was arrested on the word of another Dewsbury man, James Thackray, who claimed he had accepted the king's shilling. When Nowell did not appear at regimental headquarters at Wakefield – having never actually enlisted – soldiers turned up at the bewildered weaver's home. Despite his father rounding up seven people to attest in court to William's whereabouts far from the fair, he was thrown in jail as a deserter.

Patrick's lengthy and impassioned letter in the *Leeds Mercury* on 15 December under the pseudonym 'Sydney' laid out the facts of 'this extraordinary and cruel affair' and the anguish of the boy's parents. 'Sydney' underlined how easy it was for a man to lose his liberty to a single lie, despite a cast iron alibi.

Dewsbury was incensed and Nowell's supporters demanded a re-hearing. After fifteen more witnesses were produced, young Nowell was finally released. He had spent ten miserable weeks in jail and vowed to have Thackray prosecuted. Patrick's intervention was key. He appealed to his old sponsor, Yorkshire MP William Wilberforce, who joined the campaign, and to his old Volunteers corps officer Palmerston, now Secretary of State for War. Palmerston wrote personally to the Rev. P. Bronte from the War Office, vindicating the crusade and offering to pay Nowell's legal bills. The letter was published in the *Mercury*:

> 'Sir, Referring to the correspondence relative to William Nowell, I am to acquaint you, that I feel so strongly the injury that is likely to arise to the service from an unfair mode of recruiting, that if by the indictment which the lad's friends are about to prefer against James Thackray they shall establish the fact of his having been guilty of perjury, I shall be ready to indemnify them for the reasonable and proper expence, which they shall incur on the occasion. I am, Sir, Yours, &c
> PALMERSTON'

Thackray was indeed convicted for perjury and transported overseas for seven years. For Patrick, it was about more than the young weaver and his grateful parents. It was not even about such gratifyingly public proof of friends in high places. It was, as he wrote in the *Mercury*, that justice could prevail without insurrection, even in wartime:

> 'It is a proud reflection, and a source of consolation in these times, that while the iron hand of despotism [Napoleon] is falling fast over the Continent of Europe, we Englishmen, still enjoy the pure administration of justice; that we have laws to regulate the conduct of every man from a beggar to a king, and that no station however low, no rank however high, can screen from justice, him that doeth wrong.'

It is Pat's clearest statement of his belief in law and order, the root of his Tory leanings, and loyalty to his new home among 'we Englishmen'. Station or rank being irrelevant to fair play might account for why he startled the congregation very soon afterwards by announcing from the pulpit that he was going on strike.

Patrick often conducted services at St Peter's Church out at Hartshead-cum-Clifton, Liversedge, for the ailing curate there, taking his young assistant Joseph Tolson. They rode over side by side on horseback. Tolson was a weaver's apprentice who stood in as clerk. One Sunday John Buckworth asked his curate to cover the Hartshead services in the morning and afternoon, then take the Dewsbury service in the evening. He wanted to attend a family gathering with Rachel's relatives at their house, the Aldams. Patrick agreed but Yates explains: 'When returning to Dewsbury both were caught in a thunderstorm and drenched with rain.' Pat always had a fear of developing a chest complaint, having buried enough people who caught a chill and went straight downhill. Sopping wet and freezing cold, he went straight to the Halliley home with Joseph tagging along behind.

> 'On arriving he was met by Mr Halliley, senr. [Rachel's father], to whom he explained ... that being wet to the skin, he wished Mr. Buckworth to officiate instead. On hearing this Mr. Halliley exclaimed, and very likely in jest, 'What! keep a dog and bark himself.' Mr. Brontë saw no fun in the remark, but taking it to be a deliberate insult, was highly incensed.'

Without saying a word, Pat turned around and both men went home to grab dry clothes and a bite to eat. When Joseph reached the church he saw, ominously, 'Mr. Brontë was already there, and seemingly quite cool and collected.' Until he climbed into the pulpit to deliver his sermon:

> 'If the congregation were at all sleepy that evening, they must soon have been aroused, for he announced that it was not his intention to preach again after that evening, giving as his reason that he had been most grievously insulted.'

He said not another word on the matter, preached his sermon and left the congregation abuzz. Patrick was as good as his word, though it risked stalling his career when the Hartshead incumbent finally died. Luckily, the vicar understood why the hard-working curate, local hero and friend of Palmerston was so upset. He had surely winced when he learned what his high-handed father-in-law had said. It was the sort of thing that earned the mill owner his nickname, the King of Dewsbury.

Though Dewsbury was the mother church, like Madron to Penzance, Hartshead came with the title of perpetual curate and a small living. Pat used the professional network that allowed Evangelical Anglicans, still the minority, to find work and at the age of 33, he finally had his own church.

St Peter's Church was built by the Normans before 1120 and remodelled in the late middle ages. There were commanding views across the south Pennines from every corner of the churchyard and an ancient yew tree dating back to when the church was built. It was reputed to have been where Robin Hood took the wood for his last arrows before he died. Inside were items donated by the Armytage family, longstanding benefactors whose family seat was Kirklees Hall. It was on their land that Hood was reputed to lie buried near the remains of a mediaeval nunnery. The injured hero sought help from his kinswoman the prioress, but she was in league with villainous Red Roger of Doncaster and bled him to death instead. In 1811, it was the home of Sir George Armytage and his family. Their coat of arms may have made Patrick smile. The crest featured a bent arm holding a staff like the one he carried everywhere.

Beautiful, if crumbling, Pat's first church served several villages and had none of the pretentions of either the mother church or its vicarage. Hartshead had no parsonage at all. He found lodgings that reminded him of home, with Peter and Harriott Bedford at Lousy Farm, later called Thornbush. Lousy was an old English word for thorny, referring to the upland vegetation. The Bedfords were tenant farmers like his parents. Peter was the butler at Kirklees Hall before a terrible accident. The gig he was driving overturned. His first wife was killed and he broke both arms and one leg. By the time Patrick met him seven years later, he had remarried and they had two little sons. It is likely that Harriott also worked at the Hall and between them they knew how to make a man comfortable.

Both his home and his low-roofed church stood in a glorious position high on the moor between Cleckheaton and Huddersfield and Patrick had a short walk to work across the fields. With a lot fewer baptisms and burials to perform up in Hartshead than down in densely populated and disease-riven Dewsbury, he had time to write. Alongside his contributions in the *Mercury* he began writing letters to the *Leeds Intelligencer* on parochial matters.

In 1811, he produced another book, *Cottage Poems,* with an instructive tone 'for the lower classes of society' that includes *Verses sent to a lady on her birth-day*, evidently from the days of Mary Burder. Though she has 'eyes of startling blue, And velvet lips, of scarlet hue' his possibly misjudged birthday message includes: 'You're but a breathing mass of clay, Fast ripening for the grave.'

It is difficult to guess at Patrick's feelings when he included lines he wrote at the height of his doomed infatuation. Especially as this was around the time that Mary turned 21 and could have married without permission. It was a shame things had not worked out. Still, he was pretty pleased with the poem. Curiously, he reworked *Winter-evening Thoughts* as *Winter-night Meditations* starring a woman named Maria. Just why he chose this name for the girl reduced to prostitution and destined for Hell we cannot say, though it must at least have been a talking point later.

He placed an advertisement in the *Leeds Mercury* on 2 November 1811 for the book, priced at three shillings and sixpence. Essentially sermons in rhyme, the content was less significant than the author's name. Patrick submitted his work with an accent over the 'e' in his surname to signify its pronunciation. The printers in Halifax substituted a diaeresis (a mark that does the same thing) and Patrick Bronté the curate became Patrick Brontë the poet. The evolution of that famous name was complete.

Sadly its second outing was in a withering dismissal in *The Monthly Review* of January 1812: 'Mr Brontë courts not the favour of critics; and so far he is right, because critics and he cannot be on good terms.' It was not the best start to 1812 but Pat in Yorkshire, like Maria in Penzance, had no idea what a momentous year this would be.

When his 35th birthday rolled around on 17 March, he had a reputation as an excellent preacher, published poet and defender of the weak but was still single. Even his irrepressible friend William Morgan was on the way to domestic bliss. He was courting young Jane Fennell. Meanwhile, the social unrest that Patrick so hated was ready to erupt afresh and somehow he had landed at the very heart of it. This was to be the year that threw Maria in Penzance, Patrick in Yorkshire and the whole of England into turmoil.

For Patrick Brontë before Maria, it started with the Luddites.

In early 1812, the working people of West Yorkshire were in trouble. From the moment Patrick arrived, tension had been rising over the impact of industrialization on livelihoods. Rapid advances in manufacturing were destroying established ways of working in the wool trade. Suddenly skilled workers saw their jobs taken by new machinery, wide frames that produced inferior but cheaper cloth in mills rather than weavers' cottages and sheds. Among the worst hit on his patch were the croppers, who trimmed new woollen cloth to create a smooth surface. A well-paid family trade for generations, the huge hand-held shears were displaced by mechanical frames and many faced the workhouse.

Times were already hard as the long war with France made trade difficult and kept food prices high. Parish families caught in the middle were going hungry. Some responded by joining the Luddites, a radical movement to defend livelihoods by attacking the machines. It had begun in Nottingham the previous year, when knitters smashed up the new weaving frames with hammers. Frame-breakers were dubbed Luddites after a notional leader called Ned Ludd and protest spread across the Midlands and into the North. The army was put on high alert and Parliament moved to make frame breaking a hanging offence.

The Church of England proved itself the Tory party at prayer, with Evangelicals among the most ferocious in denouncing the protests. By the spring of 1812, the atmosphere of impending violence in the parish was palpable, not unlike it had been in County Down when Pat was younger, before the rebellion, and he joined the clergy in urging restraint from the pulpit.

One of Patrick's colleagues, former Hartshead curate Hammond Roberson, became infamous for his Hellfire warnings to anyone supporting the protests. Still, the secret night time training on the West Riding moors continued and in early April there were a series of frame-breaking attacks on mills around Huddersfield. The *Lancaster Gazette* reported: 'All these outrages, and much worse, are perpetrated without the detection even of a single individual: and thus escaping, the offenders seem, as must naturally be expected, to increase in strength and daring.'

Proof came when men from across the district gathered to drill in silence for an attack on William Cartwright's mill at Rawfolds near Cleckheaton. Cartwright openly challenged the Luddites to attack and wanted to be the one to crush them. As the dark night of the new moon approached, both sides prepared for battle.

Neither Patrick nor anyone else got much sleep on the night of 11 April 1812. The whole area thrummed with tension as upwards of 150 men with hammers, guns and axes gathered near Dumb Steeple, an unmarked obelisk in one of Sir George's fields. With covered faces, they marched across Hartshead moor not far from St Peter's and towards the mill. Cartwright was lying in wait with armed staff and militia inside.

The pitched battle that followed left at least two dead but an unknown number injured or dying. Only two mortally wounded Luddites were left behind as the rest fled, many walking wounded while others were carried. As they scattered, Hartshead cottagers gave what food and help they could as the roads were soaked with blood.

The whole parish was gripped by grief and fear. The retaliation by soldiers was swift and brutal, even among their own ranks. One poor soldier had refused to fire on the Luddites and was sentenced to a fatal flogging outside the mill. Cartwright graciously had the 300 lashes reduced to 25 to appease the appalled crowd that was forced to watch.

Meanwhile, there were bodies to bury. They were the men who had escaped the mill only to die of their injuries in the woods or while being hidden by their relatives and friends. Patrick noticed movement in the graveyard as he walked home one night but he did not investigate. Next morning, he saw freshly disturbed earth in the south-east corner nearest the road but chose not to report it. For at least seven centuries, the people of the moor had been laying their dead to rest at St Peter's. It was not for him to deny them this one consolation.

As the surviving rioters awaited execution or transportation in York cells, Cartwright became an Establishment hero and Roberson built a new church for himself, Christ Church in Liversedge.

The Luddites fought the law and the law won.

But for resilient Patrick Brontë at least, things were about to look up. William Morgan had arrived to work in Bradford just after Patrick took over at Hartshead and they picked up their friendship where they left off. William was now engaged to young Jane Fennell just as her father was organizing his new school. He needed to recruit an external examiner and his future son-in-law recommended Pat, the ex-schoolteacher who taught both church and chapel children their catechism, or Christian principles.

John Fennell remembered Pat from Shropshire and invited him round to the Grove. It was a pleasant escape from the grittier problems at home and all in a good cause. Pat agreed to be the external examiner, reporting to the school committee and Methodist Conference and would get there on foot like St Patrick.

'Mr. Brontë had a shillalagh [shillelagh] … it was his favourite stick,' reports Yates. 'When at Hartshead it, or one of the same kind, was his companion, and the mode of carrying it led to him being jocularly spoken of by Mr Atkinson [another curate] and Mr. Hammond Roberson as "Old Staff".'

Excitement seemed to follow Pat around. There was always something for Old Staff to sort out. Meanwhile, his private life bordered on monastic. It had been five long years since his bungled romance with Mary Burder and he had not found anyone else. At the farm he was getting set in his ways, eating a frugal diet of porridge, potatoes and dumplings, with cold meat with the Bedfords on Sundays. His hair was receding and he slept alone.

Peter and Harriott had what he so wanted for himself, a married life with children. Pat had baptized the youngest, baby George, and wondered if he would ever have a child of his own. Then one day in early summer 1812 William bounced in with exciting news from Woodhouse Grove. His fiancée Jane's charming cousin was up from Cornwall. She was witty, pretty, pious and available. Would Patrick like to meet her?

Pat the poet, Pat the romantic, Pat the desperately lonely bachelor most certainly would.

Chapter 4

Grove, Actually

When Jane Fennell sank into a chair to write her fateful letter to Maria in early 1812, she was almost at the end of her tether. Taking the job of launching a church school in West Yorkshire with her husband John seemed a marvellous idea at first. But within six months of opening the doors to sons of preacher men, it had all turned into a bit of a nightmare. Nine lads arrived in January 1812 but very soon were joined by dozens more and poor Aunt Jane, then almost 60, couldn't cope. In desperation, she turned to the Branwells for back-up. She needed another deputy matron. She needed the best needlewoman in the family. She needed her accomplished, easy-going and thankfully unmarried niece. She really needed Maria Branwell.

Described as a 'blest saint' by her husband, Aunt Jane needed a halo as governess of the new Wesleyan Academy at Woodhouse Grove. Today, the school is a welcoming and orderly place. In the spring of 1812, it was barely-contained chaos as the Fennells fought to meet the instant demand for a free Methodist boarding school. Places were reserved for the sons of itinerant preachers and there was no shortage of takers. These parents never stayed long in one place as they took Wesley's message across Yorkshire. Now Methodists on the move could pack their boys off to the Fennells in Apperley Bridge.

John Wesley's attitude to education was unsurprising, given his own. His mother, indomitable Susanna Wesley, had a financially hopeless husband and 19 children. Those who survived infancy were allowed to take it easy until they turned five, then expected to learn their letters the following day. Susanna had no time for slackers. At the end of the first day of their mother's home school, wee Wesleys were expected to have mastered the alphabet. Only two failed the task and Susanna took the view that they were seriously deficient.

By the time he reached university, young John did not see student life as anything other than deadly serious. He started the Holy Club at Christ Church, Oxford, and though the name was coined in mockery by his fellows, Wesley liked it. He spent his time in bible study, devotion and visiting inmates in the squalid local prisons.

Little surprise that when Wesleyans opened a school there was an absolute putting away of childish things. No little Methody man was expected to learn through play. Indeed, playing at all was expressly forbidden. Susanna's puritanical zeal put the seal on her son's approach and Wesley was clear about how to treat children, though he never had any of his own. A wise parent, he said, 'should begin to break their will the first moment it appears. In the whole art of Christian education there is nothing more important than this.'

Wesley opened Kingswood School outside Bristol in 1748 and his rigid school rules were adopted for the Grove two decades after his death. Pupils were in chapel by 6.30am and went to bed at 8pm. Every second in between was spent on academic or physical work under relentless adult supervision in the pursuit of spiritual perfection. It takes a lot to break a child's will, so flogging was also part of a Christian education. The Methodist Conference was all for corporal punishment but there's no evidence humane John Fennell was as enthusiastic about daily beatings as his successors. A Reverend John Bletsoe left in 1816 after a punishment scandal recorded by a shocked Conference as 'homicide attempts'.

Methodist leaders were facing a manpower crisis. Demand for Evangelical ministers outstripped supply and there was an urgent need to train up a new generation of preachers. Another boys' school was needed in the North just as an old Quaker mansion appeared on the market. It was on the rural outskirts of Bradford in a location they liked, well away from the temptations of town. *The Morning Advertiser* of July 1811 advertised a des res, 'the elegant mansion called Woodhouse Grove, near Apperley Bridge, about eight miles from Leeds, four from Bradford, and five from Otley, adapted for the residence of a large genteel family.

> 'The house consists of drawing and dining rooms of large dimensions, with breakfast room, study, butler's pantry, housekeeper's room, servants' hall, kitchens, and every other

convenience, on the ground floor; twelve lodging rooms, dressing room, and accommodation for servants, wash-house, laundry, brewhouse, and other offices, fitted up in a complete manner. Out-buildings comprise stabling for twelve horses, double coach-house, harness room, &c. Conveniently detached is a farm-yard, with large barn, cow house, pigging house. The whole of the buildings are of freestone, and in the best repair.'

Location, location, location was emphasized with descriptions of fashionable gardens and upscale neighbours:

'The pleasure ground and gardens contain about seven acres, well planted, and laid out with much taste and beauty, with hot house, green house, an excellent bath, a fish-pond, well stocked, and supplied by a never-failing spring of soft water. The country, for many miles round, is beautifully ornamented by the seats of many families of distinction, and the picturesque scenery of this part of Aire Dale, is equal to any in the County. In front of the house is eight acres of rich land, ornamented with large oaks, and other fine timbers. The river Aire winds in front, and the stream affords fine trout fishing; the county also abounds with game, that altogether readers this is a complete residence for a Gentleman.'

The Wesleyan Methodist Conference had other plans. Within weeks it had bought the estate for £4,575 and set up a committee to turn the elegant family residence into the school Wesley would have wanted. It was the most money the Methodists had forked out for anything, there being few rich Conference members at the time. So the stables became a chapel, the barn was earmarked as a schoolroom and most of the first floor became dormitories. The ornamental gardens were replaced with vegetable patches. The teaching staff grew to two with the recruitment of a young 'classical master' called William Burgess. Overspending was reserved for a whopping portrait of Wesley for the drawing room that left no money for books and required a hasty new appeal for funds.

As the academy's governor and governess, John and Jane Fennell greeted their first pupils from across the North in the New Year of 1812. The boys were aged between nine and thirteen. They included three sets of brothers and all had Wesleyan preachers for dads. Wesley had been dead for 21 years by the time Woodhouse Grove opened and while girls were among the first pupils at Kingswood in the 1740s, it was boys only at the Grove.

The school opened on the second wintry Wednesday of January with a service in the converted stable for the handful of pupils and rows of churchmen. As they began their stretch, with one month off a year, the sermon by the Reverend James Wood left lads in no doubt they were there only to work and to pray. The school would 'guard them from the corruption which frequently abounds in large numbers of giddy youths.'

The schoolroom for said youths, however, was not yet sorted, according to former pupil and nineteenth century school historian Josiah Slugg:

> 'When the 12th of January, the day of opening, arrived, under the circumstances we must not be surprised to find that there was considerable unpreparedness on the part of the committee as to the reception of scholars. No room had been provided which could be used for teaching. The best that could be done was to utilise the dining-hall for an hour in the morning and an hour in the afternoon. This arrangement continued for a short time, until a suitable schoolroom could be provided.'

That was to be the converted barn, but the Wesleyan Academy at Woodhouse Grove was up and running with a handful of children and congratulations all round. The low-key life of the school could not last. Word travelled fast and hard-up ministers beat a path to their door, leaving to do God's work unencumbered by young boys. One such parent was the Reverend Joseph Entwisle: 'I took my dear William and James to the school at Woodhouse-Grove,' he wrote. 'I felt much at parting with my dear boys: – grateful to God for a situation so favourable to learning and religion; yet sorrowful at parting.'

By the end of February, another 18 children had arrived. Aunt Jane watched her workload triple in six weeks, and still they came. Among these first pupils was John Stamp, who wrote to his 'Honoured Father' on 29 February, with an assurance that he and his brother were well, a list of schoolmates and details of how boys do their bit to supply the school kitchen. 'We are each to have a piece of ground about three yards long and two yards and a half broad for a garden, which we are to cultivate ourselves,' he writes. This promised fresh food for the future, if not the present. In March there were complaints about the diet at the school, though the specifics were not recorded, and the Fennells were told to make changes.

The Reverend Stamp wanted to know how the boys spent their time, beginning with the Lord's day, so John's letter home in early April reflects Wesley's direction that every moment should be filled with improving activity. On Sunday, explains Master Stamp:

> 'We rise at six o'clock in the morning, and to half-past, washing, &c; to seven, a public prayer meeting; to eight, private prayer and reading; from eight to nine, family prayer and breakfast; from nine to half-past ten, reading; from half-past ten to twelve, preaching; from twelve to half-past one, private bands [prayer groups], dinner; from half-past one to two, the chapter to be read from which the morning's text has been taken and each boy to remember a verse; from two to half-past four, preaching and reading; from half-past four to six, public prayer meeting; from six to eight, supper and family prayer and go to bed.'

And that was the day of rest. The other six days were no less regimented:

> '*Monday morning*: Rise at six; to half-past, washing, &c; to seven, a public prayer meeting; to eight, in the school at reading and exercises; to nine, family prayer and break-fast; from nine to ten, in the school at Latin; from ten to twelve, accounts and leave school, except those that learn the flute stay till half-past and learn; to half-past one, dinner, exercise; to half-past four, writing and geography. In the evening, as Sunday evening.
>
> '*Tuesday*: Morning, as Monday morning; in the afternoon, from half-past one to half-past four, writing, and those that do not learn French, spelling; the evening, as Monday, except private bands after the prayer meeting.
>
> '*Wednesday*: Morning, as Monday morning; from half-past one to half-past four, writing, accounts, and history; the evening, same as Monday evening.
>
> '*Thursday*: Morning, as Monday morning; from half-past one to half-past four, writing and accounts; in the evening, as Tuesday.
>
> '*Friday*: Monday, as Monday morning; in the afternoon, translate French fables, and lectures; the evening, as Monday evening.'

On Saturday of that week at least, it was classes in the morning but a 'holiday' in the afternoon and one night a week to look forward to. 'We have class meeting on a Tuesday evening,' he writes, 'and it is always a good season.' There was also the occasional outing: 'We all went to Bradford last Wednesday to purchase some books, and half a dozen of us drank tea at Mr Keys'.'

As the school roll continued to rise, Aunt Jane was feeling her age. Nine years older than her husband, she should have been ready to retire. Instead, she soon had the enormous job of keeping house for 59 boys. While John Fennell was excellent in a classroom full of children, he was not cut out for the management role of head teacher. Organisation was not his strong point, so he left all the practical decisions to his overwhelmed wife, with Jane junior doing her best to help out.

Though his wife and daughter were run ragged, John felt the spiritual side of things was going awfully well. 'Don't scold me for scribbling,' he wrote in a breathless letter to Joseph Entwisle in March, because he had big news. The 'wonder-working Lord is still going on with his blessed work' with the young Entwisles and their classmates. They had enjoyed a 'revival' or religious awakening:

> 'Yesterday was a glorious day among them. They spent the time from school-hours till supper in prayer to God in the school-room, where I had ordered them a fire. One of the servants put her ear to the key-hole of the door, and God smote her heart. Another of them stole unperceived into the school, and had not hearkened long before she began to cry for mercy. The third must needs see and hear for herself, and she also was deeply affected, and has set out, I hope, in good earnest.'

Not only were more than twenty boys saved, so were the servant girls spying on goings-on through the keyhole. Even if it had frightened the life out of them. 'Thus,' continues Fennell, 'by the instrumentality of these dear boys, are three thoughtless girls brought to an acquaintance with themselves, and are determined for heaven.' Certainly the Reverend Entwisle was impressed, writing immediately to his nephew in Liverpool that, 'God is raising us up more preachers!'

A school bursting at the seams with young zealots, overwrought servant girls, more housework than anyone could cope with, a constant lack of funds. How much of this did lady of leisure Maria Branwell know as she packed her trunk, 400 miles away in balmy Cornwall? She was certainly familiar with Methodist teaching methods but had never been a junior matron in an Evangelical boarding school. Woodhouse Grove was a daunting undertaking, tasked as it was with providing a new generation of Methodist preachers. It is easier to guess at the thoughts of the female Fennells. As the ones left to oversee all the distinctly inglorious work of cooking, cleaning and sewing, the two Janes were simply relieved to hear their capable kinswoman was on her way.

For 29-year-old Maria Branwell, the decision to make the long journey from Penzance to Apperley Bridge was not one to take lightly. In April 1812, more than a decade before the arrival of the railways, there were two modes of public transport – overland by horse-drawn coach or by sea in a constant trader, also known as a constant coaster, which was a regular packet ship that sometimes accepted passengers along with freight. This was usually at the discretion of the captain and few records were kept before 1815. A weekly packet did run from Penzance to the Isles of Scilly, so others may have left for Bristol and on to Liverpool.

It was the age of the sailing ship, where travellers were regularly prey to shipwreck if an Atlantic gale drove them towards the rocks. Maria had grown up with many desperate tragedies on her own stretch of coast and there were also French privateers prowling the sea lanes. Though her trunk may well have gone by sea, as we will see, and she could have sailed to Bristol or Liverpool, it is likely she made the journey largely by land.

For those without their own coach and horses, it was a case of booking a seat on a stagecoach or mail coach. Stagecoach owners practiced a pile 'em high policy, while mail coaches cost more but were less crowded and more comfortable. The first leg of Maria's journey was from the Union Hotel to Truro on the 3pm coach, where she could change for a coach to London. From London, she would set out for Yorkshire on the Great North Road.

In her biography of Charlotte Brontë, Elizabeth Gaskell observed: 'The journey from Penzance to Leeds in those days was both very long and very expensive.' It was also fraught with danger. At the time Maria undertook her journey, the newspapers were full of coaching catastrophe. The most dangerous place to travel was a cheap seat on the outside of the carriage, as demonstrated by the *Gloucester Journal* in March 1812:

'On the arrival of one of the Bath coaches at Chippenham on Wednesday morning, it was found that three of the outside passengers were in a state of insensibility on the top of the coach. In two the vital spark was completely extinguished: in the third animation was restored, but he died shortly after! Their deaths were occasioned by the inclemency of the weather, it having rained the whole of the preceding night.'

Maria could afford an inside seat, though this was not without its dangers, according to the *Bury and Norwich Post* the following month:

'Thursday last a passenger in a stage-coach, which runs daily from Chichester to Brighton, was seized, near Shoreham, with a violent fit of insanity, and bit a lady who was in the coach with him in a most shocking manner, about the face and arms. The coachman and outside passengers hearing her screams, got down, and with much difficulty rescued her from the jaws of the maniac.'

Mail coaches were a classier way to travel and had an armed guard. This was because of the highwaymen, scourge of the road in the Regency era. Attacks were frequent, such as a 4am hijack in Ireland where passengers lost £2,000 in cash and property. The *London Courier and Evening Gazette* in April 1812 reported:

'The Newry fly coach was stopped by a strong band of robbers, who, without any intimation, fired into the coach, but without injuring any of the passengers. They proceeded to hand out those in the coach, one by one, and with the most dreadful imprecations, made them deliver up all they possessed. There were two ladies, Mrs HAMILTON and daughter, whom the robbers obliged to kneel down in the road, declaring they would shoot them instantly: one of the gang, however, interfered, and even declared he would not allow their baggage to be touched. However, the captain of the banditti [robbers] ordered every thing to be carried off. Money, watches, trinkets, clothes, every particle was plundered.'

If Maria did not freeze to death, find a maniac in her coach or a highwayman's pistol at her head, the terrible state of the roads made crashes common. Sometimes wheels came off. At other times, rutted roads, spooked horses or bad weather overturned the coach. When a lynch-pin shook free in Market

Harborough in February 1812, the coach overturned and the guard's leg was smashed. In March, wrote the *Stamford Mercury*: 'The Lincoln mail-coach was overturned near Leasingham on Sunday last, in consequence of the bad management of the driver of a post chaise, who, being in a state of intoxication, drove his vehicle against the coach.'

Eight passengers escaped serious injury 'but the guard suffered severely'. In December, reported the *Exeter Flying Post*, a mail coach was upset at North Petherton, 'by which accident Mr. Robert Carpenter, an eminent grazier of Somersetshire, who was on the box with the coachman, was killed on the spot'.

Even without such dramas, travel was arduous. In the summer months, coaches could cover up to 40 miles a day so Maria's Georgian journey would have taken well over a week. Her fare did not include accommodation and each stop at a coaching inn meant finding honest porters, food and sleeping quarters amid the horses and hustlers.

If Maria did travel by sea, she could have landed in Liverpool or Hull, then gone overland or done the final leg by barge. A packet travelled along the Leeds Liverpool canal, stopping at Apperley Bridge. Slugg records the boys being taken to town on 'the Leeds Canal flowing through the valley of the Aire, not far from the Grove premises, on which barges drawn by horses glided slowly but safely'.

The most likely stop on the Great North Road was Ferrybridge, 30 miles from Apperley Bridge. One coach that did the route was called the *Eclipse* and arrived there in the evening. From Ferrybridge, she may have been met by a post-chaise hired from one of the inns either side of the eponymous Apperley bridge, the George and Dragon or the Stansfield Arms, or simply taken another coach.

Finally, the intrepid Miss Branwell was delivered to the door of the Grove. Maria rode up the steep driveway through the grove of beech and oak to be greeted like the cavalry, already with some small inkling of the culture shock to come. After a lifetime at the centre of a thriving, lively and important town she had arrived at an isolated old mansion, miles from anywhere. As she lit her way to bed with a candle on her first night, the silence compared to Penzance and the coach stops was intense. Maybe all too reminiscent of gothic fiction that was easy to dismiss when outside was the sound of the street and the quay. Outside Maria's new bedroom window there was only the darkness, the rustle of oak trees and hoot of a barn owl.

Maria and her cousin had much to catch up on since the Fennells left Cornwall, especially Jane's love life. Then Maria was introduced to classics teacher William Burgess and another young man who would become her friend during that tumultuous year.

In his leap-day letter of February 1812, young John Stamp mentions in passing: 'We expect a classical master from Aberdeen soon.' He was Joseph Abbot, who was born in Cumbria and finished his education between 1808 and 1812 at Marischal College, part of the University of Aberdeen. He was 23 when he joined the staff at Woodhouse Grove shortly after it opened. He is recorded as 'Abbott, 1812-1812' in the register of Kingswood School, which shared the admin for both schools in the early days.

Under Kingswood rules, Abbot would have been an assistant master. This meant sleeping in the boys' dormitory with little in the way of comfort or privacy. Tasked with overnight supervision as well as daytime teaching, he had a cubicle among the rows of crib beds where the pupils slept. Time off in the drawing room with the adults would have been a welcome relief. Abbot later wrote to Charlotte Brontë: 'I happened to be intimately acquainted with both your father and mother with the latter more especially as I lived for some months in the same house with her before she was married.' He describes 'the pleasant time I spent at Woodhouse-grove with your Mother and her cousin and Mr Fennel [sic] and the old 'duchess' a soubriquet given by me to Mrs Fennel from the stately cap she always wore...'

Once the introductions were over, news of Penzance imparted and Maria had rested from her voyage, the frazzled old Duchess talked her through the domestic duties. Maria quickly realised her reputation for stitching was a mixed blessing, but she was determined to be Useful. Embroidering samplers was no preparation for keeping dozens of boys presentable. The distinctive uniform consisted of dark blue jacket and corduroy trousers with a large flat cap in red and yellow. Pupils were allowed one suit every eight months, so it had to last, to say nothing of keeping all the bedding in reasonable repair. So Maria dutifully ploughed her way daily through a mountain of mending and wondered when she could make a respectable exit.

Then one day in June 1812, a tall Irishman with a shock of red hair and carrying a staff like a moorland Moses arrived at the door.

Ostensibly, the Reverend Patrick Brontë was there to double check on what was expected of him as the school's external classics examiner. In truth, he had walked a dozen miles across country at least in part to meet the much-talked-of Miss Branwell. Jane and William engineered the meeting of their eligible best friends to give Cupid a nudge. It was a blind date, or at least a blind pot of tea. As William and Jane teased each other about wedding plans, Maria would make a witty aside, or they would all talk of books, of religion, of life. Of course, what everyone noticed but nobody mentioned – at least not until later – was the instant chemistry between the Irish curate and the Cornish cousin.

After that, Patrick was at the Grove any chance he got and while Mr Brontë and Miss Branwell were devout Christians, there was more to life than going to church. Mainly, there was a lot of walking. The doors of the Grove opened out onto the path that lead down to the river Aire, across school land. At those rose-tinted moments, it was not a Spartan seminary but the still-elegant mansion. Though the grounds were not quite as superb in cash-strapped times, they had not lost their splendour. They were also free of young spies in red and yellow caps. Elsewhere the uber-regimented school day went on without them as the couple enjoyed a refined Regency romance in the adults-only areas, the grounds laid out with such taste and beauty. Unfortunately, the pretty fishpond had been partly filled in as a Methodist health and safety measure, but the large oaks and winding paths with breath-taking views were still to enjoy.

For well-to-do Maria, this environment was perfectly normal. It was still quite grand for her suitor, but doing his wooing in the rolling parkland of a Georgian mansion was just another crucial phase in the long reinvention of Pat Prunty. Neither rich nor truly poor, Maria and Patrick shared an enjoyment of the finer things when they were available.

Patrick must also have enjoyed the lack of enraged male relatives intent on ruining his chances. He was older and had his own church, but he was still courting a woman from another world. Maria's father was dead, though, and her only brother hundreds of miles away so there could be no repeat of the Jean McAlister debacle. Maria's Uncle Fennell was a good friend, unlike Mary's Uncle Burder. This time everyone approved of Patrick as a suitable match.

Though 1812 was an unusually cold summer, they took every opportunity to walk beside the Aire, which flowed sparkling and clear before the imminent arrival of polluting mills in the valley. An account by former pupil Edward Pinder waxes lyrical about the beauties of the neighbourhood at the time: 'The Grove's academic shades, with such natural attractions of scenery, and almost close to the banks of the Aire, then a pellucid stream, might be deemed fitting haunts for the Muses...'

It was certainly a fitting haunt for a courting couple. The hours spent strolling the grounds and the riverbanks together (Jane and William at a discreet distance) were a chance to swap life stories, opinions and hopes and very soon, they were smitten. While demure Maria might look dainty, she was resilient, clever and optimistic. Patrick had met his match. They discovered a great deal in common, not least a love of literature, an earnest faith and shared sense of life's possibilities.

As with any new relationship, both would have presented their best selves. Possibly Maria spoke more of her family's philanthropy and place in society than the dodgy Dunkins or banished brother-in-law. Patrick may have glossed over his humble roots, radical brother and scandal that closed his school. The past was, for both, another country. They met at an age to know who they were and what they wanted.

Maria did not think Pat odd or peculiar. Pat did not see a confirmed spinster but exactly the kind of woman he wanted to spend his life with. Both very far from where they were born, they had been brought to Yorkshire by a wider movement to shake up religion. A shared Celtic heritage was maybe part of the attraction, as their Irish and Cornish voices and stories resonated one with the other.

Also, Maria seems to have understood Patrick very quickly. Though he was a good friend, a caring priest and single-minded in his ambition, he also appears to have been gauche around potential lovers. He never really understood how badly he had behaved towards Mary Burder. Now he had finally found a woman who saw through his enthusiastic but clumsy moves to the good heart and like mind. Though Patrick's inability to empathise with how she might feel during their courtship was to exasperate Maria in the months to come.

Whenever they could, Maria and Patrick headed for Kirkstall Abbey six miles along the river from the Grove, often with Jane and William. It was a fashionable destination. The ruined twelfth-century Cistercian monastery was officially Romantic with a capital 'R', after painters such as Joseph Turner immortalized the spot in their work. Or if they simply wanted to be alone at the Grove, there was always a secluded stroll around Elam's Tower, the old folly in the woods. Both venues had pleasing echoes of the gothic romances Maria enjoyed in her *Lady's Magazine* and this time she was the virtuous heroine with a besotted beau. Though unlike Ethelinda and Clementina, she did not have to be chased by wolves or scared witless at midnight to find true love.

Falling for each other so deeply and so quickly took them both by surprise. By August, Patrick knew he had found another woman he wanted to marry and this time he was serious. He mulled it over on his regular treks to see her, twelve miles there and twelve miles back. Maria shared his commitment to education, poetry, books, Evangelical ministry and the importance of friends. Yes, she was a Methodist but chose the Church of England as schism approached. So Patrick did not have to choose between his heart and career as with poor Mary Burder, dumped for being a Dissenter. As the anguished exchange of letters to come would show, he could not bear to think of losing this one, The One.

Maria also knew whom she wanted to marry. She just wished he could afford a horse. When he set off home to parish duties and the Bedfords at Lousy Farm, she worried. The Luddites loomed large in Maria's imagination as her lover strode back and forth to see her. For this, she had her friend Joseph Abbott to thank. His account to Charlotte suggests she was already at the Grove in April, but it may actually have been his favourite anecdote, retold at the Grove a little while after Rawfolds:

> 'And I well remember how frightened she was when one night on my return from Leeds on foot – a walk of eleven miles I told her and her cousin Jane Fennel [sic] … how that I had been met on my way and stopped by a regularly organised body of men marching along with military precision. As I approached it, a man in command gave the word 'halt' when the moving body, it was too dark to distinguish individuals, became stationary and the man stepped out from it to confront me asking, in a harsh rough voice, as he did so, 'who goes there?' 'A friend', was the ready, and, under the circumstances of the case, the most prudent answer to the challenge. 'Pass friend', was the instant rejoinder, followed without even so much as a 'comma's' pause, with the word of command, 'quick march!' and the black mass of men with still blacker hearts moved on and for what fell purpose do you think? Why to make that very attack upon the Mill...'

Unrest still rippled through the West Riding but by the late summer of 1812 it would take more than secret armies to keep Maria's lover away – and not just because he had a gun in his pocket. He was always glad to see her. Patrick was ready to propose and knew just the place. On Sunday 23 August 1812, he dropped to one knee amid the beautiful ruins of Kirkstall Abbey and asked Maria to be his wife. She accepted and they returned to the Grove hand in hand, hugging their secret to themselves.

As Maria and Patrick enjoyed their summer of love, school life at Woodhouse Grove lurched on in its disorganized fashion. It is interesting to note what was happening all around Maria, because she makes no mention of any of it in the letters to her fiancé we will come to soon. Reading her correspondence, it is very easy to forget that Maria was effectively part of the school staff, as was Patrick in a peripatetic way. There is no mention of schoolchildren in her letters, no sense at all of the strict regime she has been summoned to help with. However, school records reveal a hectic backdrop to Maria's bliss and the days between dates were not spent sighing into teacups like an Austen heroine.

Grove historian and former headmaster Frank Cyril Pritchard sums up the Fennell era as 'romance and muddle' and by the time Maria was engaged, the muddle was becoming a mess. John Fennell was not a manager and the Duchess had had enough. Also, 1812 was crunch time as the Methodists decided to split from the Church of England and Evangelical Anglicans had to choose a side.

Maria much preferred to concentrate on matters of the heart, mind and soul than piles of ripped cord pants, her auntie's housekeeping headaches and uncle's career choices. Also, it was quite easy to shut them all out. While the areas assigned to young scholars and junior masters grew overcrowded and cramped, the governor's quarters retained the luxury of the original mansion. Here Maria could sit with Jane as they composed their letters in the North, much as their contemporary and social equal Jane Austen was doing in the South. Tall windows allowed natural light and a view to the pellucid river as Maria poured out her heart to the man she loved.

Chapter 5

Saucy Maria

Nine letters over four months through the late summer, autumn and early winter of 1812 are virtually all we have of Maria Branwell's own record of her life. In them she speaks volumes. Patrick's love letters of 1812 are lost or sold and we can only guess at what he wrote during their engagement, though they clearly brimmed with brio to elicit such replies. Maria's letters are suffused with the ecstasies and insecurities of her new relationship and seldom allude to the domestic trials around her. She is preoccupied instead by what Pat is thinking and feeling and their chances of staying this happy. From the day they become engaged to the day they are married, Maria and Patrick suffer equal bouts of panic that the other will have a change of heart.

From her first letter, just after accepting his proposal, Maria reveals feelings almost too overwhelming to confess. 'My dear Friend,' she writes on 26 August 1812:

> 'This address is sufficient to convince you that I not only permit, but approve of yours to me—I do indeed consider you as my *friend*; yet, when I consider how short a time I have had the pleasure of knowing you, I start at my own rashness, my heart fails, and did I not think that you would be disappointed and grieved at it, I believe I should be ready to spare myself the task of writing.'

Maria must write, though, to put his mind at rest. It is Wednesday and Patrick only left on Sunday but has written fretting that she might change her mind. She writes to say she does not regret a word she has said to her darling in the drawing room, by the river and certainly not at the ruined abbey:

> 'Do not think that I am so wavering as to repent of what I have already said. No, believe me, this will never be the case, unless you give me cause for it. You need not fear that you have been mistaken in my character.'

She is not capable of spurning even the smallest gesture of kindness, she explains, especially from him:

> 'I will frankly confess that your behaviour and what I have seen and heard of your character has excited my warmest esteem and regard, and be assured you shall never have cause to repent of any confidence you may think proper to place in me, and that it will always be my endeavour to deserve the good opinion which you have formed, although human weakness may in some instances cause me to fall short.'

These promises don't just depend on willpower, she adds, because God will help her stay true. Anyway, their engagement appears to be an open secret as the Fennells have been teasing her about the contents of his billet-doux. She writes: 'Your letter has caused me some foolish embarrassment, tho' in pity to my feelings they have been very sparing of their raillery.' Not that she cares. She just misses him. She cannot *'walk our accustomed rounds'* without, 'why should I be ashamed to add, wishing for your presence'. She hates when it is time for him to leave but is always worried she has said too much.

> 'If you knew what were my feelings whilst writing this you would pity me. I wish to write the truth and give you satisfaction, yet fear to go too far, and exceed the bounds of propriety. But whatever I may say or write I will *never deceive* you, or *exceed the truth*. If you think I have not placed the *utmost confidence* in you, consider my situation, and ask yourself if I have not confided in you sufficiently, perhaps too much. I am very sorry that you will not have this till after to-morrow, but it was out of my power to write sooner. I rely on your goodness to pardon everything in this which may appear either too free or too stiff, and beg that you will consider me as a warm and faithful friend.'

How not to be too free or too stiff, the eternal dilemma of a new relationship. One minute opening her heart, the next stepping back in a panic that she is going too far. By 5 September, Maria's confidence has grown enough to promote her man from plain friend to 'My dearest Friend' in response to his latest 'affectionate and very welcome letter'. She is in a good mood after news from Penzance: 'I had yesterday a letter from a very dear friend of mine, and had the satisfaction to learn by it that all at home are well.' She is also happy that Patrick is not wearing himself out with too much walking. Life is good and can only get better: 'I feel with you the unspeakable obligations I am under to a merciful Providence ... O my dear friend, let us pray much that we may live lives holy and useful to each other and all around us!'

Maria would have liked a bit more time to get used to the idea of such very holy matrimony, though, and takes Pat to task for blabbing to Peter and Harriott Bedford at home. 'Have you not been too hasty in informing your friends of a certain event?' she asks. 'Why did you not leave them to guess a little longer? I shrink from the idea of its being known to everybody.'

Patrick cannot stop talking about her, so Maria teases him about how much time she and Jane spend discussing boyfriends:

> 'I do, indeed, *sometimes* think of you, but I will not say how often, lest I raise your vanity; and we sometimes talk of you and the doctor [William Morgan]. But I believe I should seldom mention your name myself were it not now and then introduced by my cousin.'

Jane is agog for the gossip but Maria is reticent about revealing her big news, though it seems obvious to everyone what had happened:

> 'I have never mentioned a word of what is past to anybody. Had I thought this necessary I should have requested you to do it. But I think there is no need, as by some means or other they seem to have a pretty correct notion how matters stand betwixt us; and as their hints, etc., meet with no contradiction from me, my silence passes for confirmation.'

It's not like anyone is unhappy about the engagement and when Patrick goes public, Maria's relatives can stop pretending and start handing out advice:

> 'Mr Fennell has not neglected to give me some serious and encouraging advice, and my aunt takes frequent opportunities of dropping little sentences which I may turn to some advantage. I have long had reason to know that the present state of things would give pleasure to all parties.'

Maria is bored when Patrick is not around, especially on trips to take tea with the neighbours:

> 'I will now tell you what I was thinking about and doing at the time you mention. I was then toiling up the hill with Jane and Mrs Clapham to take our tea at Mr Tatham's, thinking on the evening when I first took the same walk with you, and on the change which had taken place in my circumstances and views since then—not wholly without a wish that I had your arm to assist me, and your conversation to shorten the walk. Indeed, all our walks have now an insipidity in them which I never thought they would have possessed. ... I have now written a pretty long letter without reserve or caution, and if all the sentiments of my heart are not laid open to you believe me it is not because I wish them to be concealed for I hope there is nothing there that would give you pain or displeasure. My most sincere and earnest wishes are for your happiness and welfare, for this includes my own. Pray much for me that I may be made a blessing and not a hindrance to you. Let me not interrupt your studies nor intrude on that time which ought to be dedicated to better purposes. Forgive my freedom, my dearest friend, and rest assured that you are and ever will be dear to Maria Branwell.'

When she grabs time to write almost a week later on 11 September, she has been to Bradford to sip tea with the Cousens, an artistic family of merchants who live in an old Barkerend Road mansion. She barely has time to dash off a note:

> 'Having spent the day yesterday at Miry Shay, a place near Bradford, I had not got your letter till my return in the evening, and consequently have only a short time this morning to write if I send it by this post. You surely do not think you *trouble* me by writing? No, I think I may venture to say if such were your opinion you would *trouble* me no more. Be assured, your letters are and I hope always will be received with extreme pleasure and read with delight.'

There is only time to warn Patrick that Jane is not very happy with him:

> 'You may expect frowns and hard words from her when you
> make your appearance here again, for, if you recollect, she gave
> you a note to carry to the Doctor, and he has never received it.
> What have you done with it? If you can give a good account of
> it you may come to see us as soon as you please and be sure of
> a hearty welcome from all parties. Next Wednesday we have
> some thoughts, if the weather be fine, of going to Kirkstall
> Abbey once more, and I suppose your presence will not make
> the walk less agreeable to any of us.'

A couple of days after their favourite kind of date, Maria writes one of her most significant letters to her future husband. On Friday 18 September, she tells Patrick she was used to freedom and domestic decision-making at home in Penzance. People came to her with problems and deferred to her judgment. How much does he already know of her life in Chapel Street and Causewayhead, living without a man? Here she spells it out:

> 'For some years I have been perfectly my own mistress, subject
> to no control whatever—so far from it, that my sisters who are
> many years older than myself, and even my dear mother, used
> to consult me in every case of importance, and scarcely ever
> doubted the propriety of my opinions and actions.'

She veils pride in her independence with a suitably pious plea for a manly steer once they are wed:

> 'Perhaps you will be ready to accuse me of vanity in mentioning
> this, but you must consider that I do not *boast* of it, I have
> many times felt it a disadvantage; and although, I thank God, it
> never led me into error, yet, in circumstances of perplexity and
> doubt, I have deeply felt the want of a guide and instructor. ...
> I shall now no longer feel this want, this sense of helpless
> weakness, for I believe a kind Providence has intended that
> I shall find in you every earthly friend united; nor do I fear
> to trust myself under your protection, or shrink from your
> control. It is pleasant to be subject to those we love, especially

when they never exert their authority but for the good of the subject. How few would write in this way! But I do not fear that *you* will make a bad use of it. You tell me to write my thoughts, and thus as they occur I freely let my pen run away with them.'

To a modern reader, this seems a shame. On one hand, she is confident of her ability to make sound adult decisions. Then she lapses into helplessness and weakness and invites Pat's control. This is an era when her promise to obey is central to the marriage contract and religious education hammered home wifely submission. And maybe Maria read one gothic tale too many of good girls gone astray in *Lady's Magazine*.

Returning to more mundane matters, Patrick has once again failed as a go-between and before she sends the long letter to be posted, highlights his blunder. The Fennells had been out when Peter and Harriott visited to discuss an order of blankets for the school. Patrick brokered the deal to bring in work for struggling Hartshead, then forgot to tell the Grove they were coming:

'I do not know whether you dare show your face here again or not after the blunder you have committed. When we got to the house on Thursday evening, even before we were within the doors, we found that Mr and Mrs Bedford had been there, and that they had requested you to mention their intention of coming—a single hint of which you never gave!'

It is unlikely that Peter and Harriott Bedford were amused at their long and wasted journey but at least the Fennells found it funny. The forgetful curate was generally agreed to be 'mazed' with love:

'Poor I too came in for a share in the hard words which were bestowed upon you, for they all agreed that I was the cause of it. Mr. Fennell said you were certainly *mazed*, and talked of sending you to York, etc [the lunatic asylum]. And even I begin to think that *this*, together with the *note*, bears some marks of *insanity*! However, I shall suspend my judgment until I hear what excuse you can make for yourself, I suppose you will be quite ready to make one of some kind or another.'

Her final news explains the upbeat tone. It is relief. Maria has finally plucked up the courage to tell her family she is getting married. She describes the long, long letter she has sent about the man she has fallen in love with – and why she is not coming home:

> 'Yesterday I performed a difficult and yet a pleasing task in writing to my sisters. I thought I never should accomplish the end for which the letter was designed; but after a good deal of perambulation I gave them to understand the nature of my engagement with you, with the motives and inducements which led me to form such an engagement, and that in consequence of it I should not see them again so soon as I had intended. I concluded by expressing a hope that they would not be less pleased with the information than were my friends here. I think they will not suspect me to have made a wrong step, their partiality for me is so great. And their affection for me will lead them to rejoice in my welfare, even though it should diminish somewhat of their own.'

It was a bittersweet letter, both to write and to receive. Maria's anxiety about telling her sisters probably accounts for her attempt to keep the engagement under wraps for as long as possible. She knew it would be hard for Jane, Elizabeth and Charlotte to read. Their life together in Penzance was over.

Maria needs Patrick to take her mind off all she is forsaking and shares how to cope with moments like these:

> 'I shall think the time tedious till I hear from you, and must beg you will write as soon as possible. … When you find your heart oppressed and your thoughts too much engrossed by one subject let prayer be your refuge—this you no doubt know by experience to be a sure remedy, and a relief from every care and error. Oh, that we had more of the spirit of prayer! I feel that I need it much.'

Meanwhile, her uncle does his best to soothe the pain of the parted sisters:

> 'Mr. Fennell has crossed my letter to my sisters. With his usual goodness he has supplied my *deficiencies*, and spoken of me in terms of commendation of which I wish I were more

worthy. Your character he has likewise displayed in the most favourable light; and I am sure they will not fail to love and esteem you though unknown.'

Patrick seems to understand what she is going through and writes to reassure her that she is doing the right thing. He loves her and she believes him: 'Accept of my warmest thanks for your kind affectionate letter, in which you have rated mine so highly that I really blush to read my own praises,' she writes in her reply of 23 September. 'Pray that God would enable me to deserve all the kindness you manifest towards me, and to act consistently with the good opinion you entertain of me—then I shall indeed be a helpmeet for you, and to be this shall at all times be the care and study of my future life.'

As Maria grapples with her mixed emotions of sorrow and excitement, there is a visit from 'a large party of the Bradford folks' and it is hard to concentrate on church chitchat: 'My thoughts often strayed from the company, and I would have gladly left them to follow my present employment.' Turning aside from the emotional turmoil, it is time to decide where they will live when they are married. Maria seems to indicate that Lousy Farm is the best place to start out and that the Fennells agree:

> 'I am by no means sorry you have given up all thought of the house you mentioned. With my cousin's help I have made known your plans to my uncle and aunt. Mr Fennell immediately coincided with that which respects your present abode, and observed that it had occurred to him before, but that he had not had an opportunity of mentioning it to you. My aunt did not fall in with it so readily, but her objections did not appear to me to be very weighty. ... My cousin is of the same opinion.'

Then we have a shrewd observation that reveals bachelor Patrick's habit of simply making plans without consulting anyone. He likes to present a fait accompli but Maria is already wise to his ways:

> 'Indeed, you have such a method of considering and digesting a plan before you make it known to your friends, that you run very little risk of incurring their disapprobations, or of having your schemes frustrated. I greatly admire your talents this

Maria Branwell Brontë: a
watercolour later copied
by her daughter, Charlotte.
(Brontë Society)

Merchants of Penzance: Maria's
father, Thomas Branwell.

Matriarch: Anne Branwell,
grandmother of the Brontës.

Cornish belle: Maria's
sister, Elizabeth Branwell.
(Brontë Society)

Above and below: Uptown girl: Maria's Georgian home in Chapel Street, Penzance.

Only way is up: the remains of Patrick Brontë's birthplace in Emdale, 1905. (Tim Harrison)

Methody man: preacher John Wesley was friends with the Branwells. (Wellcome Collection)

Assembly Rooms: Maria enjoyed similar events in Penzance in the early 1800s.

Above: Ladylike:
Elizabeth Branwell
never lost her
own snuff habit.
(Wellcome
Collection)

Right: The bachelor:
Patrick Brontë
in 1809.

Above: Elegant mansion: the Wesleyan Academy at Woodhouse Grove in 1812. (Woodhouse Grove School)

Left: Giddy youths: Maria helped with the domestic demands of the first Grove pupils, sons of itinerant preachers. (Woodhouse Grove School)

The Grove today:
Old Grovian
Hugh Knowles
and Assistant
Headteacher Donna
Shoesmith-Evans.

Gothic romance:
Maria agreed to
become Mrs Brontë
at Kirkstall Abbey.
(David Jacobson)

A regency proposal:
Pat fell to one knee
at the romantic
ruin that was an
inspiration to artists
such as Turner.

Maria's box was destroyed by 'the violence of the sea' demonstrated here by the *Spray* at Ilfracombe in 1900. (Ilfracombe Museum)

Shipwreck: The *Trader* carrying Maria's books, clothes and wedding veil was 'stranded on the coast of Devonshire' at Ilfracombe like the *Arabella* here in 1895. (Ilfracombe Museum)

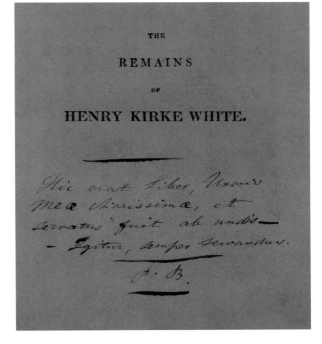

Above: The hobblers: nineteenth-century Ilfracombe fishermen who rescued people and possessions, such as Maria's 'little property.' (Ilfracombe Museum)

Right: Latin lover: Patrick inscribed, 'This was the book of my most beloved wife, and it had been saved from the waves - therefore, it must always be preserved.' (Brontë Society)

THE

REMAINS

OF

HENRY KIRKE WHITE.

Wedding day: Patrick and Maria on 29 December, 1812. Pen and ink drawing by Eleanor Houghton, 2019. (© Eleanor Houghton)

Right: Here come the brides: the double wedding of Maria and Patrick, then Jane Fennell and William Morgan took place at St Oswald's Church, Guiseley.

Below: The Brontë marriage certificate.

Protected and neglected: Grade II Listed Thornbush (Lousy) Farm in Liversedge.

Luddites and the Lord: St Peter's Church, Hartshead, supposedly scene of a secret burial while Patrick was curate.

Clough House: Spen Valley birthplace of the first Brontë sisters. (David Jacobson)

Above left: Labours of Thornton: Maria gave birth to Charlotte, Branwell, Emily and Anne Brontë before the fireplace at Thornton Parsonage, now *Emily's* café. (Bob Smith Photography)

Above right: Family of letters: Patrick Brontë's writing desk in Thornton. (David Jacobson)

Below: Tea with Mrs Brontë: Kipping House, home of diarist Elizabeth Firth. (David Jacobson)

Above and left: Bell Chapel: St James Church, Thornton, as the Brontës knew it and today, with Steven Stanworth of the Old Bell Chapel Action Group. (David Jacobson)

Ponden Hall: home of the powerful Heatons in 1820. (David Jacobson)

Final journey: Haworth Parsonage and the coffin gate. (David Jacobson)

Story in stone: memorial at St Michael And All Angels Church, Haworth. (David Jacobson)

Maria's daughters: Anne, Emily and Charlotte Brontë.

way—may they never be perverted by being used in a bad cause! And whilst they are exerted for good purposes, may they prove irresistible!'

There are more immediate plans to be made: 'I hope nothing will occur to induce you to change your intention of spending the next week at Bradford.' Maria and Patrick sometimes met on visits to Bradford, notably when Patrick addressed the Bible Society. He has also committed some more unspecified 'blunders' and while she understands his excuses, is not sure others will:

'I already feel a kind of participation in all that concerns you. All praises and censures bestowed on you must equally affect me. Your joys and sorrows must be mine. Thus shall the one be increased and the other diminished. While this is the case we shall, I hope, always find 'life's cares' to be 'comforts'. And may we feel every trial and distress, for such must be our lot at times, bind us nearer to God and to each other!'

As so often, Maria pens an earnest description of their future union as both passionate and pious:

'My heart earnestly joins in your comprehensive prayers. I trust they will unitedly ascend to a throne of grace, and through the Redeemer's merits procure for us peace and happiness here and a life of eternal felicity hereafter. Oh, what sacred pleasure there is in the idea of spending an eternity together in perfect and uninterrupted bliss! This should encourage us to the utmost exertion and fortitude. But whilst I write, my own words condemn me—I am ashamed of my own indolence and backwardness to duty. May I be more careful, watchful, and active than I have ever yet been!'

Patrick should have been more careful, too. 'Let me hear from you soon,' Maria ends but she did not and on 3 October there is an abrupt departure from the billing and cooing, the gentle reproofs about forgotten notes and being mazed. When Maria picks up her pen on Saturday, she is furious:

'How could my dear friend so cruelly disappoint me? Had he known how much I had set my heart on having a letter this afternoon, and how greatly I felt the disappointment when the bag arrived and I found there was nothing for me…'

Often ascribed to pre-wedding jitters, this outburst paints a telling scene. Either Maria was having a bad day or the combined stress of planning a wedding, persuading Patrick to consult her on where they should live or the hours and hours of sewing, had got to her. Finding no cheering letter in the postbag was the final straw, though she quickly reins in her fury. Maybe the bride-to-be took a walk around the room and stared out of the window for a while, to compose herself before carrying on:

'But whatever was the reason of your not writing, I cannot believe it to have been neglect or unkindness, therefore I do not in the least blame you, I only beg that in future you will judge of my feelings by your own, and if possible never let me expect a letter without receiving one.'

It is an insight into conducting a romance long before speedier forms of communication were invented. Maria suffers the equivalent of being told 'I'll call' only for the phone never to ring. She might suspect a modern boyfriend of losing her number or lying. When her nineteenth-century suitor's letter fails to appear, has it gone astray or was it never written? Is he already reneging on his promises? She is rattled and needs him to understand that this is important. She cannot let it go:

'You know in my last which I sent you at Bradford I said it would not be in my power to write the next day, but begged I might be favoured with hearing from you on Saturday, and you will not wonder that I hoped you would have complied with this request. It has just occurred to my mind that it is possible this note was not received; if so, you have felt disappointed likewise; but I think this is not very probable, as the old man is particularly careful, and I never heard of his losing anything committed to his care. The note which I allude to was written on Thursday morning, and you should have received it before you left Bradford. I forget what its contents were, but I know it was written in haste and concluded abruptly. Mr Fennell talks of visiting Mr Morgan to-morrow. I cannot lose the opportunity of sending this to the office by him as you will then have it a day sooner, and if you have been daily expecting to hear from me, twenty-four hours are of some importance.'

She devotes quite a lot of this letter to not receiving a letter and while it looks like an over-reaction she cannot stop herself:

'I really am concerned to find that this, what many would deem trifling incident, has so much disturbed my mind. I fear I should not have slept in peace to-night if I had been deprived of this opportunity of relieving my mind by scribbling to you, and now I lament that you cannot possibly receive this till Monday. May I hope that there is now some intelligence on the way to me? or must my patience be tried till I see you on Wednesday?'

This neediness on both sides is underpinned by anxiety. Their headlong fall into love over such a short time is part of the problem. Maria is taken aback at the ferocity of her feelings, the sheer panic at not hearing from him:

'Surely after this you can have no doubt that you possess all my heart. Two months ago I could not possibly have believed that you would ever engross so much of my thoughts and affections, and far less could I have thought that I should be so forward as to tell you so.'

She goes as far as to half-contemplate calling the whole thing off: 'I believe I must forbid you to come here again unless you can assure me that you will not steal any more of my regard.'

As soon as she has written the words, she is in two minds about sending the letter and underlines the next sentence: 'Enough of this; I must bring my pen to order, for if I were to suffer myself to revise what I have written I should be tempted to throw it in the fire, but I have determined that you shall see my whole heart.'

Then… 'I have not yet informed you that I received your serio-comic note on Thursday afternoon, for which accept my thanks.' So she vented her spleen before the note arrived and decided to send it anyway. Just to bear in mind next time he promises to write, presumably. Serio-comic is not what she needs. Luckily, he is invited to join an outing to Kirkstall Abbey the following week for Jane's birthday and a reference to his poetry lightens the mood: 'My cousin desires me to say that she expects a long poem on her birthday, when she attains the important age of twenty-one.'

A final, underlined postscript scribbled on Sunday morning reveals a last stab of worry, possibly prompted by getting ready for church, that she cares too much about the here and now and not enough about spiritual matters:

> 'I trust in your hours of retirement you will not forget to pray for me. … I feel that my heart is more ready to attach itself to earth than heaven. I sometimes think there never was a mind so dull and inactive as mine is with regard to spiritual things.'

The birthday outing is a great success, all the talk of the future. The excited couples have decided to share their wedding day, applying for a special license to marry in a double ceremony at Guiseley Parish Church on 29 December. Patrick and William will take turns as minister and bridegroom, while Maria and Jane will do likewise as bride and bridesmaid. They walk and talk, best friends making wedding plans together. The Duchess and Uncle Fennell chipping in with benign advice. The next letter is dated 21 October and Maria is in much better spirits: 'With the sincerest pleasure do I retire from company to converse with him whom I love beyond all others,' she begins.

> 'Could my beloved friend see my heart he would then be convinced that the affection I bear him is not at all inferior to that which he feels for me—indeed I sometimes think that in truth and constancy it excels. But do not think from this that I entertain any suspicions of your sincerity—no, I firmly believe you to be sincere and generous, and doubt not in the least that you feel all you express. In return, I entreat that you will do me the justice to believe that you have not only a *very large portion* of my *affection* and *esteem*, but *all* that I am capable of feeling, and from henceforth measure my feelings by your own.'

How else, she asks, could she abandon her beloved Penzance? Where she lived comfortably and happily, surrounded by the people and places she loved. She never intended to leave forever and this underlying sense of loss, and even loneliness, surely has a role in the sudden storms of emotion in some of her letters. He can never entirely understand what she is giving up, her sunny, leisured and independent life before him. The kind of life he has never lived, the beautiful place he has never seen, the dear people he has never met. Maria is choosing Patrick above all else:

'Unless my love for you were very great how could I so contentedly give up my home and all my friends—a home I loved so much that I have often thought nothing could bribe me to renounce it for any great length of time together, and friends with whom I have been so long accustomed to share all the vicissitudes of joy and sorrow? Yet these have lost their weight, and though I cannot always think of them without a sigh, yet the anticipation of sharing with you all the pleasures and pains, the cares and anxieties of life, of contributing to your comfort and becoming the companion of your pilgrimage, is more delightful to me than any other prospect which this world can possibly present.'

More than a sigh, one suspects, for the book club and assembly room balls, the azure sea and exotic flowers. By now, surely, Patrick expects a reproach over his slow replies, though Maria now pretends it is a good test of her patience:

'I expected to have heard from you on Saturday last, and can scarcely refrain from thinking you unkind to keep me in suspense two whole days longer than was necessary, but it is well that my patience should be sometimes tried, or I might entirely lose it, and this would be a loss indeed!'

Maria also professes to embrace a degree of inner turmoil:

'Lately I have experienced a considerable increase of hopes and fears, which tend to destroy the calm uniformity of my life. These are not unwelcome, as they enable me to discover more of the evils and errors of my heart, and discovering them I hope through grace to be enabled to correct and amend them.'

Her resilience comes of this endless wrestling with life-changing decisions and attempts to understand the divine plan for her life. Though she is practical too. In an age when a chill was something to take very seriously, she reports her fellow bride-to-be Jane has a 'very serious cold' and cough. 'I take all possible care of her, but yesterday she was naughty enough to venture into the yard without her bonnet!' Meanwhile, the nights are growing colder and her uncle is still in pursuit of blankets for the boys: 'Mr Fennell requests Mr Bedford to call on the man who has had orders to make blankets for the Grove and desire him to send them as soon as possible.' Maria writes often and fulsomely about her powerful religious sentiments and the full text of her letters is in Appendix 1. However, while saving souls is one thing, saving lives often came down to bonnets and blankets.

In perhaps her most intimate letter, on 18 November 1812 Maria gives a hint of the sexual attraction they keep strictly to themselves. She opens with, 'My dear Saucy Pat, Now don't you think you deserve this epithet, far more, than I do that which you have given me?' Was she addressed as his dear saucy Maria? Looks like it. Jane and William tease Maria about the content of these letters she lives for: 'Both the Dr and his lady very much wish to know what kind of address we make use of in our letters to each other – I think they would scarcely hit on *this*!!'

Sauciness aside, Patrick has sent torrid prose in response to some criticism. Maria pretends to be taken aback but is clearly quite gratified:

> 'I really know not what to make of the beginning of your last; the winds, waves, and rocks almost stunned me. I thought you were giving me the account of some terrible dream, or that you had had a presentiment of the fate of my poor box, having no idea that your lively imagination could make so much of the slight reproof conveyed in my last. What will you say when you get a *real, downright scolding*? Since you shew such a readiness to atone for your offences, after receiving a mild rebuke, I am inclined to hope, you will seldom deserve a severe one. I accept – with pleasure your atonement, and send you a free and full forgiveness.'

All is well again, with a return to the familiar who-loves-whom-the-most contest:

> 'But I cannot allow that your affection is more deeply rooted than mine ... As to the other qualities which your partiality attributes to me, although I rejoice to know that I stand so high

in your good opinion, yet I blush to think in how small a degree
I possess them. ... I do not, cannot, doubt your love, and here
I freely declare I love you above all the world besides.'

Maria has sent to Penzance for her most precious belongings, including her
books, volumes of magazines and some items of her trousseau, including
a veil. They were packed up and sent by sea, but never made it. This is 'the
fate of my poor box' mentioned earlier. The ship has come to grief and
almost everything lost:

'I suppose you never expected to be much the richer for me, but
I am sorry to inform you that I am still poorer than I thought
myself. I mentioned having sent for my books, clothes, etc.
On Saturday evening about the time you were writing the
description of your imaginary shipwreck, I was reading and
feeling the effects of a real one, having then received a letter
from my sister giving me an account of the vessel in which she
had sent my box being stranded on the coast of Devonshire, in
consequence of which the box was dashed to pieces with the
violence of the sea and all my little property, with the exception
of a very few articles, swallowed up in the mighty deep.'

The vessel was the *Trader* and she was driven onto rocks in north Devon
on 23 October 1812 by the sudden Atlantic gales that plagued shipping in
the busy Bristol Channel. The scant record in *Lloyd's List* reports only the
bare facts of the disaster: 'The Trader, Dennis, from St. Ives and Penzance
to Bristol, run on shore near llfracombe 23d inst. Cargo landing.'

The powerful tidal bore of the channel made it even more dangerous
in a winter storm and ships would often seek refuge at Ilfracombe. Some
did not make it past rocks near the harbour mouth, including the 57-ton
sailing ship transporting Maria's precious box. 'Cargo landing' would
be thanks to the self-employed boatmen known as hobblers (see plates
section), who guided or towed ships to shore and helped in an emergency
such as the *Trader*.

An identical fate befell the *Arabella* in October 1895, when she became
wedged in Britton Rock (see plates section) after being driven ashore by a
midnight gale. The *Cornishman* reported: 'The *Arabella* ... was wrecked
near Ilfracombe early on Wednesday morning, and her crew, of four,
drowned. Two boatmen, who attempted a rescue, also perished.'

It was these brave boatmen of north Devon who would have salvaged what they could of Maria's 'poor box' in 1812. Its reputation as a harbour of refuge – from wild weather and predatory privateers – made Ilfracombe a centre for boatbuilding, repairs and loading up on supplies. 'Dennis' in the press report refers to William Dennis, who built *Trader* there in 1805 with William Huxtable. It was one of the smaller constant coasters, trade ships that sometimes carried passengers. So the hobblers may have also rescued any such victims along with the crew before turning to the cargo. The *Trader* was repaired and refloated in its home harbour, sailing out of the Brontë story to serve on until the late 1830s.

Her sister must have revealed more details about what happened on that stormy night but Maria, who could devote pages to an absent letter, does not share the whole 'account of the vessel ... being stranded' until she sees her fiancé in person. Without the wreck, Maria might never have mentioned all her 'little property' from Penzance, thus highlighting seawater stains as tell-tale indications of her life before Yorkshire. Maria puts on a brave face as she continues her letter to Patrick:

> 'If this should not prove the prelude to something worse, I shall think little of it, as it is the first disastrous circumstance which has occurred since I left my home, and having been so highly favoured it would be highly ungrateful in me were I to suffer this to dwell much on my mind.'

Most people would dwell a little and she must have done so in private. Her sisters had sent a wedding veil for her to wear but it had not survived the disaster and was lost. It seems likely there were several items for her bottom drawer that were now at the bottom of the Atlantic. Still, she has to be practical and ends by inviting Patrick on a shopping trip to Leeds the following week. Clothes claimed by the mighty deep must be replaced.

Then on 5 December with just three weeks to the wedding, the future Mrs Brontë is having a mini meltdown. As ever, she is in a spate about Patrick's periodic silences and this time is openly sarcastic:

> 'So you *thought* that *perhaps* I *might* expect to hear from you. As the case was so doubtful, and you were in such great haste, you might as well have deferred writing a few days longer, for you seem to suppose it is a matter of perfect indifference to me

whether I hear from you or not. I believe I once requested you to judge of my feelings by your own—am I to think that *you* are thus indifferent? I feel very unwilling to entertain such an opinion, and am grieved that you should suspect me of such a cold, heartless, attachment.'

Just as abruptly, she halts her insecure rant in favour of a touching confession:

'But I am too serious on the subject; I only meant to rally you a little on the beginning of your last, and to tell you that I fancied there was a coolness in it which none of your former letters had contained. If this fancy was groundless, forgive me for having indulged it, and let it serve to convince you of the sincerity and warmth of my affection. Real love is ever apt to suspect that it meets not with an equal return; you must not wonder then that my fears are sometimes excited. My pride cannot bear the idea of a diminution of your attachment, or to think that it is stronger on my side than on yours. But I must not permit my pen so fully to disclose the feelings of my heart, nor will I tell you whether I am pleased or not at the thought of seeing you on the appointed day.'

Maria's letters are often written in stages, at different times of the day and often overnight before 'the old man' comes for the letters. In this one, she moves from lashing out, to frank apology, to guest lists and wedding cakes. Plans for the big day are well underway:

'We intend to set about making the cakes here next week, but as the fifteen or twenty persons whom you mention live probably somewhere in your neighbourhood, I think it will be most convenient for Mrs. B. [Harriott Bedford] to make a small one for the purpose of distributing there, which will save us the difficulty of sending so far. You may depend on my learning my lessons as rapidly as they are given me. I am already tolerably perfect in the A B C, etc. I am much obliged to you for the pretty little hymn which I have already got by heart, but cannot promise to sing it scientifically, though I will endeavour to gain a little more assurance.'

Maria and Jane live and work together and spend every spare moment planning their wedding. They also sit writing to their fiancés together and discussing their relationships:

> 'Since I began this Jane put into my hands Lord Lyttelton's *Advice to a Lady*. When I read those lines, 'Be never cool reserve with passion joined, with caution choose, but then be fondly kind, etc.' my heart smote me for having in some cases used too much reserve towards you. Do you think you have any cause to complain of me? If you do, let me know it. For were it in my power to prevent it, I would in no instance occasion you the least pain or uneasiness.'

It is difficult to see too much reserve in Maria's honest and adoring letters. In this, her last before they are married, she offers devotion:

> 'I am certain no one ever loved you with an affection more pure, constant, tender, and ardent than that which I feel. Surely this is not saying too much; it is the truth, and I trust you are worthy to know it. I long to improve in every religious and moral quality, that I may be a help, and if possible an ornament to you. Oh let us pray much for wisdom and grace to fill our appointed stations with propriety, that we may enjoy satisfaction in our own souls, edify others, and bring glory to the name of Him who has so wonderfully preserved, blessed, and brought us together.'

She has recovered from her opening fury:

> 'If there is anything in the commencement of this which looks like pettishness, forgive it; my mind is now completely divested of every feeling of the kind, although I own I am sometimes too apt to be overcome by this disposition. Let me have the pleasure of hearing from you again as soon as convenient. This writing is uncommonly bad, but I too am in haste. Adieu, my dearest. —I am your affectionate and sincere Maria'

And those are the last words we have of Maria as Miss Branwell. Without this precious bundle of letters, cherished by Patrick and later handed to their daughter Charlotte, we would know nothing of Maria's true character. Her letters are alive with her passion, loyalty, intelligence, wit and learning along with her faith and her fears. Like Pat, she can lose her temper if she suspects a slight. We know how much she loved her Cornish life and the pain she endured when abandoning it for an entirely different life with him.

It was a whirlwind romance, two people swept up in each other and quickly realizing this was the real thing. The letters reveal both the dizzying delights of such a breakneck romance, but also the inevitable mood swings. Was it all real? Could they really love each other so intensely so quickly? And always, the nagging fear that it could vanish as quickly as it began. That second thoughts, a late letter or niggle could break the spell. Maria's feelings are beautifully expressed as she freely lets her 'pen run away with them'. Through her we have Patrick's and though second-hand, they are no less vivid. He makes her 'really blush to read her own praises' and when they quarrel, his make-up words are 'the winds, waves and rocks' that 'almost stun' her.

When Maria Branwell met Patrick Brontë, each had found the love of their life.

Chapter 6

Becoming Mrs Brontë

Maria Branwell's big day would give a modern wedding planner a fit of the conniptions. Letters to her lover were not the only missives Maria was dashing off in time to catch the old Grove postman. She and Jane each wrote to their intended, then to their darling Charlotte in Penzance. Maria's little sister was now engaged to Joseph Branwell and the brides-to-be in Yorkshire and Cornwall hatched a plan to be married on the same day, at the same hour, several hundred miles apart. It was to be a triple Regency wedding.

Becoming Mrs Brontë was more complicated than it looked.

On Tuesday 29 December 1812, Maria and Jane would be wed at Guiseley Parish Church, while Charlotte would go to Madron like so many Branwells before her, including Aunt Jane. This was all co-ordinated by Maria and her family and may account for at least some of her more stressed outbursts. Meanwhile, one of the bridegrooms was writing frantic letters of his own. Patrick Brontë was desperate for a parsonage for St Peter's at Hartshead and had been trying to convince the governors of Queen Anne's Bounty to pay for one.

The central church fund helped to support poor clergy and Pat wanted a home built to share with his wife. It did not have to be as grand as the Buckworths' medieval manse in Dewsbury, or Healds Hall occupied by scourge of the radicals Hammond Roberson, but even William Morgan would take Jane home to a house in Bierley near Bradford. Patrick wrote several letters asking for enough money to build a new parsonage in Hartshead, including during his engagement in October 1812, but these fell on deaf ears.

It was to be a Lousy honeymoon but as she made clear in her letters, Maria did not mind. Though a short romance it was not a shotgun wedding. Unlike her mother, Maria was not pregnant on her wedding day – she did not have to get married. Harriott Bedford did her best to provide a bridal suite at the farm and baked cakes for the parishioners as the nuptials went ahead as planned.

Uncle John and Aunt Jane led the wedding party as they set off to the ceremony three and a half miles away in Guiseley. Maybe Grove schoolboys lined up to wave them off but given the strict regime, maybe not. The Fennells had just celebrated their own anniversary and there was time to reminisce about the wedding Maria recalled in Madron when she was a child, like the one Charlotte was walking to right at that moment. Sorrow at the absence of her parents was eased by her kindly uncle, who took on the role of father to both brides.

They were all accustomed to walking to church for the banns to be read. They left the house and went through the grounds, past the holly bushes and old gothic folly. Then they followed the track though rolling countryside to the parish church. John Wesley himself had compared the area to an Italian island dotted with villas. Former pupil Josiah Slugg wrote:

> 'On the higher side of Apperley Bridge, the landscape is, or was, however, yet more exquisitely beautiful; and no one, who in youth approached Esholt Hall [a country house en route] through the splendid avenue of trees, or skipped across the Aire, running parallel to it, by the stepping stones, between which its irritated silver waters brawled as they glided on, or proceeded to Guiseley through the glades of the wood, whose giant limbs swept the sward, while among their boughs the nimble squirrels lilted like birds or butterflies, can be surprised that John Wesley should have set down that sylvan spot as the "Caprera of Yorkshire".'

The fifth day of Christmas in Apperley Bridge was colder than Sardinia and it was an hour's walk to the parish church of St Oswald for the hardy group.

Brontë dress historian Eleanor Houghton has imagined the wedding outfits for Maria and Patrick in the plates section of this book. Miss Branwell could afford a new dress, which would then become her best one for other special occasions. During the early nineteenth century, white was a fashionable colour for gowns and not reserved for wedding dresses, so Maria's muslin dress would have been of a stylish shape and shade. It had a skirt full enough to allow for walking, being held out of the mud over one arm until she reached the church. Houghton points out that military details were in vogue, hence the frogging on the eau de nil spencer (little jacket). Ostrich feathers were de rigueur as fashion plates in *The Lady's Magazine* attest, hence the matching bonnet with plumes. The veil was borrowed after hers went down in the shipwreck. Typically, it would have been attached to the bonnet, hanging down at the back after it was lifted from her face following her vows. Meanwhile, Patrick's attire would have consisted of a sombre black wool coat and breeches, a white shirt and black hat. Low-crowned clerical hats were slowly becoming outmoded and Houghton gives him a top hat, sometimes worn in this period by low church clergymen such as Patrick.

If Maria and Jane were close, so were Patrick and William. Since their meeting in Wellington, their friendship had only deepened. When Pat was the first to leave the Madeley circle three years earlier for Yorkshire, William gave him a leather-bound collection of sermons and homilies as a token of enduring friendship. It was a touching prophesy as they would indeed support each other through the joys and sorrows of the coming fifty years. As they dressed for their joint winter wedding in 1812, they were each other's best man and also best friends.

At the church, the carefully co-ordinated dance began. The Duchess took pride of place in the front pew as, effectively, mother of the brides while John Fennell walked his daughter and his niece down the aisle. At the altar rail, Maria and Patrick stood side by side with Jane her bridesmaid while the Reverend Morgan said:

> 'Forasmuch as Patrick and Maria have consented together in holy wedlock, and have witnessed the same before God and this company, and thereto have given and pledged their troth either to other, and have declared the same by giving and receiving of a ring, and by joining of hands, I pronounce that they be man and wife together...'

Then they all swapped places and the Reverend Brontë took the Book of Common Prayer to marry his friends William and Jane. Maria took her place as bridesmaid, though now technically a married matron of honour.

Then Maria walked out into the winter light with her new husband, not as Mrs Prunty but as the first, last and only Mrs Brontë.

It was a Celtic wedding on Yorkshire soil with two Cornish brides, Maria married to an Irishman and Jane to a Welshman. And in faraway Madron Parish Church, the youngest belle of Penzance went from Miss Branwell to Mrs Branwell at exactly the same time. The letters flying between the wedding planners, carried by the mail coaches that had carried Maria, paid off. Charlotte's daughter, also called Charlotte Branwell, wrote: 'Perhaps a similar case never happened before or since: two sisters and four first cousins being united in holy matrimony at one and the same time. And they were all happy marriages.' Then that word again, the one Pat might have hoped to leave behind with Old Staff: 'Mr. Brontë was perhaps peculiar, but I have always heard my own dear mother say that he was devotedly fond of his wife, and she of him.'

Never more so than during that first blissful year of 1813, which began at Lousy Farm accompanied by an announcement in the February issue of *The Gentleman's Magazine*:

> 'At Guisely, [sic] near Bradford, by Rev. W. Morgan, minister of Bierley, Rev. P. Bronte, B.A. minister of Harshead cum Clifton, to Maria, third daughter of the late T. Bromwell, [sic] esq. of Penzance. And at the same time, by the Rev. P. Bronte, Rev. W Morgan, to the only daughter of Mr. John Fennell, headmaster of the Wesleyan academy near Bradford.'

Despite the misspellings, Maria's marriage was recorded alongside those of Lucia Bartolozzi (later a celebrated singer and theatre impresario) in London, an heiress in Brighton and the eldest daughter of a lieutenant general in Bath. The English gentry had been informed. For a lady raised in polite society, as Jane Austen observed the following year, 'one may as well be single if the Wedding is not to be in print'.

Despite this middle class contentment, the outside world was still a far from happy place. The winter of 1812 had been particularly brutal for labouring families. The French wars were sucking the country dry, the industrial revolution was laying waste to traditional employment and a series of poor harvests combined with high taxes to increase food prices and hunger among the poor.

Maria moved to Hartshead in January 1813, just as the last Luddite prisoners were deported or hanged for their crimes in York. It was the aftermath of rebellion in the raw. Pat had seen it all before, while Maria had been sheltered by class and geography. A sense of unease still pervaded the area. Just days after the wedding, the *Morning Chronicle* of 4 January reported: 'The depot of arms mentioned to have been seized by the Magistrates near Halifax, amounted to eight muskets and six pair of pistols.'

The authorities were tipped off by an informer and William Hall, a Luddite leader from Liversedge, also turned king's evidence to save his neck. Many who escaped a criminal colony or the gallows left the area to start again. The corpses were cut down from the York gibbets as machines in mills continued to replace croppers in sheds, but the open revolt was over. The industrial revolution could not be halted.

After a life in bustling Penzance then a few months at the Grove, Maria was sometimes nervous at the isolated farm. Yet she was soon made welcome. Patrick was popular across the parish after his fight to clear the name of young William Nowell in Dewsbury. Unlike some of his fellow clergy, he had not displayed vengeful wrath from the pulpit during the frame-breaking crisis. The new couple had plenty of friends, including a fellow Nowell campaigner, Marmaduke Fox. He was friends with Pat and among the first to take his wife to call on the new Mrs Brontë.

Maria wrote often of her intention to be a helpmate to Patrick once they were married. Now she was a clergy wife with a very different role than she was used to, in a poor and troubled West Riding parish. She too tended to the flock, attending services and visiting the sick.

When they were together, though, Maria and Patrick were entirely wrapped up in each other. Married life was good for Pat's writing. Much better and more upbeat poetry written since he fell in love appeared in his collection *The Rural Minstrel* published that year. For Maria's 30th in April he wrote *Lines, Addressed to a Lady, on her Birth-day*. They were a lot more cheerful than the ones he wrote to Mary Burder on her 18th and then reworked as a warning against prostitution. The hundred and seventeen lines of verse Patrick wrote to his bride are a testament to his deep love for her and echo her letters to him. It is the only thing we have that Patrick wrote for Maria and includes:

'Maria, let us walk, and breathe, the morning air,
And hear the cuckoo sing,–
And every tuneful bird, that woos the gentle spring.
Throughout the budding grove,
Softly coos the turtle-dove,
The primrose pale,
Perfumes the gale,
The modest daisy, and the violet blue,
Inviting, spread their charms for you.
How much enhanced is all this bliss to me,
Since it is shared, in mutual joy with thee!'

Another, *Kirkstall Abbey, A Fragment of a Romantic Tale*, was inspired by their courtship amid the riverside ruins. In both poems Patrick reveals his great love of the Yorkshire landscape. Having her beside him only makes everything better. They had known each other for barely a year and were still besotted. On the tabletop moor there were walks through the morning air, there was poetry and there was sex. By Mazey eve 1813, Maria Brontë was pregnant.

It seems likely that this was when Maria and Patrick moved from Lousy Farm to Clough House in the village of Hightown. With his £62 a year and her £50, they could just about afford to rent the handsome Georgian house half a mile away. It bore an uncanny resemblance to dear old 25 Chapel Street and felt more like home than the lonely, windswept farm. Like at Rotterdam Buildings, the front door opened onto a wood-panelled hallway. The door itself had a huge inside metal bolt more than capable of keeping a stray Luddite at bay.

On the ground floor there was a large hall and two front rooms, with a small kitchen for cooking leading to an outside wash kitchen for laundry. On the first floor there were six rooms for sleeping, studying and dressing. Two large attic rooms were intended as servant quarters, or a nursery like in Penzance. Below the kitchen was a cold cellar used as a food larder, with a large stone table and shelves.

For Patrick, too, it was a welcome change. He was 36 years old and had been a lodger since leaving Ireland. He had never lived in his own home, so a longer walk to his church was worth it. The parents-to-be could furnish their first home together, getting everything ready for their baby behind their own front door.

Living in a village made it easier for friends to call on the Brontës. Maria and Patrick visited John and Rachel Buckworth in Dewsbury and William and Jane Morgan remained close. Meanwhile, the Fennells had quit Woodhouse Grove. Maria's uncle decided against following the Methodists when they split from the Church of England. John remained within the established church and prepared for ordination as a minister in Bradford. The Duchess was simply glad of a rest.

Maria's friend Joseph Abbott was also off Methodism for life after the austere academy. He too was ordained an Anglican and moved to Canada where he was a high churchman with a dislike of Dissenters generally and itinerant Evangelists in particular. He remained interested in education and held a series of senior roles at McGill University in Montreal. It was from there he wrote to Charlotte Brontë about his brush with the Luddites. His son John Abbott became the Prime Minister of Canada in 1891.

At Clough House in late 1813, Maria could finally relax and prepare for the baby. Among her belongings at Brontë Parsonage Museum is a pair of knitting sheaths made of brown wood. These tapered, flattened sticks were a kind of knitting needle found in the North and could be used to knit quickly while standing up or walking around. They were often of great sentimental value and carved or decorated sheaths were handed down in families. Maria's are inscribed with M.B. in black letters, which suggests they were a wedding gift. Everybody's favourite aunt and an ex-matron to scores of boys, Maria was to have children of her own, born and bred in Yorkshire. So nimble-fingered Mrs Brontë began knitting baby clothes.

A wanted pregnancy was both a delight and a worry in 1813 when mortality rates were high. Patrick owned a copy of *Domestic medicine; or, A treatise on the prevention and cure of diseases by regimen and simple medicines*, by William Buchan. His advice for pregnant women included: 'They ought to avoid all flatulent food, and to wear a loose easy dress.' Also that: 'Breeding women are very subject to the tooth-ach, especially during the first three or four months of pregnancy.' They were also prone to constipation-induced headaches, which '…may generally be removed by keeping the body gently open, by the use of prunes, figs, roasted apples, and such like.' As the birth grew near, Maria began her lying-in, an extended period of bed rest. She was attended by a local midwife and doctor when she went into labour.

Maria gave birth to a healthy little girl in early 1814 (her birthday is unknown) and the delighted parents named their firstborn after her mother. The baby was healthy but the single biggest danger for a new mother was puerperal – or childbed –fever. Blood poisoning (sepsis) caused by bacterial infection of the birth canal killed many women and deaths spiked in 1812, 1813 and 1814. It usually developed three days after the birth and led to a horrible death within eleven.

It was most common in poor homes where the custom was to make the lying-in room like a darkened cave with a fire. Sealing the mother into an overheated, airless and unhygienic space and insisting on her lying flat and still long after the birth created dangerous conditions where bacteria spread. Surgeon and 'man midwife' Charles White died in 1813 after a career campaigning against unhygienic practices:

> 'When the woman is in labour, she is often attended by a number of her friends in a small room, with a large fire, which, together with her own pains, throw her in profuse sweats; by the heat of the chamber, and the breath of so many people, the whole air is rendered foul…'

He advocated cleanliness, plenty of fresh air and moving around after the delivery. Well-read Maria would have followed his advice. She recovered well and a few weeks later may have been 'churched' at St Peter's. This was a special service to give thanks for a safe delivery and return to health of the mother.

Little Maria Brontë was christened at St Peter's on 23 April 1814, a week after her mother's birthday. William Morgan did the honours at the stone font, made in 1662 from a section of an original Norman pillar that had been hollowed out and inscribed with the year. Afterwards, the mothers of the congregation held a christening tea. They were decidedly fond of their peculiar parson and his new little family.

Within a month of the christening, Maria was pregnant again.

As Maria looked after the baby and began knitting for another, Patrick continued to network with his Evangelical friends in Bradford where John Fennell and William Morgan now worked with the vicar of Bradford, John Crosse. He got to know the Reverend William Atkinson, nephew of Hammond Roberson (they of the Old Staff joke) and perpetual curate of Thornton, a village on the outskirts of the parish.

His new friend had a startling proposal. Would Patrick like to swap jobs with him? Atkinson was wealthy so not interested in the money. He was interested in courting Frances Walker of Lascelles Hall, near Huddersfield and not far from St Peter's. As one parishioner put it to journalist William Yates: 'He had a bird to catch, near Hartshead.'

It was an exciting offer. Thornton was a bigger chapelry so came with a living of £140, more than double what he was earning at St Peter's. Even better, the job came with a parsonage. Maria liked the idea. Thornton was closer to her family, with Aunt Fennell and Jane Morgan in Bradford. Mr Brontë went to see Mr Atkinson and told him it was a deal.

Patrick and Maria welcomed their second daughter, Elizabeth Brontë, on 8 February 1815 and named her after her sociable auntie in Penzance. The move to Thornton was planned for May and appeals for help once more flew from Yorkshire to Cornwall. Maria asked her sister Elizabeth to come help with the babies and the house move. So Aunt Branwell made the epic journey north for the reunion. The sisters had not seen each other for three years and Elizabeth had never even met Patrick or the children. The capable Cornishwoman surveyed the situation and started organising the packing.

One day Charlotte Brontë would go to school in Dewsbury and later write *Shirley* inspired by family stories of frame-smashing, Evangelical clergy and the kings and queens of Dewsbury. In May 1815, though, just four Brontës and Aunt Branwell rode away from their restless, rural corner of the parish and headed for Thornton.

Chapter 7

Mothering Heights

The elegant Branwell sisters arrived in Thornton with their little namesakes and impeccable manners to discover polite society was waiting. Maria made friends among the wealthy women of the area and settled into a delightful social round with echoes of Penzance. After the Hartshead hiatus she could once more take tea in drawing rooms and talk about books and instructing the poor, though this time she was usually pregnant. Maria found a familiar milieu, the bluestockings of Bradford parish.

Thornton Parsonage was the birthplace of Charlotte, Branwell, Emily and Anne Brontë. It was also where their mother made her own stab at being a lady of letters.

Like Lousy, the name Thornton, more obviously, derives from the hardy thorn trees around the hillside village above Bradford. At Whitsuntide 1815 it was a small but thriving place where most people worked in weaving or farming, while some were employed in stone quarries on the moor at Thornton Heights and coal mines in the valleys.

The Brontës' house was built in 1802 by John and Sarah Ashworth, commemorated by the date and their initials chiselled over the door. It was bought by the Church of England in 1807. Thomas Atkinson lived there for at least some of his eleven years as curate before trading places with Pat. Larger than the other houses along the street, it stood on the busy main road through town. Of the 23 buildings in Market Street, three were pubs catering for locals and travellers. The Black Horse, the White Horse and the Bull's Head lay en route to the industrial hubs of Bradford one way and Halifax the other. The children would grow up near a little shop selling 'spice', the old Yorkshire word for sweets.

They arrived on 19 May 1815 after the eleven-mile journey from Clough House. Maria, Patrick and Elizabeth took the girls inside then explored the new place. The ground floor had a hall leading to a large drawing room to the left and a dining room to the right. At the rear was a scullery with stone steps leading upstairs for the use of servants. A flight of wooden steps for the family ran from the hallway.

On the first floor were two large bedrooms to the left, the largest for the children and the other for their parents. To the right of the staircase was a small narrow room for Elizabeth and later the maids. To the rear rose steeply sloping farmland and open country, though no garden. The church terrier – property record – for 1817 also records the Parsonage 'having a stand for a cow and a horse at one end and a cottage at the other...' Pat could not afford a horse, but his visitors could.

This was the first Brontë Parsonage, though it was also known as the Glebe house. Pat was again perpetual curate, so until he moved on or died they had the security of a home. Now he had a pay rise, Maria's money allowed her to go shopping. They acquired a new mahogany dining table, plus eight chairs with black horsehair upholstery. The set was made in a provincial workshop and each chair had a number from one to eight carved under the seat.

The drop-leaf table and four of the chairs now stand in the Parsonage at Haworth. This was where the Brontë sisters later gathered to write, discuss ideas and plot how to get published. In Thornton, the furniture was simply to allow Maria's rapidly expanding family to eat together. Though church records are mainly what survive of these years, such things are testimony to ordinary family life. Maria and Pat enjoyed everyday pleasures such as picking out furniture for their new house.

By far the most imposing building on the street was not the Anglican parsonage but the chapel of Thornton's large Nonconformist community. The Independent (Congregationalist) Chapel of Kipping was built in 1769 and grew from an influential Puritan community established in the 1640s, or even earlier. Meetings were originally held in a barn near Kipping House – soon to play a huge role in Maria's life – but relocated in the eighteenth century when religious persecution abated.

By contrast, Pat's church was a dilapidated old building behind Thornton Hall. St James' chapel-of-ease was an outpost of the vast parish of Bradford run from the church of St Peter (now Bradford Cathedral) in the city centre. It was known locally as the Old Bell Chapel because of the small bell-house on the top containing a single bell cast in 1664. Inside it was dark and damp and paved with slippery gravestones. Poorly planned burials beneath the church floor caused subsidence and a faint but foetid smell pervaded the interior.

There had been a chapel there since at least 1560, originally dedicated to St Leonard and complete with secret underground passage from Thornton Hall. It had two cryptic date stones. One read:

'THIS CHAPPELL WAS BUILDED BY [blank] IIIIII [blank] E FREEMASON IN THE YEARE OF OUR LORDE 1612.'

The name had been removed with a chisel. Or rather, most of it had. The work was a restoration rather than a rebuild and the mason clearly fell out of favour, probably for joining the Dissenters. Thornton historians William Preston and Alan Whitworth suggest the missing freemason was churchwarden Richard Lillye. The person ordered to remove the name may have left a clue by disguising some letters and keeping the E.

Another stone was carved 1587, though there is no record of why. Freemasons remained influential members of the congregation, witnessed by ornate masonic gravestones. In 1872 the new church of St James opened across the road. William Cudworth writes:

'The foundation-stone was laid with Masonic honours by the Marquis of Ripon, the Grand Master of the Order, on which occasion a large number of the craft were present.'

Kipping was king among Thornton Dissenters, but Methodists also had a longstanding presence. They met in houses or outside in summer and were known as Click-'ems. Click meant snatch and that was the Wesleyan way, snatching people from sin before it was too late. The Branwells in Penzance had just helped to build the new Methodist Chapel in Chapel Street, opened in 1814. So Elizabeth could have made informal contact with her fellow Wesleyans, while attending her brother-in-law's church for propriety's sake. Maria might have abandoned the Click-'ems but her big sister had not.

Once the unpacking was done, Maria and Elizabeth (and Pat) were ready to make their entrance. On 7 June 1815, Elizabeth Firth of Kipping House paid them a courtesy call and on 9 June they were all invited to Allerton Hall, in one of the villages under Pat's auspices. It was the home of cotton baron Benjamin Kaye and his wife Mercy. He employed many of the cottage weavers in the area and traded the finished goods in Manchester. Elizabeth, who was 18, was there with her widowed father, the wealthy doctor and churchman John Firth.

Maria was always charming, as Patrick attests later when writing to Mrs Gaskell. 'She was an excellent wife and mother, and a highly respected member of Society.' She had 'sound sense,' an 'affectionate disposition' and 'delicate tact and taste'. There was no danger of her failing to impress.

It was the beginning of a series of friendships that would endure for the rest of her life. Through Elizabeth she met Fanny Outhwaite, daughter of Bradford doctor and philanthropist Thomas and his wife Frances. Fanny and Elizabeth met at the exclusive Crofton School near Wakefield. Elizabeth was also the cousin of Frances Walker of Lascelles Hall, the object of Thomas Atkinson's determined courtship.

Maria had stepped straight into a ready-made social life, made all the easier by having a stylish sister beside her. Maria and Elizabeth were daughters of a wealthy Cornish merchant. They knew themselves to be Elizabeth's social equal. Though their Penzance homes had not been *quite* on the scale of Kipping House or Allerton Hall and their private incomes could not compare, they were of the same class.

It was easy to talk up their own backgrounds with the kind of sparkling stories and repartee that Aunt Branwell would later rehearse in her dotage, discreetly flashing a gilt-edged smelling bottle or two. How that reminded them of the assembly room balls and evenings at the playhouse... did Miss Firth enjoy the theatre? Sip of tea. No need to mention being removed to another, rather less central, house when dear Father died.

One thing was immediately apparent to every lady weighing them up across the china. The newcomers were at home in upper class company. The former belles of Penzance maintained their taste, elegance, conversational skills and social ease. As tea was served, it would be easy to drop in the latest news of their brother in Penzance. Their brother the former mayor, chief magistrate and Lieutenant in the Volunteers. Or allude to their dear childhood friend, *Sir* Humphry Davy. Pat could chip in with his friends in Parliament if necessary.

Elizabeth Firth was living exactly the kind of life Maria had lived at her age, that of an educated young woman doing the social rounds. She even resembled her. The young mistress of Kipping was petite too, only a shade over 5ft 3in tall and weighing just over seven stones.

After three years of lodging and rented houses and Luddites on the doorstep, Maria felt back where she belonged – among the gentry.

Pat needed a good professional relationship with Dr Firth, an important man in the district, but the two families rapidly became close friends. Three days after the Allerton soiree, Maria and her sister called on Elizabeth at home and were soon exchanging regular visits.

Maria's existence was proscribed by the expectations of the age, pregnancies and a domestic sphere populated by demanding small children. Her life of the mind was at the mercy of her life as a mother. Yet she did have one. Her social and intellectual life centred on Kipping House and for its details, albeit sketchy, we have Elizabeth Firth to thank. Miss Firth's role in history stems entirely from her diary. Without it we would know virtually nothing about Maria's life in Yorkshire or the early years of her astonishing children.

In the late Regency era there were several female diarists of note, though they recorded their lives in different ways. In Madeley Vicarage the elderly Mary Fletcher recorded her strange dreams, such as the one where her dead husband appeared with a warning about John Kingston.

In London, Welsh-born Hester Thrale Piozzi documented life among the literary elite (and lived in Penzance for a spell in 1820). Her younger friend Fanny Burney also wrote shrewd diaries detailing literary, theatrical and court life. In Chawton, Hampshire, Jane Austen critiqued her world in ground-breaking novels and literary commentaries.

Just seven miles away in Shibden Hall near Halifax lived Maria and Elizabeth's West Yorkshire contemporary, Anne Lister. Dubbed 'Gentleman Jack' she was among the first British women to live an openly gay life. Her detailed diaries were so explicit she wrote parts of them in code.

In Thornton, there was Elizabeth Firth. She kept a diary from the age of 14 but birth, death or a trip to the dentist, it was all the same to the daughter of Kipping House. In 1815 her new copy of *The Ladies' Own Memorandum-Book, or Daily Pocket Journal* has more space allowed to recording how she spends her annual £50 pocket money and dress allowance than her inner life. As to her thoughts as a witness to history, little warrants more than a single line in her diary. She seldom worries about syntax and never about diareses.

For those interested in the lives of the Brontës, it is possibly the most annoying document of the nineteenth century. Yet it is also invaluable, peppered with clues to their daily lives for more than five years. Though sparse on detail, it is an anatomy of a middle class lady's life in Regency Thornton, a life she shared with the young Brontës and her close friend, their ladylike mother.

Of particular interest is her reading material. This takes on added significance when attempting to discover the literary influences of the mother of the Brontë siblings. A fascinating snapshot of literature doing the rounds among the Thornton ladies is provided by Elizabeth's diary of 1815, when she first met Maria.

Just as we can reasonably infer Maria's choice of books from the Penzance Ladies Book Club records, so her friend's reading list throws a light on the books she discussed in Thornton when the gossip ran out. The opinions of the parson's well-read wife would have been important to the younger woman. The books mentioned in the diary that year include *Pride and Prejudice* by Jane Austen, *The Corsair* by George Byron and *A Journey to the Western Islands of Scotland* by Samuel Johnson.

She read a range of works by female writers, from the conservative moralist Jane West to members of the eighteenth-century Bluestocking circle such as Elizabeth Carter, Elizabeth Montagu, Elizabeth Vesey and Catherine Talbot. She also read Elizabeth Smith, a leading biblical scholar, and Sophia Lee, who wrote romances and used the money to open a girl's school near Bath. When Elizabeth went 'to sit with Mrs Bronte in the evening' in August she began *A Compendium of Geography* by Richmal Mangnall, her school teacher at Crofton Hall.

Kipping House was built in the seventeenth century and was a fine residence fit for the gentry. It had a library and large sunny drawing room looking out over a huge sloping garden to the Pinch Beck Valley. It was just minutes from the Parsonage, down old Kipping Lane below Market Street. Maria loved to visit the lovely big house, away from the clutter of babies and Pat's papers.

The Brontës had only been in Thornton a month when, at long last, the Napoleonic Wars came to an end. On 18 June Arthur Wellesley, Duke of Wellington, claimed a decisive victory at the Battle of Waterloo. After 23 years, Napoleon was finally defeated. Maria's country had been at war since she was ten years old. On 20 June the Brontës were invited to a celebratory dinner party at Kipping.

Conversation around the table would have flowed easily. It was dizzying for Maria to recall that it had only been three years since she lived in Penzance as redcoats thronged the harbour and her brother drilled with the Volunteers. Maria's life had changed beyond recognition in some ways but returned to a kind of equilibrium in others. If Elizabeth Branwell was there she may have thought of cousin Thomas, the young Royal Navy officer who never came home.

Of the nationwide celebrations Elizabeth Firth records nothing except the Sunday service on 23 July 1815. 'A collection was made for the widows and orphans of those who fell at the Battle of Waterloo.'

Soon it was August and baby Elizabeth had still not been christened. This was organised for the 26th and Maria's newly-ordained uncle presided at the Old Bell Chapel 139-year-old octagonal stone font. The families were now on godparent terms: 'Mr Bronte's 2nd daughter was christened Elizabeth by Mr Fennel [sic] my Papa was Godfather Miss Branwell and I were Godmothers'. Once again Maria handed her baby to be splashed with holy water with another already on the way. She was at least a month pregnant with her third child. When she found out, her sister agreed to stay on to see her through the next birth.

With the end of summer came a seismic change, at least for Miss Firth. Since her mother's death, she had worn black. Elizabeth Firth the elder had died the previous year in an horrific accident outside their home. On 2 July 1814, young Elizabeth had written one of her lengthier sentences:

> 'My ever to be lamented Mother was thrown out of the gig and killed on the Spot by a blood vessel breaking in the head; aged 56 years the accident happened in the lane opposite the Kitchen windows.'

On Sunday 3 Sept 1815 she notes, 'We gave over wearing black for my dear Mother.' Which made room for another woman to join the Kipping circle, 53-year-old Anne Greame. Elizabeth had recorded a 'tete ah tete' [sic] with Miss Greame on 27 February that year when it can be assumed she learned of her father's marriage proposal. There is nothing to reveal Elizabeth's feelings about this, seven months after her mother's sudden death. Nor 72 hours after mourning ended in the entry for 6 Sept. 'My Papa was married to Miss Greame at Bradford Church by Mr Morgan the bridal party dined at Exley and came here in the evening.'

It can only be assumed that the Brontës made the guest list. Elizabeth's new step-mother was the twin sister of Fanny Outhwaite's mother, Frances. She came from a landowning family at Exley near Halifax. Anne takes her place in the diary as Mrs Firth and appears to have endeared herself as she begins to appear as Mother.

In December 1815 in faraway Madeley, Mary Fletcher died, aged 76. In many ways she was the invisible architect of the Brontë family. If she had not recommended John and Jane Fennell for Woodhouse Grove, William Morgan for Bradford and Pat for Dewsbury, Maria may never have met her husband and the Brontë sisters and their brother would never have been born.

As Maria's 33rd birthday drew near in April 1816, so did her due date. The drawing room towards the back of the house was prepared as her lying-in room, away from the noisy carts of Market Street. Here Aunt Branwell saw her new niece into the world on 21 April 1816. She was named Charlotte after another aunt. Maybe she had a look of her. Charlotte Brontë wrote after a visit from Cornish cousin John Branwell Williams, 'the moment he saw me he exclaimed that I was the very image of my Aunt Charlotte.'

The baby was duly christened at the Old Bell Chapel on 29 June 1816 by William Morgan. Then it was time for Elizabeth Branwell to go home. Maria was clearly going to have one baby after another. Her sister needed to get back to her own life in Penzance. She and Maria went for tea at Kipping together for the last time. On Sunday 28 July Elizabeth Firth wrote at the length usually reserved for a death in the family, 'I took leave of Miss Branwell she kissed me and was much affected. She left Thornton that evening.'

And with that, she was gone. Elizabeth Branwell caught the stagecoach from Bradford and began the long trek home.

Maria missed her immediately, though Elizabeth Firth visited the very next day. With a baby and two toddlers to care for alone, Maria suddenly had her hands full. Pat advertised for a nursemaid among the pupils of the School of Industry in Northgate, Bradford. The charity was founded in 1807 as a school for the instruction of poor children in education, industry and the doctrine of the Church of England. Vocational training was free but came at the price of draconian school rules. Girls were obliged to wear their hair very short, cropped almost to the skull, and punishments for the slightest transgression were harsh.

Nancy Garrs was a 13-year-old pupil when fate picked her out for a role in the most famous family saga in literature. She was one of twelve children. Her father Richard was from a French migrant family called De Garrs that dropped the 'De' during the Napoleonic Wars. Patrick hired Nancy as a nursemaid and she moved in to the Parsonage. Though a child herself, 13 was a normal age to begin work for a girl of her station. She was met with kindness, remaining devoted to her employers for the rest of her life.

Nancy looked after the children, a Thornton lady called Mrs Feather did the laundry and Maria had time to go out for tea and take walks with her friends. She missed her sister, had more free time with a live-in maid and her husband was enjoying his writing life. Maybe this was when she decided to join him.

For Patrick, the plus side of running a poor second to the Nonconformists in terms of numbers was time freed up for writing. Dissenters did not trouble him for baptisms and even many Anglicans chose to marry in Bradford.

In 1816 the (modestly) well-known writer in the family was the Reverend Brontë and he published *The Cottage In The Wood, or the Art of Becoming Rich and Happy*. The art is in feeling spiritually rich and therefore happy in a Christian sense. Wisdom and understanding are better than silver and gold, biblically speaking.

In the foreword Pat makes clear that literature has a serious job to do and has no time for writing simply to entertain:

> 'The sensual novelist and his admirer, are beings of depraved appetites and sickly imaginations, who … are diligently and zealously employed in creating an imaginary world, which they can never inhabit, only to make the real world, with which they must necessarily be conversant, gloomy and insupportable.'

He dismisses the 'romantic author' too, as he (never she) arouses sympathy for fictional characters from readers who show none towards people in real life.

Maria Brontë agreed and made another significant decision. She decided to try her hand at being a published writer, if only for a local magazine. In public at least, Maria had put away romantic things and wanted to add her voice to the Evangelical literature. Her genre was not to be gothic but do-good. Her oeuvre must also be Useful. The result was Maria Brontë's only known work intended for publication, *The Advantages of Poverty in Religious Concerns* which appears in full in Appendix 2.

This was probably written for William Morgan after he launched *The Pastoral Visitor* for Bradford in January 1815, though could have been intended for *The Cottage Magazine, or, Plain Christians' Library*, a similar enterprise by John Buckworth out of Dewsbury. With Pat enjoying a purple patch and for other reasons we will come to, it seems likely that 1816 was when Maria became the first female Brontë to take up her pen.

Morgan's religious pamphlets, known as tracts, were privately printed every month, largely at his own expense, and intended to work like a pastoral – home – visit by a minister. Tracts were much favoured as a way to proselytize among poor people who could read. He invited submissions and authors used pen names or initials. William Morgan liked the sound of his own voice, both in the pulpit and in print. His natural verbosity was at odds with his intention to speak plainly and simply. Hence each issue cost a penny and his articles ran over several issues.

MOTHERING HEIGHTS

When Maria was growing up poverty had been a Methody problem, though one that happened to other people. The advantages of having barely enough to eat and the constant fear of unemployment were not ones she ever enjoyed herself. What did 'poor' look like to Mrs Brontë? She had her £50 a year, Patrick his £140. While not rich, they paid no rent and he had a job for life with a house attached. The broad threshold income for a middle class family was around £100.

No-one had replaced the clergy with factory machinery and none of their new friends were on the breadline. An income exceeding around £500 a year qualified someone as rich, a bracket easily attained by the Firths of Kipping. Maria had been used to such a life herself, cushioned by moderate wealth for the first twenty-nine years of her life.

There were workhouses in Thornton and at Dean House near Allerton Hall. The inmates were often those too sick or disabled to work, widows, unmarried mothers, destitute families and the elderly. Workhouse regimes were little different to prisons. The Thornton accommodation varied, according to reporter and historian William Cudworth in the *Bradford Observer* of 1874:

> 'Its position ... was subject to change, there not being a special building for the purpose, and a practice existed of renting small houses, or hovels, in various places for the paupers.'

The end of the war with France signalled a rise in unemployment as servicemen returned to find work in a post-war economic slump. A new Corn Law in 1815 made bread expensive. Faced with low wages, high food prices and no vote, radicals regrouped to agitate for social and political reform.

The summer after Charlotte was born and Elizabeth returned to Penzance, the weather was terrible. Ash trapped in the atmosphere by an enormous volcanic eruption in the Dutch East Indies, now Indonesia, the previous year continued to cause cold and rainy days. Hence 1816 was dubbed 'the year without a summer'. Harvests failed as a result, increasing hardship across Britain just as the *Visitor* was in full swing trying to raise money for bibles. While Mary Shelley responded to the gloom by beginning work on a gruesome afterlife in *Frankenstein,* Maria urged keeping one's attention on a wholesome alternative in Heaven.

Maria's arguments in *Advantages* are broadly in line with themes in printed sermons and magazines addressed to cottagers – that is, the actual poor. They argued for acceptance of a hard life lived piously in anticipation of an eternity of ease with God. There are shades of Wesley's translation of *The Christian's pattern: or, a treatise on the imitation of Christ* by Thomas à Kempis that she first read in Penzance. Maria's message, like that of the monk and her husband, was that being poor does not mean God does not care. In fact, it keeps things simple not to have material comforts to distract from spiritual understanding. Despair over your appalling circumstances is simply giving in to the voice of the devil.

'Poverty is generally, if not universally, considered an evil; and not only an evil in itself, but attended with a train of innumerable other evils,' she begins. A reader might concur, but Maria argues 'this a mistaken notion' springing from worldly thinking and is 'improved and corrected by an acquaintance with the holy Scriptures...' though she does allow:

> 'Perhaps some who are daily and hourly sinking under the distresses and privations which attend extreme poverty, should this paper fall in the way of any such, may be ready to say that the writer never experienced its horrors, and is therefore unqualified to judge of its effects...'

They may. Maria does not consider herself unqualified to comment, though, and presses on. In essence, *Advantages* rehearses the arguments of the deserving and the undeserving poor. Those who suffer extreme poverty usually have themselves to blame:

> 'Such a wretched extremity of poverty is seldom experienced in this land of general benevolence. When a case of this kind occurs, it is to be feared the sufferers bring it on themselves by their own excess and imprudent folly; but even when they reap the fruit of their doings, they are not permitted long to suffer. The penetrating eye of Christian charity soon discovers, and its hand is as soon stretched out for their relief.'

The deserving poor are likewise saved by the benevolence of charity such as the hovels scheme:

> 'The poor but honest and industrious Christian, for whose benefit this humble attempt is made, is scarcely ever suffered to languish in extreme want, yet he may be exposed to great

distresses, which at times he is tempted to consider evils hard to be endured: at most repines at his lot, and thinks that the God who is declared to be *merciful to all* and whose *tender mercies* are said to be *over all His works,* has forgotten to be gracious to him. Dismiss these unworthy thoughts, my Christian friends; they come from the enemy of your immortal interests and the father of lies.'

This was the view from the Parsonage between tea parties. It was never published and Pat later added a note on the end. 'The above was written by my dear wife, and sent for insertion in one of the periodical publications. Keep it, as a memorial of her.'

Each issue of *Visitor* had a section called *Answers to Friends and Correspondents* flagging up forthcoming content, thanking contributors and promising future publication. It is just possible that the brief 'B. is unsuitable' in August 1816 referred to Maria Brontë's submission being spiked, omitting the M to avoid embarrassment, though it is much more likely she was informed via Pat. The rejection must have stung. Especially as Jane Morgan had a list of dire warnings about not taking communion published, directly under an article by Pat. William, Jane and Pat were allowed to preach in the pamphlet but Maria was not. She was deemed *too* preachy, even for them. There must have been some degree of awkwardness next time they all met across a teapot.

Yet *Advantages* is no better or worse than the acres of such sentiment that did make it into the *Visitor*. Patrick's own *On Conversion* details 'the views and feelings of an awakened sinner' over several instalments. Like the *Methodist Magazine*, there are reports of exemplary deaths, such as the poor woman who declares, 'Oh, dear Sirs, I would not change this dying bed to be queen of England!' Instructions in *An Address to Persons Employed in Manufactories* include 'Having your Master's interest at heart continually, as if it were your own…'

The significance of Maria's writing lies not in its content, but in its existence. No other family in English literature suggests a genetic element to literary genius as powerfully as the Brontës, though nature was bolstered by nurture at the Glebe house in Market Street. As Nussey notes:

'This fragile delicate little woman found time in the midst of her young family & busy household to write poetry & small articles for a Cottage Magazine in which her husband was interested & also a contributor.'

Leaving aside until later Maria as fragile and delicate, this is a significant marker in the origins of the Brontës as writers. From their earliest days, the eldest saw their mother with a pen in her hand and the youngest were told about it. It was not just men who could write. Women wrote too. Big Pat and little Pat were also accustomed to the women in their lives writing letters, opinion pieces and poetry. Educated and expressive women were the norm during the children's formative years.

So what of the poetry Nussey refers to? The plural 'articles'? If she is right, they are lost or buried in private collections. Maybe Maria took umbrage and sent her unsigned work much further afield. But it would be easy to overstate Maria's writing life. It seems unlikely her journalistic output extended much beyond *Advantages,* especially if it caused friction with friends. The many letters she would still have been writing to friends and family would be a better guide to her real life and concerns.

Maria's beliefs were sincerely held and her piety unfeigned. They suffused both her love letters and her religious tract. In this, she shared the outlook of Henry Kirke White, Pat's Cambridge friend and the author of her shipwrecked book. As Robert Southey said of White's student poetry, 'I plainly saw the Evangelicals had caught him.' This is not to denigrate religious themes but to be realistic about Maria's influences. She was not a rich and liberated lesbian writing all her own rules like Anne Lister. Neither was she a celebrated satirist who moved in aristocratic circles in London and Bath like Fanny Burney. Nor was she left alone for hours to write about secular love and manners like child-free Jane Austen.

Maria's influences were other female writers on a Christian mission. They included other clergy wives such as the late Mary Fletcher. The divine diva of Madeley was also born to wealthy parents and married an Evangelical parson. Elizabeth Firth's diary again proves illuminating, placing prolific Georgian writer Hannah More on the Thornton reading list.

More was a member of the London Bluestockings and wrote improving tales for her own *Cheap Repository Tracts*. On 12 June 1816, Elizabeth Firth writes, 'Read Black Giles the Poacher.' This was *Black Giles the Poacher: with some Account of a Family who Had rather Live by their Wits than their Work*. It was written by More in 1796 about a deeply undeserving clan:

> 'Giles fell into that common mistake, that a beggarly looking cottage, and filthy ragged children, raised most compassion, and of course drew most charity. But … it is neatness, housewifery,

and a decent appearance, which draw the kindness of the rich and charitable; while they turn away disgusted from filth and laziness...'

More was greatly admired by Maria and the Thornton set. Six days after Elizabeth read the *Black Giles* tract she wrote, 'Mr & Mrs Bronte & Miss Branwell came to tea' and it must have been discussed with the parson, his wife and her equally devout sister.

The list of useful books recommended in Morgan's *Visitor* describes *Cheap* tracts as 'entertaining and instructive' for the young and the poor. 'Nor can the most refined mind peruse them without pleasure and profit.' Maria had much in common with this contemporary, another Westcountry woman. More had also enjoyed a fashionable social life in her youth. She made her name as a playwright for the London stage but as she grew older, focused on instructive Evangelical writing for the poor.

She churned out three editions of *Cheap* tracts every month for three years in the late 1790s, selling six million at a penny each. She also argued for female education and against slavery, becoming friends with Pat's patron William Wilberforce. She supported the established order, where the labouring classes were encouraged to improve their education and religious practice while not challenging their God-given station in life.

More, who was 71 in 1816, never signed her tracts with 'H.M.' but a more anonymous 'Z.' Maybe the poems and other articles ascribed to Maria by Nussey remain disguised by her own version of Z. After all, her daughters started out in print as Currer, Ellis and Acton Bell.

The least intriguing but most likely explanation for the paucity of published evidence of Maria's literary career is her ever-growing family. English writer Cyril Connolly later observed, 'There is no more sombre enemy of good art than the pram in the hall.' In Maria's day, there were no prams – or perambulators – as such. Baby baskets on wheels were used by a few members of the aristocracy but were pulled by a pony or goat. The littlest Brontë would have slept in a bassinet and been carried by adults or older siblings outdoors.

It was not the pram or bassinet that stopped women like Maria from writing, it was the babies inside. Like every fertile Georgian wife with a fertile husband and no contraception, Maria was in the grip of her childbearing years. A pregnancy a year was Maria's lot. The choice between writing and rearing children was made for her. Patrick, on the other hand, could escape to his church, study or library to write.

The real landmark literary event of 1816 was the birth of Charlotte Brontë, author of *Jane Eyre*, *Shirley*, *Villette* and *The Professor*. But in the year without a summer, she was simply the latest occupant of the 'pram' in the Parsonage hall.

By January of 1817 Maria was carrying her fourth baby. In March Elizabeth's diary reveals a new companion staying with the Brontës for a couple of months, a Miss Thomas. She joined in with tea parties, visits and walks. Juliet Barker suggests this was a family friend on a visit from Penzance. Nancy Thomas lived in Chapel Street next door to one of Maria's cousins by marriage, another Jane Branwell.

Received wisdom holds that Maria and Patrick were both desperate for a boy, though they welcomed and cherished each of their daughters. When Maria gave birth on 26 June 1817 it was to a son and, the law being what it was, an heir. He was named Patrick Branwell Brontë but came to be known by his Cornish middle name. Possibly he was introduced as Branwell when Elizabeth visited the same day, as she recorded his name as Branwell Patrick 'born early in the morning'.

The next day Elizabeth was at home to a crowd of her female friends and included the three little Brontë sisters, to give their parents time with the new baby. Little Pat was a redhead like his father and had his moment at the Old Bell Chapel font a month later. He was baptized by John Fennell, with John and Anne Firth for godparents.

Pat never felt blasé when Maria was having a baby and its gender was the least of his worries. At the time, almost a fifth of children were buried before their first birthday and one in every 200 mothers died while giving birth or soon after. The curate visited dying mothers and distraught fathers, buried their babies.

Neither infant nor maternal mortality was a respecter of class. Five months after Branwell was born, 21-year-old Princess Charlotte, daughter of the Prince Regent, died hours after giving birth to a stillborn son, what the *Leeds Intelligencer* described as a 'Royal and National Calamity'. The old bell was muffled to mark the strange, night-time state funeral in Windsor on 19 November. The *Morning Chronicle* described the procession where eight black horses drew the hearse towards St George's Chapel, followed by ninety-nine royal servants bearing torches:

> 'The serenity of the night, the moon shining in unclouded majesty, blending its tranquil rays with the artificial glare of the funeral flambeaux, threw an awful, a religious, and an interesting effect on the whole of this sepulchral pageant.'

The mood of the country seemed quite gothic enough when on 20 December 1817 Jane Austen's brother published *Northanger Abbey*, five months after the author's death. Her satire on gothic fiction had actually been written in 1799, when Maria was devouring such stories in the *Lady's Magazine*.

Austen was both a fashionable author and daughter of a Church of England vicar. *Sense and Sensibility* was bought by Maria's book club before she left Penzance and *Pride and Prejudice* was in the Kipping House library. Austen was always on the Thornton bluestocking radar. It is possible, probable even, that Maria did read the novel sending up the whole gothic genre. In *Northanger*, Austen spoofs such blockbusters as *The Mysteries of Udolpho* and takes a swipe at that favourite page-turner in Penzance, *The Castle of Wolfenbach* by Eliza Parsons.

As a curate's wife and the mother of four with a fifth on the way, did Maria too disdain the 'foolish love stories' (Patrick) or 'horrid romances' (Austen) of her youth? She still had her volumes of *Lady's* to flick through when the children were asleep and Pat was out, but she was no longer a suggestible teenager like Catherine Morland in *Northanger*.

For Maria, sex life went on. Around the time that the young Princess Charlotte died after giving birth in Surrey, Mrs Brontë had conceived for a fifth time in Yorkshire. In February 1818 Patrick published his longest book, *The Maid of Killarney; or, Albion and Flora: a modern tale; in which are interwoven some cursory remarks on Religion and Politics*. This time the peasants are Irish and their sufferings smack of first-hand experience. The happy ending comes thanks to religious conversion.

Maria celebrated her 35th birthday with her customary bump but as she began her lying-in in July 1818, there was bad news from Penzance. Her only brother Benjamin had died at 43, leaving Mary a widow at 41. They had six children, the youngest only two years old. On 25 July 1818 the *Royal Cornwall Gazette* reported:

> 'On Wednesday last, at Penzance, after a lingering illness, Benjamin Branwell, esq. one of the Magistrates of that borough, leaving a wife and large family to deplore his loss.'

Letters of condolence to Cornwall crossed letters of congratulations to Yorkshire when five days later on 30 July 1818, Emily Jane Brontë was born in front of the Thornton fireplace. There were plenty of Janes in their life, but Emily's name alone was unique to her immediate family. It would have been rude to ignore the name of the last living Branwell sister, but it was pushed into second place.

Maybe this baby, the future poet and author of *Wuthering Heights*, simply seemed different. Certainly there has never been anyone like her before or since. She was bigger than the others, with the long limbs of her father and 'very beautiful eyes, kind, kindling, liquid eyes, sometimes they looked grey, sometimes dark blue…' according to Ellen Nussey.

Maria now had five children under five and one nursemaid still only 16. The Brontës needed more help and Pat went back to the Bradford School of Industry to recruit Sarah Garrs, Nancy's 12-year-old sister. The younger girl arrived with her cropped hair and few belongings to be the new nursemaid. Nancy was promoted to cook and assistant housekeeper. Sarah moved in beside her big sister across from the children's bedroom and grew to love the Brontës too.

With things calmer at home, Pat organized a long-overdue renovation of the Old Bell Chapel beginning in the autumn of 1818. The roof leaked and wooden pews were starting to rot. A month before Emily arrived he had received a faculty, church planning permission, to make improvements. Pat replaced the roof, rebuilt the south wall and put in bigger windows. The bell was housed in a cupola, an ornate small tower with open sides. Afterwards, a painted board was erected to record the work by Pat and his churchwardens – 'This Chapel was repaired and beautified A.D. 1818.' The only truly beautiful element was viewed by Elizabeth on 10 November. 'Went to look at the Angel in Thornton Chapel.' Though she does not say whether the angel was a mural, a painting or a statue.

A writer's inheritance can take many forms. As Nussey observes of Mrs Brontë:

> 'Her intelligence and cultivation were such, there can be no doubt that the Brontë family were, as is usually the case, eminently indebted to their Mother for their manifold excellencies if not for their talents likewise.'

In early 1819, little Maria turned five years old and if anyone seemed talented, it was this eldest child. Patrick enjoyed discussing the leading topics of the day with her, with as much pleasure as with an adult. The doting father said his firstborn possessed 'a powerful intellectual mind.' Just a year behind her was Elizabeth, growing into a more practical person who 'had good solid sense' according to her father. The potential of the Brontë sisters most influenced by their mother was never to be realized, though the friendships Maria forged in Thornton would have a role in her family's life long after she had departed it.

As the children grew, Thornton Parsonage seemed to shrink. Five boisterous little Brontës, two parents and two servants under one roof made for a crowded house. Maria dearly wanted a garden so the older children could play safely outside. Then, in 1819, as winter turned to spring, there came another fateful turn in her life story.

The Reverend Henry Heap, vicar of Bradford, offered Patrick a new job six miles away in Haworth. The Reverend James Charnock had died and there was a vacancy for a perpetual curate. Accepting the move meant saying goodbye to their friends but improving their living conditions. Haworth came with a bigger rent-free home and was an Evangelical stronghold. It was a plum beat for an ambitious parson like Pat.

Haworth was famous in Evangelical circles thanks to its legendary curate a century earlier, known as Mad Grimshaw. Though he had been dead for decades, the wild-eyed Reverend William Grimshaw left an indelible impression on his flock, not least for his habit of herding people out of the pub and into church with the aid of a horsewhip. He would also drag anyone caught riding on the Sabbath down from the horse and onto their knees to pray.

A fiery preacher, he was second in line to inherit the Methodist leadership. Though tipped to succeed John and Charles Wesley, he died first in 1763. Known as the Apostle of the North, he would have been a hero to the Branwells in Penzance, who were Wesley's friends in the South when Maria was a child.

From a professional point of view, Haworth was a prestige posting for an ambitious low church Anglican. From a personal point of view, it was a timely offer. With five growing children and two growing maids, they were struggling to pay the bills and Maria suspected there was a sixth baby on the way. The first Brontë Parsonage was bursting at the seams. They needed to move. The pay rise and bigger house in Haworth seemed the answer to all their prayers. Pat grabbed at the job with both hands.

What he and Maria did not know – and Henry Heap did not tell them – was that the mill town high on the moor had a long history of deciding on its own parson. Saying yes to a promotion in May 1819 proved to be the easy bit.

Chapter 8

The Resistance

Haworth in 1819 was not a place to put much store by being told what to do. Not by the Church of England, not by an offcumden curate and most certainly not by Bradford. When Maria and Patrick Brontë decided to make the independent and outspoken Yorkshire town their family's new home, the fun had really started.

You can always tell a Yorkshireman but you can't tell him much, so the Brontës and their brood could not simply pack up and move. First Patrick and Maria had to endure a year long, ludicrous and at times quite frightening fight to be accepted by the people of Haworth. Some offcumdens – anyone not born there – fared better than others and it tended to depend on the methods used by the outsider to either ingratiate or impose himself. The ones Patrick had to court were the all-powerful Haworth Church Land Trustees. Under an Elizabethan agreement, from December 1559, they paid the curate's wages out of the income from farmland at Stanbury.
    Or not.
    If the trustees did not choose him they could give the money to the poor instead. As they also owned the land the parsonage stood on, they were not handing it rent-free to any reverend but their own. So while technically the vicar of Bradford chose the man for the job, it was actually the gentleman farmers and mill owners of Haworth. Henry Heap could nominate Patrick all he wanted but unless the six trustees approved, it was never going to happen. The men were from the oldest families of the chapelry. At Oxenhope, two miles south of Haworth, lived William Greenwood of Moorhouse, John Beaver of Buttergate Sykes and William Rushworth of Mouldgreave. James Greenwood lived at Bridgehouse in Haworth. In Stanbury, a mile and a half west of Haworth, were Stephen Taylor of the Manor House and Robert Heaton of Ponden Hall.
    When Patrick accepted the job in May 1819 he and Maria were blithely unaware of this perennial power struggle. They had no idea what they were taking on but they soon found out. The trustees had not been consulted

on Mr Brontë so when Mr Heap went to Haworth to take the service on Whit Sunday, the church doors were slammed in his face. The vicar was vexed, the battle lines were drawn and it was all duly reported in the *Leeds Intelligencer* on 14 June 1819:

'We hear that the Rev. P. Brontë, curate of Thornton, has been nominated by the vicar of Bradford, to the valuable perpetual curacy of Haworth, vacant by the death of the Rev. James Charnock; but that the inhabitants of the chapelry intend to resist the *presentation*, and have entered a caveat at York accordingly.'

The leaders of the resistance were a powerful bunch. Patrick took out his trusty staff and set off to do battle, a two-hour walk over six miles. He invited himself over to Stanbury to meet Stephen Taylor, father of Mercy Kaye of Allerton Hall, and his fellow freedom fighters. It was futile. They had nothing against him, the trustees said, but would not be told what to do by Bradford. Even the appointment of famous hellfire preacher William Grimshaw in 1742 had caused ructions, though for the opposite reason. He was nominated by the trustees and opposed by Bradford. Haworth won and put its own man in the pulpit.

Patrick tried to resign in early July 1819. Mr Heap warned that the archbishop of York, the Most Reverend Edward Harcourt, would be most furious. His Grace was prepared for Patrick to hold both Thornton and Haworth until the row was settled. Patrick wrote to tell Stephen Taylor that he was caught between a rock and a hard place. He admitted not knowing 'the circumstances of the case' (running battle with Bradford) when he accepted the nomination and now he could not back out because, 'I should run the greatest hazard of seriously displeasing the Archbishop, who had received and approved my nomination'. Patrick had no choice but to plough on. 'I do think that Providence has called me to labour in His vineyard at Haworth, where so many great and good men have gone before me.'

Unfortunately, until Providence had approval from the trustees, Patrick and Maria could not move to the roomy, rent-free parsonage with garden and spectacular views. Evenings at home in Thornton were consumed by wondering what to do. Mr Brontë may have been taken aback by the stand-off between Bradford and Haworth but for his wife it was nothing new. Unseemly squabbles between a chapel and its mother church had been a familiar story back in Penzance. Charles Valentine Le Grice, her neighbour and man of letters, was perpetual curate of St Mary's Chapel behind her house in Chapel Street and had a high-profile spat with the vicar of Madron in 1808, the year her father died. Le Grice insisted on the chapel keeping its own separate registers of baptisms and burials, much to his boss's fury at Madron. The curate held out until 1812, when an Act of Parliament gave him official registration rights. There were regular rows over who called the shots because the curate was chosen by Penzance Corporation but the vicar in Madron had to agree.

It was a turf war pure and simple, not dissimilar to the one between Bradford and Haworth. The lesson from Cornwall was that the chapel won. Until Haworth wanted the Brontës, the Brontës were going nowhere.

Something happened in July 1819, when Maria was three months pregnant, that made Patrick feel it was hopeless, most likely a protest when he took the service on the 12th. The trustees would not budge. They alone chose the perpetual curate of Haworth and they had not chosen Patrick. On 14 July Patrick wrote to Stephen Taylor to admit defeat. 'I have just written to the Archbishop and the vicar of Bradford to acquaint them with my resignation of my nomination to the living of Haworth.'

All of a sudden, the trustees were not so sure. An imperious invitation was issued to say he could audition with a sermon the following Sunday. Despite his domestic pressures, Pat was polite but firm. 'My conscience does not altogether approve to a circumstance of exposing myself to the temptation of preaching in order to please,' he replied. Instead, he suggested the trustees make a surprise visit to see him in Thornton any time they liked. 'It is an easy matter to compose a fine sermon or two for a particular occasion,' he said, but turning up unannounced would give them a better idea of his preaching and his character. The miffed churchmen cast around for another candidate to put to York.

Violence was in the air again in 1819, with the Peterloo massacre in August sending fresh waves of unease through the professional classes. The simmering people power Patrick so feared surfaced in Manchester when more than 40,000 unarmed men, women and children gathered to demand parliamentary reform and universal suffrage. They were dressed in their Sunday best and many wore red 'caps of liberty' inspired by the French revolution thirty years earlier. People carried banners calling for everything from the vote to love and were accompanied by bands playing music.

This good-natured protest was met with slashing sabres in a murderous cavalry charge by the army and local militia. At least eleven protestors died and hundreds more were terribly wounded. The calls for reform did not go away. Without a voice in parliament, the poor felt powerless in the face of growing unemployment and high bread prices imposed by the hated Corn Laws. They wanted fairer taxes and better use of public money.

Meanwhile, local parish politics concerning the Brontës were no less volatile. The stalemate over at Haworth continued and services were being run on an emergency rota of visiting ministers. Patrick could not dodge his turn forever and at the beginning of October the archbishop ordered him over to lead the worship. Patrick wrote an anxious note to his fair-weather friend Stephen Taylor. 'I hope you will receive me in a friendly manner tomorrow, as I am obliged to go to you, in compliance with the wishes of the Archbishop.'

Patrick maintained a dignified silence about how he was received on Sunday 10 October but friendly it was not. He resigned again and this time, it was accepted. Henry Heap's indignation knew no bounds and he decided to show who was really boss of St Michael and All Angels in Haworth. He offered the job to the Reverend Samuel Redhead, curate of Horton chapel in Bradford, and a friend of Patrick and Maria.

The trustees agreed to this only if Mr Redhead accepted a joint nomination with themselves and the vicar. Redhead declined and lived to regret it, as revealed in his papers after his death. Diary entries from that awful autumn in the rebel town were shared in a letter from his son-in-law to the editor of the *Leeds Intelligencer* in April 1857. They begin with the first farcical Sunday of his three-week incumbency, 31 October 1819:

'Went to Haworth in a post-chaise, accompanied by Mr. Rand [a churchman from Bradford], and had an interview with the churchwardens to whom I produced my license, &c., upon which they caused the church doors to be opened for divine service. We proceeded to the church, where I was informed by the clerk that the churchwardens refused to allow the bells to be rung. Began the service without them to a small congregation, which gradually increased to more than 500 persons, who, in an apparently attentive manner, joined in the prayers. Immediately on entering the pulpit, the whole church became one scene of confusion, the congregation leaving their pews and rushing out of the church in great disorder (on the signal given by the churchwardens, trustees, &c.), calling aloud "Come out, come out." Great disorder prevailed in the churchyard, and even within the doors of the church during the sermon, without any attempt on the part of the officers to restrain it; and on leaving the church Mr. Rand and I were pursued and hooted and insulted by considerable numbers out of the village.'

Things were no better the following Sunday, 7 November 1819. Locals were just getting warmed up. They had their orders, including pre-arranged signals:

'Went to Haworth, accompanied by Mr. Crosley, one of the churchwardens of Bradford. Considerable numbers were assembled near the church, and with some slight insults we got into it. The congregation was large, and expressed some disapprobation by restlessness and inattention, and towards the close of the prayers many directed their attention to the churchwarden's pew, as if waiting for some signal, and again upon going into the pulpit the churchwardens left their pew, and instantly the utmost confusion prevailed. After a time the churchwardens returned, but there was great disorder in the churchyard and about the doors of the church by persons going out and coming in, with a total disregard to all decency and order, and without any exertion on the part of the officers to repress it. I expostulated with the churchwardens, but to no purpose. The afternoon service commenced in the midst of uproar and confusion, all decency seemed thrown aside, and laughing, talking, and noise frequently interrupted the prayers. After the second lesson, I proceeded to read the articles; the tumult increased, the churchwardens were not in the church, and about the middle of the articles all became uproar and confusion, great numbers leaping over the tops of the pews, throwing to the pew doors with great violence, stamping with their feet, shouting and rushing out in the most outrageous and tumultuous manner. The whole scene was perfectly indiscribable [sic], and to the end of the prayers nothing but tumult prevailed. Having retired to the vestry after service, I again expostulated with the churchwardens: the church filled with unruly people, they pressed round the vestry, which was soon filled, the shutters of which were closed by persons without and, for my personal safety, I put myself under the protection of the churchwardens as the guardians of the peace. The crowd was then removed from the vestry and the door shut, but all was uproar in the church. The churchwardens told me they were unable to repress the tumult. I replied that if they were so, they were required to call in to their assistance the respectable inhabitants of the town. Their answer was, that the respectable inhabitants of the town would not act, as there was but one feeling amongst them in common with the people at large on the subject of the vicar of Bradford's appointment to their church.'

Amid this unholy riot, the Toothill family had to bury their 64-year-old loved one, James, and the 'animosity and rage' was paused to allow the dead local, at least, some dignity:

'The funeral service was performed in comparative stillness, but immediately after, the same violence and tumult in the churchyard occurred, and we were pursued out of the town in the midst of hootings and pushing and shouting and insult.'

Redhead was rattled and appealed to the archbishop, who sent a stern warning to the hooligans. He threatened to close the church and refer the whole matter to the Lord Chancellor if they did not behave. Redhead returned the following Sunday with his wingman Crosley and 'some expectation of a more peaceable reception, from the Archbishop's remonstrance'. Alas:

'When we entered the village we were saluted with shoutings and insults, and pursued with the most indecent insolence. The same irreverent conduct was displayed all the way to the church, and we had no prospect but of the greatest disorder. Indecency and impiety marked their conduct during the prayers, and when I entered the pulpit all was uproar and confusion. I felt obliged to close the service without preaching. I gave directions to the churchwardens to shut up the church till they received instructions from the Archbishop, as I should lay the whole matter before him on the following day. I further told them that I should expect their protection through the town, with which they complied, and we went as we came, pursued more like wild beasts than human beings. Their shoutings continued, and we heard them for more than a mile and a half. The day after, Monday, 15, I wrote to the Archbishop and obtained his consent to my resignation.'

Who could blame him. J. Hodgson Ramsbotham said his late father-in-law had accepted the appointment 'without any idea of the uproarious reception he should meet with' and it was only '*with considerable difficulty*' that he persuaded the archbishop to release him. Henry Heap had proved who was the boss of St Michael and All Angels in Haworth and it was not him.

Over in Thornton Patrick and Maria opened their *Intelligencer* on Monday 22 November to read what they already knew, the unnamed correspondent likely to have been ousted Samuel himself:

> 'We regret to learn from a Correspondent, that scenes, scarcely possible in an heathen village, have been witnessed on three successive Sundays, in the church of Haworth, merely in consequence of the minister officiating under the appointment of the vicar of Bradford, and the license of the Archbishop of York. The churchwardens are certainly liable to a prosecution for the willful neglect of their duty and deserve to feel, that the house of God, and the hallowed ground of a church yard, are not proper places in which to allow, by disturbance and howlings, the loudest and lowest marks of the irreverence and insult. The highly respectable clergyman alluded to, has, we also hear, resigned the situation.'

The trustees won the battle and Patrick was still on the covering clergy rota. Each appearance required a twelve-mile round trip across the wild, wintry moorland in the slanting rain. He had to make an awkward return on 17 November 1819 to baptize month-old baby Margrett Wilson, the daughter of Sally and Thomas, a wool comber, of Spring Head. The routine moment of signing the register signalled the official arrival of Patrick Brontë at St Michael's, though he had no idea whether it would ever be permanent. Every service was conducted in the febrile atmosphere of a chapel at war with the mother church. At least he was paid two shillings a time in expenses.

On 17 January 1820 Maria went into labour and the children were herded away to spend the day at Kipping House. It was another girl, named Anne for her Cornish grandma and auntie who died long ago, but was soon known as Annie. Sarah Garrs cut a curl from the baby's head. The doting young maid kept a lock of hair from Maria and all of her children, now kept in the Brontë collection in Haworth.

With the exquisite face of a china doll, Ellen Nussey later described Anne as 'quite different in appearance to the others' and with a gentleness about her. 'She had lovely violet blue eyes, fine pencilled eye-brows, a clear, almost transparent complexion.'

That made ten people in the parsonage and something had to give. In the end, the ecclesiastical clash over Haworth was resolved because Patrick was forced to go cap in hand to the archbishop. The Brontës were broke. Two weeks after the birth of Anne Brontë, Patrick wrote again to the governors of Queen Anne's Bounty, with a copy to the archbishop.

He was forced to spell out why he and Maria just could not manage on what they had coming in, though he judiciously left out her £50 a year legacy. Her money arrived every quarter, rain or shine, it was the local contribution to his curate's wages of £140 that had to be wrung out of his parsimonious flock. They included fees for marriages and burials of about five pounds 'and a voluntary contribution, frequently made under exceedingly unpleasant circumstances – amounting for the most part to seven or eight pounds'.

Patrick was having trouble parting Yorkshire people from their money. Specifically, the many Nonconformists who objected to paying towards a church they did not attend. They needed a top up or even Maria's sewing skills could not keep him out of rags:

> 'If I were a single man, I might find what I have sufficient, but
> I have a wife, and six small children, with two maidservants,
> as well as myself to support, without I can obtain something
> more, in a just and honourable way, I greatly fear, that with the
> most rigorous economy, I shall be unable, any longer to uphold
> in appearance the due degree of Clerical respectability.'

They had outgrown Thornton Parsonage and could barely make ends meet (though the ends encompassed two live-in servants). The family desperately needed the house and the living at Haworth, though the wave of hostility towards them was unsettling.

Patrick's begging letter forced the archbishop to act, insisting that the reluctant Henry Heap meet with the Haworth trustees and reach a compromise. After another ill-tempered powwow, Mr Heap and the Haworth grandees finally agreed to a joint nomination, possibly out of pity for the cleric who now had six children to feed. In the first week of February 1820, Patrick was appointed to the cure of 6,000 souls at Haworth. The trusty *Leeds Intelligencer* reported the truce on 13 March:

> 'The Rev. P. Brontë, A. B. of Thornton, has been licenced, by his Grace the Archbishop of York, to the living of Haworth, near Keighley, on the nomination of the Rev. H. Heap, vicar of Bradford, and J. Beaver, W. Greenwood, J. Greenwood, S. Taylor, and R. Heaton, trustees of Haworth church lands.'

Honour was served and the resistance stepped down, but such animosity does not vanish overnight. Patrick spent the next two months commuting between Thornton and Haworth, a two-hour walk each way, to make sure the peace held, before he risked moving Maria and the children. He also had to get the parsonage ready. It had stood cold and empty since his predecessor James Charnock died in May 1819, ten months earlier and his widow Grace had had to move out.

Thornton Parsonage was home to his happiest years with Maria and preparing to leave their many friends was painful. Still, Haworth Parsonage was an exciting prospect for them both. For Maria, it was where she expected to watch her children grow up, building a happy home for the fourth time.

January to March 1820 was incredibly busy. There was a new baby to care for, Patrick was shuttling backwards and forwards between both chapels, and consulting with Maria over the practicalities of the move. Meanwhile, the wider world was as turbulent as ever. On the 29 January George III died and the Regency ended, as the flamboyant Prince Regent became George IV. The funeral was held on Ash Wednesday in mid-February and declared a national day of mourning. Everywhere closed and churches held special services.

At Windsor Castle the king lay in state as crowds gathered to view the body. This did not go as well as one might have hoped, reported the *Leeds Intelligencer*:

> 'The crush on these occasions, required the utmost exertions of the police-officers and soldiers on duty, to prevent the most serious mischief. The screams of the women and children were dreadful; and many were extricated in a fainting state while others were altogether deprived of their senses.'

Things were far more dignified around Patrick's crepe-draped pulpit. Maria was unlikely to have been up and about by then, but Elizabeth Firth bought a black spencer, hat and gloves to bid the old king goodbye.

The following month there was a happier gathering at the little old church. On 25 March 1820, ten-week-old Anne Brontë, the baby with the violet eyes, was christened. William Morgan conducted the service while Elizabeth Firth and Fanny Outhwaite were godmothers. Amid the celebrations, however, there was doubtless conversation about the mood of the country. The extravagant lifestyle of the new king, which did not alter a whit when he took the throne, could not have been more out of step with his subjects. Since the massacre in Manchester, the public mood had darkened, with unrelenting post-war inflation and food shortages.

The government was deeply unpopular and a plot to kill off the cabinet had been uncovered the week after the royal funeral. The Cato Street conspiracy in London was led by revolutionary Arthur Thistlewood, who intended to assassinate ministers as they dined together in Grosvenor Square. The radicals planned to lead a popular uprising, but the authorities were tipped off, the murder plot was foiled and the ringleaders hanged and then beheaded, the last felons in the country to meet this end.

By March, Scottish radicals were calling for strikes and protest plans spread to the West Riding. Dubbed the Radical War, one such uprising was rumoured to happen just six days after Anne's christening, at Huddersfield on March 31, Good Friday. Patrick was convinced that they must all be on their guard in Thornton and terrified the Firths with talk of his enduring fear, militant uprisings. That night Elizabeth wrote an unusually expressive line in the diary. 'We sat up expecting the Radicals.'

In the event, they could have slept easy, according to the *Yorkshire Gazette:*

> 'During the last week we are happy to say, that no acts of outrage have been resorted to in this district. The failure of the intended attack on Huddersfield, on the 31st ult.; and the still more complete discomfiture of the hopes and prospects of the Radicals, in the abortive attempt to effect a rising on the 12th inst. have, *for the present*, occasioned a pause in the execution of those plans of rebellion, which we cannot doubt were formed.'

Meanwhile, Maria had a house move to organize. On 5 April Elizabeth Firth went to say her goodbyes before she left on holiday. Five days later Patrick conducted his last funeral and then handed the cure of those dear and difficult Thornton souls to the Reverend William Bishop.

So with the arrival of spring in 1820, Maria's happy, hectic Thornton years came to an end. In the third week of April it was all change. God had called them to Haworth and Haworth had finally relented. But for all of the Brontës, this would be different. The new parsonage would never be the crowded, lively little house in Thornton. Maria would not dart around after her babies, take tea with her best friends across the road or write anything considered worth keeping.

With moving on came other, invisible changes in the wind. If Maria was finding it harder to recover from the birth of Anne than her other children, at least she had the capable Garr sisters to help her pack and plan. On 15 April 1820, Maria turned 37. It was to be her last happy birthday, at the close of their most perfect years as a family. Though six-year-old Maria and five-year-old Elizabeth would have some memories of Thornton, their little brother and sisters would not recall their birthplace. Charlotte turned four as they left, Branwell was not quite three, Emily was 21 months old and Anne just three months. It was their father who would never forget. Years later, Patrick wrote simply, 'My happiest days were spent there.'

Stephen Taylor made amends for the recent hostilities by sending two flat carts with horses and drivers from Stanbury to move the family. Everything, including the eight chairs, mahogany table and bookshelves, were loaded on. Then all ten of them climbed aboard and headed across the Pennines to Haworth. Maria and Patrick, Sarah and Nancy, little Maria and Elizabeth, Charlotte, Branwell, Emily and baby Anne.

As Maria travelled up Main Street she saw it was much as Chapel Street was at home, the artery of a busy working town. In Penzance the principal road ran to and from the quay, in Haworth it was an artery of the wool trade. Stores, pubs and workshops lined the steep thoroughfare that was part of the trans-Pennine turnpike road from Bradford to Colne in Lancashire. It was paved with setts (larger and flatter than cobbles) partly to give horses' hooves some purchase as they laboured up the one-in-six hill. As Ellen Nussey put it, 'the horse's feet seemed to catch at the boulders as if climbing.' The whole town ran on worsted, the long-fibred woollen yarn made by wool-combers and weavers who worked by hand in their own cottages or, increasingly, in the large mills of the Worth Valley.

Just as Penzance was mistakenly believed to be a remote corner cut off from the world, so Haworth was not the isolated village of myth but known locally as 'the city on the hill'. Like Chapel Street and its mule train, Main Street was also an odorous place, with open sewers running down the sides. Fortunately, Maria still had her delicate china bottle to stave off the smell.

She had been terrified for Patrick's safety during the Luddite rebellion roiling around his ears in Hartshead and more recently fretted about radicals in Thornton. Now her whole family was arriving where, until very recently, it was not wanted. She knew what this congregation was capable of if it took against her husband. It was a tough crowd and only five short months had passed since Mr Redhead and friend had been chased out of town like wild beasts. Patrick had fared little better. The atmosphere was still tense, despite the veneer of acceptance.

It may have felt more like the new sheriff clip-clopping into town in the wild west of America than a new parson arriving at a West Yorkshire church. No-one watching from a shaded window could guess that the little Brontës held close by Maria would have an everlasting impact on their ancient and stubborn town.

Chapter 9

Pursued by Death

As the lead horse and cart toiled away up the hill, they passed many of the three hundred crowded homes that had one privy per dozen families. Turning left past the Black Bull Inn and up past the King's Arms, Mrs Brontë and her children caught their first sight of their new home. Maria was now mistress of this elegant Georgian house with its own privy, set above and apart from the town. The horses were brought to a halt and the children lifted down, one by one. To the rear lay the endless mysteries of the moors, the big skies of a wild paradise. Here three of the Brontë sisters would create masterpieces of English literature but their mother would never read them. Maria had arrived at her long journey's end.

The parsonage with its classical façade was built in 1779 from the moor itself, with millstone grit from the nearby quarry. Nine windows looked out across the graveyard and church, then beyond to the Worth Valley. Windows at the rear opened west onto the gorgeous South Pennines that would lay claim to Emily's imagination in *Wuthering Heights*. The old road led off to the hamlet of Stanbury two miles away and Ponden House (later Hall), home of the Heaton family.

The house at the top of Parsonage (now Church) Lane was considerably bigger than the one in Market Street, but there were still only four bedrooms for Patrick, Maria and six children. The parents moved into one of the two large bedrooms at the front of the house, with a cradle for baby Anne. It is probable that the eldest girls, Maria and Elizabeth, shared a room while Charlotte and Emily shared another and Branwell had a small one to himself. Sarah, 14, and Nancy, 17, were billeted in the servant's room next to their employers.

The ground floor was flagged in stone, the walls covered in off-white distemper and the windows had inside wooden shutters but no curtains. Patrick had buried too many blaze victims and saw curtains as a fire risk. Once the furniture was unpacked and the children settled, life fell into a familiar routine. Maria took charge of domestic matters while Patrick began his new job, each determined to make a success of their new life.

The inhabitants of this hilltop town were hard working, hard drinking and hard to impress. Strangers were a common sight but to stay they had to earn their place. Patrick knew they had to tread carefully, as he explained later in a letter to John Buckworth over in Dewsbury:

> 'When I first came to this place, though the angry winds which had been previously excited were hushed, the troubled sea was still agitated, and the vessel required a cautious and steady hand at the helm.'

Mr Brontë did not have a horsewhip like the fundamentalist Mr Grimshaw. Instead Patrick was that rarity in a revival-prone generation, a quiet Evangelical. He had to prove the mini civil war in the parish had been worth it.

On their first family Sunday Patrick left early to prepare for the service, letting himself into St Michael's by the old priest door. Bell-ringers arrived to toll Great Tim and two other bells, the chimes resounding through the Parsonage as Maria and the Garrs readied the children for church. Then Maria straightened her hat, took a final glance in the mirror and prepared to make her debut. She led the five children and carried the baby out of the Parsonage door, down the lane and into the gloomy church as locals took their first proper look at the controversial new parson's wife.

Mrs Brontë ushered her little ones into the parsonage pew with its green baize seats, under the organ loft and beneath the imposing three-tier pulpit. It was a tight squeeze. The old-style square box pew could only really seat three facing the action. The rest had their backs to the congregation. The church interior was dark, thanks to six stone pillars and serried ranks of black oak box pews, each with the name of the family who paid to sit there painted on the door. The towering pulpit dwarfed the simple altar of oak chest on a small carpet, with a velveteen blue cover and ancient silver chalice.

The parish clerk sat on the lowest level, while Patrick went to the second level to conduct the service, then to the top for the sermon, usually a parable explained in simple style. It was still the season of Easter and he would have preached on Christ's resurrection. Above his head was a sounding board installed by Grimshaw to help his voice carry. An inscription from Paul's first letter to the Corinthians read, 'I determined not to know anything among you, save Jesus Christ, and him crucified.' Then, 'For to me, to live is Christ, and to die is gain' from his first letter to the Philippians.

Those filing into the church that morning were the same people who had so enjoyed leaping over pews, stamping their feet and hooting to drive out Patrick, then poor Samuel Redhead, just a few months earlier. Maria, her husband and their children were only there because they had allowed it. Now they were back on their best behaviour, such as it was. Ellen Nussey described one such service where many people who could not read only really paid attention to the sermon:

> 'The people assembled, but it was apparently to *listen,* any part beyond that was quite out of their reckoning. All through the Prayers a stolid look of apathy was fixed in the generality of their faces, then they sat or leaned in their pews … The sexton with a long staff continually walked round in the aisles, 'knobbing' sleepers when he dare, shaking his head at and threatening unruly children, but when the sermon began there was a change, attitudes took the listening form, eyes were turned on the speaker. It was curious now to note the expression, a rustic untaught intelligence gleamed in their faces, in some a daring doubting questioning look as if the lips would like to say something defiant.'

Patrick may have considered that simply the default Haworth look, especially as the Church of England did not command all the Christians of Haworth. The town had an unusually large number of places to worship given its size, so competition was stiff. Grimshaw foresaw the eventual split of the Methodists from the established church and opened a Wesleyan chapel in 1758. Other Dissenters did well and there was not one, but two Baptist chapels. The West Lane chapel was built in 1752 and when the Brontës arrived in 1820 a breakaway group was drawing up plans for Hall Green chapel, four hundred yards away.

There was yet another place people went to communicate with the other, the end house in Acton Street, two minutes' walk from St Michael's. It was the home of the Haworth wise man, Jack Kay. Maria would have been aware of his fame as a soothsayer because people came from across northern England to consult him on mystical matters. Just as superstition still ran deep at home in Cornwall, so a belief in magic was prevalent enough to keep Kay in business here in Yorkshire.

He offered customers weather forecasts, fortune telling, astrology and charms to ward off bad luck. He also professed to be something of a witchfinder, diagnosing illness in people or animals as due to the evil eye, then providing charms to reverse the curse. His most popular service was gazing into a crystal ball to divine the face of a future husband or wife. When the Brontës arrived in 1820, the wise man of Haworth was 54 years old and had his own faithful flock.

Nonconformists (and maybe covert crystal-ball gazers) were common among the church land trustees, who qualified more through their local clout than beliefs. These included mill owner James Greenwood, who was a leading Baptist, and several Methodist men of business. Maria must have felt relatively at home in this mix, with many of her new neighbours supporting both church and chapel. She had done the same at home. The Methodist merchants of Haworth had much in common with her late father and wealthy relations in Cornwall. Though Patrick would always have a good relationship with his Nonconformist colleagues, especially regarding health and education, plenty of people still needed his church for the rites of passage.

In truth, the church did not dominate the lives of Haworth folk in 1820. The reproving, improving Victorian era was still some way off (as was Patrick's Committee for the Suppression of Vice) and Georgian pleasures still held sway.

In many ways, the bustling Haworth Maria encountered had more in common with Penzance than had Hartshead or Thornton. There were beer shops and whist shops for a drink and a flutter, along with inns and cockpits for more raucous nights out. Haworth Fair and feast days brought the whole town together as they had for generations.

For the men and women of Haworth, the parson might be consulted in a medical or legal emergency. Doctors and lawyers were expensive. They also used his graveyard to dry their laundry on washdays. Mainly, he was there to introduce them to God at the font as babies, to each other in marriage and to heaven when they died and were buried. Everything in between was a matter for themselves. Except for clerical recruitment, where they had made themselves plain. Mrs Gaskell records the opinion of one man who rated his parson a 'rare good one' because 'he minds his own business, and ne'er troubles himself with ours'.

It is hard to know what their reaction was to the gunshots heard at the Parsonage every morning. Every night, the new parson loaded his pistol and laid it by the bed. Every morning, he got rid of the bullets by firing out of the window. Presumably Maria was used to it but this wild west behaviour may have done his reputation no harm as they struggled to be accepted by a place accustomed to operating fairly free of outside interference.

Maria and Patrick knew that taking up residence did not mean they were home and dry. There was the matter of the lesser-known proviso on the trustees' charter. They could also withdraw the parson's pay if they became dissatisfied *after* he took on the job. One way and another, the Brontës had to get out there and schmooze.

For Patrick that meant carrying out his duties with dogged devotion, the heavy workload of baptisms, marriages and, especially, funerals, alongside regular services and visits to the sick. For Maria it meant once more making her social savvy Patrick's secret weapon. Maria was the perfect counterpoint to her self-made man of God. Her ease in polite society had won them influential friends in Thornton. Now they needed a charm offensive among the movers and shakers of their new patch.

It would have made sense to start with the powerful Heatons of Ponden. In 1820, Robert Heaton lived at the imposing family seat out at Stanbury with his unmarried younger siblings, Michael, Harriet and William. The Heatons were landowners and industrialists, making money from cotton, corn and wool with their mills in the Worth Valley. As the daughter of a wealthy merchant, Mrs Brontë was the social equal of Miss Heaton and her brothers and the mixed company made a visit perfectly acceptable. An invitation to tea at the sixteenth-century mansion would have held no terrors.

A round of social calls was how the Brontës eased themselves into the good books of Haworth bigshots. Mr Brontë had always courted the support of useful members of the ruling classes. Now he had Mrs Brontë by his side, a bona fide gentlewoman. They were a formidable team.

Maria maintained the elegance she was noted for throughout her life. As a girl in the Tonkin portrait she wore a dress with a scoop neck edged with a frill. In her only other portrait, she appeared in profile as the grown woman Patrick knew (see plate section). She is wearing an Empire line dress in palest blue, with a ribbon under her bosom and the frilled neck she favoured. The neat matching bonnet edged in lace has flowers on the front, above the curls framing her face and brown eyes.

On social calls Maria dressed to impress in the chic shawl she owned. It was made of cashmere with stripes of claret and gold and an intricate paisley design at the border. Such an item was invaluable for a lady embarking on a social call on a chilly day, worn draped over the shoulders and held in the crook of the arms. Only society ladies wore softest cashmere and hers was probably made in Thornton, famous for such luxury shawls.

Heatons were at the heart of everything connected to Patrick's church and always had been. An Andrew Heaton was one of the original two land trustees named on the charter of 1559. In 1744 a Michael Heaton was in the thick of the fight to install Grimshaw, in defiance of Bradford vicar Benjamin Kennet. A letter from Michael to his brother William reveals a certain relish in their trump card:

> 'I desire you, and so doth the Trustees of the Church, that you would send down the writings of above said Church that we may look them over, and I do believe that we shall go to counsel with them, and Mr. Kennet will not give Mr. Grimshaw the nomination so we must consider whattodo [sic]. You may send rules and writings together and we will take care to bring them again when this mater is sided. Do not menshon to nobody. But the writings gives the Trustees the nominacion. I am throng plowing or I shud a com'd myself But shall let you now more in a little time.'

Whattodo indeed. If the Heatons did not like someone, they would certainly do something. Patrick and Maria most likely went to call on the Heatons in the early summer of 1820. Robert Heaton was a land trustee and a churchwarden to boot. In the Brontë quest to win friends and influence people, it would have been a crunch meeting. The Heaton parents were long dead and the house was filled only with young people. Robert Heaton was 33, Michael was 29, Harriet was 25 and William was 22. Robert was engaged to be married to Alice Midgley from Oldfield, so wedding plans would have made for suitable small talk.

It is likely the ice was truly broken, however, when Maria and Patrick discovered that the Heatons shared their passion for reading. If Robert invited the scholarly parson and his wife to see the impressive library, as he doubtless would, it would have been a thrilling moment for the bookish couple. Robert's great-grandfather created a classic Georgian gentleman's library, added to by each generation, in an upstairs room with wood-panelled bookshelves and seats for reading at the mullioned windows.

Maria and Patrick would have beheld more than 1,000 books on every conceivable subject, both fiction and factual, from a first folio of Shakespeare's plays to books of satire, sport and medicine. Among the many volumes of poetry sat two copies of *The Seasons* by James Thomson, earlier editions than Maria's sea-stained one. Love of the written word had always been one of Maria and Patrick's strongest bonds. Their unfeigned excitement when they discovered this treasure house on the doorstep can only have endeared them to their hosts.

In later years the children of Alice and Robert would become friends to those of Maria and Patrick. Charlotte, Emily, Branwell and Anne Brontë visited Ponden when they were growing up, with Emily drawing inspiration for Cathy and Heathcliff from both the building and Heaton family history. Haworth was not an easy place for Maria and Patrick to make home but if they travelled back over the moorland road to the children on a summer's day in 1820, they had made a good start. All would seem well. God was in his heaven, the trustees were in their halls and the Brontës were finally in the Parsonage.

One episode from their married life around this time has been argued over for a century and a half. Mrs Gaskell, insisting she had the story from Charlotte, wrote of an ugly scene at the Parsonage when Patrick supposedly cut one of Maria's dresses to shreds in a rage. Nussey later mentioned the fashionable frock had been a gift, so it may have come from Penzance. As soon as it appeared in 1857, Gaskell's version was challenged in a letter to the *Bradford Observer* from Patrick's friend William Dearden, with 'the true history of this little affair as given by Nancy':

> 'One morning Mr. Bronte perceived that his Mrs. had put on a print gown, which was made in the fashion of that day, with a long waist, and what he thought absurd-looking sleeves. In a pleasant humour, he bantered her about the dress, and she went up-stairs and laid it aside. Mr Bronte shortly after entered her room, and cut off the sleeves. In the course of the day Mrs Bronte found the sleeveless gown, and showed it me in the kitchen, laughing heartily at Mr. Bronte's treatment of the offending garment. Next day, however, he went to Keighley, and bought the material for a silk gown, which was made to suit Mr Brontë's particular taste.'

For Charlotte to have any recollection at all of a disagreement, it most likely happened in Haworth towards the end of 1820 or the first few weeks of 1821, when she was four. Patrick could not bear any suggestion that he mistreated his wife and wrote to Mrs Gaskell. It was not the style of the dress that worried him but the fabric. He revealed Maria was short-sighted and he worried for her safety:

> 'With respect to tearing my wife's silk gown, my dear little daughter must have been misinform'd. This you will be

140

convinced of when I assure you, that it was my repeated advice to my wife and children, to wear gowns and outward garments, made *only of silk or wool* as these were less inflammable, than cotton, or linen – On account of my wife, and children all being near-sighted, I had an exccentric [sic] dread of accidents by fire.'

The big sleeves of a print gown made of cotton could easily catch on a candle, fireplace or stove. Buying her silk for a dress 'made to suit Mr Brontë's particular taste' meant simply sticking to fire-retardant clothing. Add to this Maria's laughter and her remark once to Sarah Garrs, 'He never gave me an angry word.'

The Firths were invited over to dine in the first week of September 1820 and Patrick would stop by at Kipping House when work took him to Bradford, enjoying time with his old friend John. Then in December 1820, in his early 60s, John Firth developed bowel problems and went rapidly downhill, both physically and mentally. Five days before Christmas, Elizabeth wrote in her diary: 'My dear Papa suffered great depression of mind.' Patrick went over the following day and soothed his friend, reading to him from his favourite psalms. When Patrick left the doctor was 'more happy' and the next day 'In holy Ecstasies...'

Comforted by Patrick he remained 'very cheerful' on Christmas Eve as he faced the end. On 27 December he died at 2.30am, his wife and daughter beside him as 'he breathed his last without a struggle'. Patrick conducted the funeral on 2 January 1821, staying on for two days to comfort the family.

In between the doctor's death in the old year and the funeral in the new, the Brontës marked their ninth wedding anniversary. Despite sadness over their friend, there was plenty to be thankful for after nine months in their new home. Mr and Mrs Brontë were able to go for walks in the long summer evenings, then watch the sun set over the back of the house when winter set in, looking west across the heights. It was all so beautiful.

When her mother was Maria's age she had already lost five children, while she was blessed with six hale and hearty little people. They were a long way from Cornwall and Ireland, but Maria and Pat had everything they wanted – a home, a family and each other.

Then on 29 January 1821, twelve days after Anne Brontë's first birthday and a week before Elizabeth turned six, everything changed.

Maria was already feeling unwell when Patrick left to baptise month-old Mary Leach of Cullingworth. He came home to find Maria had suddenly keeled over, falling to the floor in the hall of the Parsonage. Doubled up with a pain in her abdomen she was carried to bed and Patrick sent for the town doctor, Thomas Andrew. Dr Andrew's verdict came as a hammer blow. Maria had an internal cancer and would soon die. There was nothing to be done.

Though often thought to be uterine cancer, modern understanding would make it questionable for a woman of Maria's age, slight build and history of childbearing. Most cases of uterine cancer occur in women over 50, with most in their late seventies. Risk factors include having no children and being overweight. It is more likely that Maria had cervical cancer. This tends to affect younger women and the risk increases after having five full-term pregnancies. It often remains symptomless until at an advanced stage.

Cancer can, of course, defy any broad grouping of its victims but whatever the origin of the tumour, it was killing her – and the Parsonage reverberated with shock.

Of the little that has been written about Maria Branwell there tends to be the assumption that she was delicate because she was small. In fact, all the evidence on Maria's health before 1821 reveals the direct opposite. She was a strong and healthy woman. She had been raised in a comfortable home with good food, sea air and access to doctors. She had dodged whatever had carried off her seven siblings. The three-year-old Elizabeth and four-year-old Thomas, then the babies, second Thomas and both Alices before she was born, adult sisters Anne and Margaret when she was a child. Maria made the arduous solo journey from Penzance, had six healthy pregnancies and survived childbirth. She walked everywhere.

Elizabeth Branwell was also petite but strong well into her sixties. Maria's offspring, apart from Emily, who was tall like her father, may have resembled little dolls in stature but they too were healthy in their early years. Maria did not fall ill because she was always frail. In 1821 as today, a robust constitution was no defence against an aggressive and incurable disease.

Though clearly terminally ill, Maria did not die immediately as feared. Overwhelmed and desperate to do his best for her, Patrick employed a nurse. Martha Wright was a 28-year-old Haworth woman who had much in common with her patient. She was married in the same year, 1812, to her husband Joseph and they had a little girl called Mary Ann who was almost the same age as little Maria Brontë. She was also an educated woman and a Wesleyan and the women quickly became friends.

A glimpse of this comes from her attempt to give Maria some small comfort with a reminder of home. The patient would beg to be propped up in bed so she could watch her nurse clean the fireplace grate, Martha said, 'because she did it as it was done in Cornwall.' Something about those moments reminded Maria of the hob-cheeked fireplaces of Chapel Street.

Through the long and fitful nights it was Patrick who insisted on tending the 'beloved sufferer' alone in their bed, now home to whispered words of comfort and silent despair. When morning came he would make life as normal as possible for the children, attempting to maintain the structure of their lives even as its foundations crumbled. Routines often ascribed to Aunt Branwell later were actually already in place. An account of these days of Maria's dying was given by Sarah shortly before her own death in 1899. She spoke to Mary Virginia Terhune, writing as Marion Harland, for *Charlotte Brontë at Home*:

> 'I have had direct from Sarah De Garrs the story of one day in the overshadowed home, a routine laid down and carried out by the father – for all these months sick-nurse, tutor, breadwinner, and bread-dispenser to the little flock already virtually motherless.'

It is a picture of a devoted father trying to distract his children from the tragedy unfolding upstairs. Even prosaic details on heating economy spoke of the medical bills piling up in Patrick's study:

> 'The six children, always neatly dressed by their nurse, met their father in his study for morning prayers, and, these over, accompanied him across the hall to breakfast. The fare was plain, but abundant, – porridge and milk, bread and butter, for the morning meal seven days in the week. The furniture of the parlour was scanty, yet well kept. The grate was economically contrived to burn the least quantity of coals consistent with enough warmth to save the occupants of the room from actual suffering; there were two small windows, both looking toward the burial-ground.'

Patrick tried to keep the children quiet as they ate, 'lest the clamour of tongues might break the quiet of the sick-room overhead'. The servants took the baby while Patrick herded the other five into his study for lessons, followed by an hour's sewing for the girls. The midday meal was meat and potatoes followed by bread pudding, rice pudding or custard. In the afternoon, Patrick left for his parish duties and the children were taken out on the moor. Here they could escape the crushing atmosphere of dread in the house and play 'with zest'. Back home, it was tea with Patrick, more lessons and sewing.

They could only be distracted for so long, though. Overhead Maria 'lay in bed all day, suffering intense pain at times, and so miserably unnerved that the house must be kept perfectly quiet when she "had her worst turns".' On her better days, the children were taken to see Mama for a few minutes before bedtime: 'While she could listen to them, the little ones said their nightly prayers at her bedside, kissed her "good-night", and stole away softly…'

Winter ended and spring arrived, but April had none of the usual air of family celebration. When Maria's 38th birthday dawned, all there was to celebrate was that she had made it through another night. Little Maria turned seven and Charlotte turned five. Soon after, a letter arrived from Elizabeth in Thornton and the following week Patrick went to Kipping House, possibly to update the Firths.

Then things went from bad to worse. The children succumbed to scarlet fever just when Maria seemed about to die:

> 'One day, I remember it well; it was a gloomy day, a day of clouds and darkness, three of my little children were taken ill of a scarlet fever; and, the day after, the remaining three were in the same condition. Just at that time death seemed to have laid his hand on my dear wife in a manner which threatened her speedy dissolution. She was cold and silent and seemed hardly to notice what was passing around her.'

Death kept its distance a little while longer, thanks to the tireless ministrations of Patrick, Sarah, Nancy and Martha:

> 'This awful season however was not long of duration. My little children had a favourable turn, and at length got well; and the force of my wife's disease somewhat abated.'

It was a reprieve but only that. Maria was wasting away, her good days scarcely better than her worst. Death had only retreated a little to close in again and Patrick could not face it alone. He wrote, like Aunt Fennell before him, to summon help from Penzance. Again, it was dependable Aunt

144

Branwell to the rescue, though with nothing to look forward to this time. It was not to Thornton, where she could renew her friendship with Elizabeth Firth and Fanny Outhwaite. It was to somewhere she had never visited and knew only from the unflattering accounts of the life of Grimshaw in her Methodist magazines. She answered Patrick's cri de coeur on the strict understanding that it was a temporary arrangement. Elizabeth had no desire to be stuck on the Pennines forever like her sister. She was 45 years old and made the epic road trip north again, promising her Cornish friends and family to be back. She packed her magazines, books, sewing equipment, smelling salts and snuff box. This time she knew to take her pattens for cold floors, too.

It was the third time she had covered the 400 miles that separated her comfortable home in Cornwall from the guest bed crammed into a corner in Yorkshire. She knew what an arduous and lonely coach journey lay ahead. When she arrived it would be to the chillier climes she loathed and a sister on her deathbed. What she did not know is what Maria had not known, either. Maria set off from her Cornish home in 1812 with no idea that she would never return. Elizabeth Branwell surely felt a pang of unease as she waved everyone goodbye and once more headed north.

Just as Maria had once received a hero's welcome at Woodhouse Grove, Elizabeth was exactly who Patrick wanted to see in Haworth. Describing her arrival after the scarlet fever crisis, he wrote:

> 'A few weeks afterwards her sister, Miss Branwell, arrived, and afforded great comfort to my mind, which has been the case ever since, by sharing my labours and sorrows, and behaving as an affectionate mother to my children.'

Elizabeth saw her hopes for a swift return home fade immediately. Maria was not the lively young mother she had left in Thornton. She was pale and thin and in constant pain. Young Maria and Elizabeth were no longer toddlers and the baby she saw into the world, Charlotte, was now five years old. There were three more children she had never met. Patrick was a different man too. No longer the poet and doting papa, now he was distraught, trying to hold everything together as each day looked like Maria's last.

As to the Thornton circle, after years of writing in her diary since she was a schoolgirl, *The Ladies Polite Remembrancer for 1821* has long, silent gaps as if this was the year 23-year-old Elizabeth Firth could not bear to record, even in her staccato style. No sooner had she lost her father and was finding life 'trying' on 21 January, than her friend was in the ghastly throes of a protracted death. No more 'Tea with Mrs Bronte' like the old days. There are no entries for either the day of Maria's collapse or the day after, but a visit to see 'very poorly' Maria on 9 February. She dined at the Parsonage on 21 February, wrote to Patrick on 17 April and ten days later he stayed overnight at Kipping.

When Aunt Branwell arrived she quickly joined forces with her old Thornton friends. Maria needed round the clock care, Patrick was worn out and the eldest children were old enough to know what was going on. So on 26 May Elizabeth Firth and Fanny Outhwaite hired a post-chaise for 10 shillings (£30 today). They rode over to Haworth and took young Maria and Elizabeth off to Kipping House for a month. They gave each little girl a new skipping rope to play with in the garden, where they could make as much noise as they liked. Charlotte was left behind with the youngest children. Not only was Mama not able to spend much time with her but adored big sister Maria – her 'little mother' – had disappeared for a month too.

Amid the stressed and sorrowing household, Charlotte was taking in more than anyone realized. She told Ellen Nussey that, 'she began to analyze character when she was five years old, and instanced two guests who were at her home for a day or two, and of whom she had taken stock, and of whom after-knowledge confirmed her first impressions.' The trauma of her mother's illness coincided with the emergence of an intense assessment of the players in her little world, of weighing up who people were and what they might do.

Retreating into her imagination, she tried to run away from home to somewhere light and happy, too little to understand why. Ellen Nussey later related the story as one Charlotte told 'with great amusement' from 'when she was about five years old'. But there was nothing funny about it at the time, when one of the Garrs found that a child was missing outside in the dark near a busy road:

> 'She had familiarised herself with the description of the "Golden City" in the Book of Revelation and she had also read "The Pilgrim's Progress". She heard the servants ... talking much of Bradford, a town ten miles off, as a place that afforded them every conceivable delight – her imagination seized upon the idea that Bradford must be the "Golden City" she had read about, and she must walk to it as the Pilgrims did; off she went and had gone

about a mile, and was rising the hill opposite the Parsonage, when she was all at once thrown into a deep shadow by the approach of a team of horses drawing a huge waggon-load; the tramping of the horses and the engulphing darkness, as she thought, terrified her so, that she sank down on the road-side, and there she was found by the maid who had followed in search of her...'

The dreadful year of 1821 was a formative time for the future author. Charlotte could only recall her mother dimly as an adult, remembering once seeing her playing with Branwell in front of the fire. Charlotte compartmentalised events around her mother's lingering death, always specifying her age at the time but seeming not to connect her memories to herself as a distressed and grieving five-year-old.

When Aunt Branwell arrived, Martha Wright left. The expensive nurse was no longer needed and would have remained a footnote to Maria's story had not Mrs Gaskell found her more than thirty years later when compiling her biography of Charlotte. She was the 'good old woman' referred to as the source of anecdotes that painted Patrick as an eccentric tyrant. The assumption has always been that Martha and Patrick – or Martha and Elizabeth – clashed or that she felt unfairly sacked and took her revenge by bending the ear of Mrs Gaskell decades later.

Yet this is not the Martha her friends recognised when she died aged 92 in Burnley, where she had lived for forty years. She was 'widely known and highly respected' according to her obituary in the *Burnley Express and Advertiser* of June 1883, and 'she occupied the position of friend and nurse during the last illness of Mrs. Brontë':

> 'An early acquaintance with sorrow [the death of Mary Ann at 22, who was buried by Patrick] gave her a stern and somewhat dignified bearing, but those who knew her best loved her most. Mrs Wright was a woman of strong mind, sound judgement and broad sympathies, with a large fund of anecdote and folk lore.'

Mrs Gaskell tapped into this fund but it seems at least possible that she embroidered Martha's stories, as she was wont to do. The fact that Martha never again spoke to a biographer may indicate dismay at the uproar *The Life* caused among Patrick's friends and former servants. She always maintained that Maria was her friend, whose suffering she tried to ease with insightful palliative care. For the rest of her days, she was regarded as a kind woman. Burnley historian Ken Spencer records that everyone spoke well of Martha, with 'her bright beaming face and gracious smile'.

As the summer of 1821 arrived it was Elizabeth who cared for her sister through the day, devising a round-the-clock relay with her brother-in-law. There was no chemotherapy, no radiotherapy and no pain relief as the cancer advanced relentlessly through Maria's emaciated frame. Patrick consulted the doctor almost daily and between nightly vigils and his clerical duties, combed his medical books. He took out his well-thumbed Buchan's *Domestic Medicine,* reading of cancer treatments such as carrot poultices and mercury pills, blood-letting and hemlock, though 'no certain remedy is yet known'.

Little Branwell had his fourth birthday in late June while Emily turned three at the end of July, in the muted surroundings of a home waiting on death. As the occupants in the Parsonage shared the vigil at Maria's agonized bedside, so the whole country awaited news of Queen Caroline, who was 'in excrutiating pain' with a bowel obstruction.

Caroline was as popular as her husband was despised, after resisting his attempts to divorce her. The press camped out at Brandenburgh House in London. She died on 7 August and the *Stamford Mercury* broke the news in a final dispatch:

> 'The struggle is over! The Queen is no more! About five minutes ago, a Moorish domestic of her Majesty burst into the vestibule; and at the same instant a loud and lengthened shriek from the female servants, as they rushed towards each other from their several apartments, rendered all explanation unnecessary.'

The country went into mourning as Patrick dreaded the day his own wife's struggle would end. Meanwhile Maria lay confined to her bed, her window overlooking the rows of tombstones in a sad circularity. She had looked out onto the graveyard at the end of the garden from her nursery window in Penzance. Now she was forced to end her days watching another. Everyone must die but few must watch so many being lowered into their graves as they inch towards their own.

When there was a death in town the passing-bell would be rung in the church tower. The bell rang three times with three strokes for a man or three times with two strokes for a woman, followed by a toll for each year of his or her life, then a repeat of the three times two or three. Since the day of Maria's collapse and terminal diagnosis in January, Patrick had conducted seventy funerals knowing she could be next. Nussey describes how the business of death surrounded Maria:

> 'The Passing-bell was *often* a dreary accompaniment to the day's engagements, and must have been trying to the sensitive nervous temperaments of those who were always within sound of it as the Parsonage inmates were, but *everything* around, and in *immediate vicinity* was a reminder of man's last bourne, as you issued from the Parsonage gate, you looked upon the Stone-cutter's chipping shed which was piled with slabs ready for use, and to the ear there was the incessant sound of the *chip, chip*, of the recording chisel as it graved in the In Memoriams of the departed.'

The ordeal of seeing Maria suffer the end stages of cancer in September was made even worse by her mental torments. She would cry out: 'Oh God, my poor children!' over and again. It spoke not of a triumphal step into paradise but of rage and despair. Patrick wanted to believe in a good death, the kind of death that Dr Firth had, where his final words were 'all's well, all's happy'. The kind expected in Evangelical circles, such as Grimshaw's 'the signs of death are on me, but I am not afraid'.

But neither William Grimshaw nor John Firth had been only 38 years old, consumed by the anguish of leaving six very young children behind. They had not died in extreme physical pain like Maria. Patrick knew all this and made his peace with it, deciding the devil was circling during the final battle between life and death but that her faith endured to the exhausted end:

> 'During many years she had walked with God, but the great enemy, envying her life of holiness, often disturbed her mind in the last conflict. Still, in general she had peace and joy in believing, and died, if not triumphantly, at least calmly and with a holy yet humble confidence that Christ was her Saviour and heaven her eternal home.'

There was nothing good about Maria's death when it finally came on 15 September 1821. Patrick and Elizabeth sat either side of her and the children

149

stood at the end of the bed with the servants. By then, Maria's tiny, wasted frame was bent double. Sarah Garrs was the witness who described Maria's final hours for Charlotte biographer Marion Harland:

> 'Charlotte Brontë was but five years old when the six children were led, in solemn ceremony, to their mother's room to see her die. ... Yet enough vitality remained in the emaciated frame to make death a struggle. So hard was it that, as an eye-witness told me, the knees were drawn up rigidly against the body, and could not be straightened when life was extinct. She had expressed the wish to her husband that "all the dear faces should be about her when she died," and the faithful Sarah carried Baby Anne in her arms when the summons came. The husband did not leave his post at his wife's pillow until ... "Her soul departed to her Saviour."'

When death came for Maria Brontë she wanted to stay in the world, her heart still more ready to attach itself to earth than heaven. Her distress was for those she left behind. Distraught Patrick endured her lament as it cut through him a final time, 'Oh, my poor children!' Poor Maria, only seven. Poor Elizabeth, only six. Poor Charlotte, only five. Poor Branwell only four. Poor Emily, only three. Poor Anne, only 20 months old.

And oh, her poor Pat, whose grief was unbearable.

Elizabeth Firth recorded only the bald fact in her diary for that day. 'Mrs Bronte died after an illness of 8 months.' When it was over, Maria's body had to be laid out at the Parsonage. The corpse was washed, prepared and dressed for the grave by a woman who worked as the local shroud-maker and 'layer-outer'. With Maria, curled into a ball, there was also the grim wait for rigor mortis to recede so that her legs could be straightened. Maria's was the first Brontë body to lie in the Parsonage with pennies on the eyes, mouth held closed with a scarf, hands over the chest. The coffin was probably made of oak and her shroud of satin, a cut above the pine and muslin used by poorer families. Visitors called to pay their respects while biddings – black-edged funeral invitations – were issued.

Maria lay dead at the Parsonage for seven days, longer than was usual at the time. There was more to do than dig a hole in the graveyard. As the parson's wife she was to be buried inside the church in the chancel, the altar area. A vault had to be dug eight feet down and lined with stone before the funeral could take place. Patrick would have trusted his sexton, William Brown, to oversee the whole distressing project. Brown was a stonemason and could have excavated the church floor himself. He was likely to have created the stonework for the tomb lining and covering slabs.

Maria died on Saturday and digging could not begin on a Sunday, especially with five baptisms already booked in for the covering cleric William Anderton. There was a wedding and a churchyard burial at St Michael's on the Tuesday so digging up the floor for the Brontë tomb must have begun or resumed on the Wednesday after Maria died. Measuring roughly six feet by six feet, it was a double-width space for family members. A wall down the middle and ledges for covering stones allowed for future coffins to be placed on top and to the side, separate spaces rather than the gothic room with shelves of popular imagination.

On Saturday 22 September 1821 the simple vault was ready and Maria could finally be laid to rest. A small coffin gate between the garden and the church was opened to allow all the Brontës, Elizabeth Branwell and fellow mourners to escort Maria through on her final journey. The gate (walled up in the 1940s by Canon William Dixon) was only used when there was a death in the family at the Parsonage.

Patrick asked their old friend William Morgan, who married them and christened four of their babies, to conduct Maria's funeral. It seems certain that Jane, who took turns with Maria to be bride and bridesmaid, and her parents joined the solemn funeral procession from the house to St Michael's. It might be hoped that the ladies of Thornton were there, though Elizabeth Firth leaves the three days around the funeral as blanks in her diary.

William met the coffin at the gate and led the mourners to the church door, saying, 'I am the resurrection and the life, saith the Lord. ... We brought nothing into this world, and it is certain we can carry nothing out...' Outside on the moor, the heather bloomed. Inside the dark church Maria was lowered into the brand-new tomb as Patrick, Elizabeth and the children tried to comprehend a life without her.

Before or after a Haworth burial came a funeral feast known as an arvill. Maria's may have been held at home before the burial like the one for John Heaton, the brother of Richard out at Ponden Hall. He was the eldest son but died at the age of 23 in 1807. His was a lavish affair. Biddings were issued and black gloves and scarves were handed out to wear in the procession behind the coffin slung between two horses.

Less likely is an arvill for Maria at a local pub, such as the Black Bull Inn, popular for toasting the dearly departed. After the Heaton funeral, the gentlemen sank 24 gallons of ale and four quarts of rum. More recently, eighty people had attended an arvill at the pub for the previous curate James Charnock. Guests would have been given traditional arvill-cake or arvill-bread and drinks. As the bill for the old parson's arvill was paid by friends it seems likely the same happened with Maria's.

Back home Patrick, a widowed father of six at 44, succumbed to a searing sense of loss, 'the innocent yet distressing prattle of my children' serving only as a reminder of their mother. He could hear that *chip*, *chip*, of the recording chisel as the stonemason carved 'Here lie the remains of Maria Bronte, wife of the Rev. P. Bronte, A.B., Minister of Haworth. Her soul departed to the saviour, Sept. 15th, 1821, in the 39th year of her age.' Then the verse Patrick chose from Matthew's gospel, a source of hope of being reunited with the dead, 'Be ye also ready: for in such an hour as ye think not the Son of Man cometh.' After another seven days, he was back at work. On 29 September the newly widowed Pat christened babies Mary Townend and James Hird. His thoughts can only have strayed to his baby Annie and bereft children at home.

Those who had known and loved Maria wrote letters of condolence and one from John Buckworth, Patrick's friend and former vicar, touched him deeply with its kindness and Christian reflection. Rachel would have shared this sympathy from Dewsbury, where the couples had become friends not so many years before. On the 27 November Patrick sat down at his desk to write a reply. Composed only two months after he was widowed, it is a first-hand account of the most harrowing year of his life and infinitely more affecting than his books of verse.

He begins with the uneasy truce in Haworth and then describes losing Maria Branwell Brontë, the remarkable woman he loved. Patrick arranged his paper and ink on his desk, sharpened his quill with a little penknife and wondered how to begin.

It was just nine years, almost to the day, since he had received another moving letter at his bachelor digs at Hartshead. That one had been from his adored fiancée at Woodhouse Grove, full of life and written in her elegant, forward-slanting hand. How glad he had been to read that she shared his vision of a long life together: 'I think, if our lives are spared twenty years hence, I shall then pray for you with the same, if not greater, fervour and delight that I do now.'

But she had not been spared. She had been taken from him before even half those years had passed and all her delight was gone. Just as their love had appeared suddenly, so too her death. He laid the whole pitiful tale out for his friend as 'a brief narrative of facts, as they have succeeded one another, in my little sphere for the last twelve months'.

Patrick begins with their arrival in Haworth, navigating the tricky first few months after the nomination debacle, 'I looked to the Lord and He controuled [sic] the storm and levelled the waves and brought my vessel safe into the harbour.' Then his own harbour had given way:

> 'But no sooner was I there than another storm arose, more terrible than the former – one that shook every part of the mortal frame and often threatened it with dissolution. My dear wife was taken dangerously ill on the 29th of January last; and in little more than seven months afterwards she died. During every week and almost every day of this long tedious interval I expected her final removal.'

He had been frightened and lonely, feeling isolated from the town and far from his friends. In his hour of need, Haworth had not rallied around him:

> 'For the first three months I was left nearly quite alone, unless you suppose my six little children and the nurse and servants to have been company. Had I been at Dewsbury I should not have wanted kind friends; had I been at Hartshead I should have seen them and others occasionally; or had I been at Thornton a family there who were ever truly kind would have soothed my sorrows; but I was at Haworth, a stranger in a strange land. It was under these circumstances, after every earthly prop was removed, that I was called on to bear the weight of the greatest load of sorrows that ever pressed upon me.'

He had done everything in his power:

> 'At the earliest opportunity I called in different medical gentlemen to visit the beloved sufferer; but all their skill was in vain. Death pursued her unrelentingly. Her constitution was enfeebled, and her frame wasted daily; and after above seven months of more agonizing pain than I ever saw anyone endure she fell asleep in Jesus, and her soul took its flight to the mansions of glory.'

Then a piercing description of how it felt to watch, helplessly, as his Maria died:

> 'Do you ask how I felt under all these circumstances? I would answer to this, that tender sorrow was my daily portion; that oppressive grief sometimes lay heavy on me and that there were seasons when an affectionate, agonizing something sickened my whole frame, and which is I think of such a nature as cannot be described, and must be felt in order to be understood.'

As he stared around the Parsonage, still trying to imagine this life without her, friends such as William Morgan helped in the most practical way they could. They dug deep to pay the medical bills that had piled up. Along with everything else, Patrick had lost Maria's £50 annuity on her death:

> 'And when my dear wife was dead and buried and gone, and when I missed her at every corner ... I had incurred considerable debts, from causes which I could neither forsee nor prevent, he [God] raised me up friends to whom I had never mentioned my straitened circumstances, who dispensed their bounty to me in a way truly wonderful, and evidently in answer to prayer.'

Though his financial burdens were eased, he was still a man trying not to drown in grief by clinging to his faith and trying to get back to normal. He describes his feelings on that winter's day, 73 days after the worst day, the day Maria died:

> 'I would also answer to this, the edge of sorrow, which is still *very keen* is somewhat blunted. The tide of grief, which once threatened to overwhelm me, has I trust been at its height, and the slowly receding waves often give me a breathing time though there are periods when they swell high and rush momentarily over me; yet I trust through the mercy of the Lord that time will produce its effects, and that I shall be enabled to pursue my ministerial labours with the necessary degree of alacrity and vigour.'

There was never anyone to replace Maria in his heart and that tide of grief would recede and swell for the rest of his life as he lost her children, too, one by one. As he finished his letter in November 1821, he knew only that Maria was gone and he had to find the strength from somewhere.

Their six singular children needed him.

Decades later no-one who knew the austere old gentleman eating his porridge, with spectacles perched on his nose and yards of white silk wound round his throat to keep warm, would know that once he had been everything to a clever and loving society lady who had exchanged wealth and comfort for a life by his side. Her dear friend, her saucy lover, who outlived her and all of their gifted children to die aged 84. With Pat died the Brontë name he had invented as an ambitious young man in 1802, given to an extraordinary family and taken to the grave in 1861.

All that remains of Maria's mind and heart to contemplate with our own eyes is one solitary love letter and the books that followed her from one life to another, surviving the stormy sea, consoling the ones she left behind. Maybe they are the best keepsakes of a life lost in the shadows for 200 years, because they are composed of words. For all her adventures, her joys and her suffering, Maria Branwell's legacy has come to be her daughters. The wise and fierce words of Charlotte, Emily and Anne Brontë burn in the world as brightly today as when they were written. Most of their mother's words are scattered to the four winds but one letter in her own hand survives the centuries. The letter that speaks of it all. Not of sorrow but of love. Not of death but of a passionate life. Of shipwrecks real and imagined. The one that begins, *My dear saucy Pat...*

Epilogue

'Oh God, my poor children' could equally have fallen from Pat's lips as their mother slipped from his arms forever. For those children, the loss of their mother and enduring grief of their father would make an indelible mark on their consciousness and surface often in their writing. That loss is plain to see in the Brontë novels, most glaringly in that their characters so often grow up motherless. Among these are the eponymous heroines of Charlotte's *Jane Eyre* and *Shirley*, Cathy and Heathcliff in Emily's *Wuthering Heights* and Helen Huntingdon in Anne's *The Tenant of Wildfell Hall*.

All the surviving Brontë sisters inherited something of their mother. Maria's most unworldly daughter, Emily, saw the world as a gothic blend of the seen and the unseen, bringing a layered understanding of the dead and the territory they claim to *Wuthering Heights* and her poetry. Her Celtic roots and the wild landscapes of Yorkshire seeming to combine in shaping her sensibilities. The only characters in Emily's one novel that she allows a happy(ish) love affair – Hareton and Cathy Linton – are fictional contemporaries of her parents.

Meanwhile Anne Brontë includes a tribute to Cornish thinking by featuring Sir Humphry Davy's *Last Days of a Philosopher* in the library of Wildfell Hall. When she was dying she felt the deep call of the sea and was buried in Scarborough, the only Brontë not to share the family vault. In her last days Anne held the little china smelling bottle with M.B. in gold, a small link to the mother she never knew. Maria's affable son struggled to make his mark but was known to his many friends by his middle name of Branwell, his mother's name before she took his father's.

Little Maria and Elizabeth Brontë joined their mother in her tomb while they were still children of eleven and ten. All that remain are their samplers, completed on their birthdays between her death and theirs. When tuberculosis also killed Branwell in September 1848, Emily two months later in December, and Anne the following May, all Patrick had left was Charlotte, the daughter who most resembled her mother. Just before Valentine's Day

1850, Patrick allowed the last of his children to read Maria's love letters from that breathless summer of 1812. Charlotte was only a little older than her mother had been when she wrote them. She wrote to Ellen Nussey:

'A few days since, a little incident happened which curiously touched me. Papa put into my hands a little packet of letters and papers, telling me that they were mamma's, and that I might read them. I did read them, in a frame of mind I cannot describe. The papers were yellow with time, all having been written before I was born. It was strange now to peruse, for the first time, the records of a mind whence my own sprang; and most strange, and at once sad and sweet, to find that mind of a truly fine, pure, and elevated order. They were written to papa before they were married. There is a rectitude, a refinement, a constancy, a modesty, a sense, a gentleness about them indescribable. I wish she had lived, and that I had known her.'

Also strange was Charlotte's powerful response to her first sight of the sea. Of an old coastal clan, her Branwell side surfaced at the age of 23 when she visited Bridlington in 1839. Ellen was there and as soon as they were 'near enough for Charlotte to see it in its expanse, she was quite overpowered, she could not speak till she had shed some tears'. Like Maria, she would never forget the sights and sounds of the ocean. 'Charlotte's impressions of the Sea never wore off; she would often recall her views of it, and wonder what its aspect would be just at the time she was speaking of it.' Five years after reading her mother's love letters, Charlotte too was gone. She died at 38, the same age as Maria, and Patrick lost the last member of his extraordinary family.

Few lives were so altered by Maria's death as that of her sister, a lady of cosmopolitan Penzance trapped in Haworth. Losing Maria broke Patrick's heart but the prospect of raising six children alone made him desperate. He cast around wildly for a new wife as his sister-in-law held the fort. Three months after the funeral he proposed to Elizabeth Firth, who was so affronted she stopped speaking to him. He made another doomed approach to Isabella Dury, the sister of his friend Theodore who was vicar of nearby Keighley. Patrick thought Mary Burder a candidate. She soon put him straight.

No-one wanted the penniless curate with six small children and Elizabeth watched her hopes of going home dwindle to nothing. She stayed to help raise the Brontës and paid her own board. There was no question of anything more. The church considered them as kindred and as such, marriage a kind of incest. Instead they were great friends, talking about books over a cuppa from her William Grimshaw memorial teapot. Nussey records:

> 'In Summer she spent part of her afternoon in reading aloud to Mr Brontë, and in winter the evenings, she must have enjoyed this, for she and Mr Brontë had sometimes to finish their discussions on what she had read when we all met for tea, she would be very lively and intelligent in her talk, and tilted argument without fear against Mr Brontë.'

Maria stayed in Yorkshire for the love of a man, Elizabeth for the love of six small children. Maria lived with Patrick Brontë for nine years, Elizabeth stayed for more than twenty. When she suffered a twisted bowel at the age of 66, the age her mother died, Aunt Branwell left her money to her Yorkshire nieces and Eliza in Cornwall. The Brontë sisters used the money to finance their first publication in 1846, *Poems by Currer, Ellis and Acton Bell*. Thus the Branwell inheritance earned in the free trade era launched the literary careers of Maria's daughters of genius – Charlotte, Emily and Anne Brontë.

Appendix 1

The Letters of Maria Branwell

'It was strange to peruse now for the first time the records of a mind whence my own sprang...'

Charlotte Brontë

To
the Rev. Patrick Brontë, A.B., *Hartshead*.
Wood House Grove, August 26th, 1812

My dear Friend,—This address is sufficient to convince you that I not only permit, but approve of yours to me—I do indeed consider you as my *friend*; yet, when I consider how short a time I have had the pleasure of knowing you, I start at my own rashness, my heart fails, and did I not think that you would be disappointed and grieved at it, I believe I should be ready to spare myself the task of writing. Do not think that I am so wavering as to repent of what I have already said. No, believe me, this will never be the case, unless you give me cause for it. You need not fear that you have been mistaken in my character. If I know anything of myself, I am incapable of making an ungenerous return to the smallest degree of kindness, much less to you whose attentions and conduct have been so particularly obliging. I will frankly confess that your behaviour and what I have seen and heard of your character has excited my warmest esteem and regard, and be assured you shall never have cause to repent of any confidence you may think proper to place in me, and that it will always be my endeavour to deserve the good opinion which you have formed, although human weakness may in some instances cause me to fall short. In giving you these assurances I do not depend upon my own strength, but I look to Him who has been my unerring guide through life, and in whose continued protection and assistance I confidently trust.

I thought on you much on Sunday, and feared you would not escape the rain. I hope you do not feel any bad effects from it? My cousin wrote you on Monday and expects this afternoon to be favoured with an answer. Your letter has caused me some foolish embarrassment, tho' in pity to my feelings they have been very sparing of their raillery.

I will now candidly answer your questions. The *politeness of others* can never make me forget your kind attentions, neither can I *walk our accustomed rounds* without thinking on you, and, why should I be ashamed to add, wishing for your presence. If you knew what were my feelings whilst writing this you would pity me. I wish to write the truth and give you satisfaction, yet fear to go too far, and exceed the bounds of propriety. But whatever I may say or write I will *never deceive* you, or *exceed the truth*. If you think I have not placed the *utmost confidence* in you, consider my situation, and ask yourself if I have not confided in you sufficiently, perhaps too much. I am very sorry that you will not have this till after to-morrow, but it was out of my power to write sooner. I rely on your goodness to pardon everything in this which may appear either too free or too stiff, and beg that you will consider me as a warm and faithful friend.

My uncle, aunt, and cousin unite in kind regards.

I must now conclude with again declaring myself to be yours sincerely,

Maria Branwell.

To
the Rev. Patrick Brontë, A.B., *Hartshead.*
Wood House Grove, September 5th, 1812.

My dearest Friend,—I have just received your affectionate and very welcome letter, and although I shall not be able to send this until Monday, yet I cannot deny myself the pleasure of writing a few lines this evening, no longer considering it a task, but a pleasure, next to that of reading yours. I had the pleasure of hearing from Mr Fennell, who was at Bradford on Thursday afternoon, that you had rested there all night. Had you proceeded, I am sure the walk would have been too much for you; such excessive fatigue, often repeated, must injure the strongest constitution. I am rejoiced to find that our forebodings were without cause. I had yesterday a letter from a very dear friend of mine, and had the satisfaction to learn by it that all at home are well. I feel with you the unspeakable obligations I am under to a merciful Providence—my heart swells with gratitude, and I feel an earnest desire that I may be enabled to make some suitable return to the Author of all my blessings. In general, I think I am enabled to cast my care upon Him, and then I experience a calm and peaceful serenity of mind which few things can destroy. In all my addresses to the throne of grace I never ask a blessing for myself but I beg the same for you, and considering the important station which you are called to fill, my prayers are proportionately fervent that you may be favoured with all the gifts and graces requisite for such a calling.

O my dear friend, let us pray much that we may live lives holy and useful to each other and all around us!

Monday Morn.—My cousin and I were yesterday at Calverley church, where we heard Mr Watman preach a very excellent sermon from 'learn of Me, for I am meek and lowly of heart.' He displayed the character of our Saviour in a most affecting and amiable light. I scarcely ever felt more charmed with his excellences, more grateful for his condescension, or more abased at my own unworthiness; but I lament that my heart is so little retentive of those pleasing and profitable impressions.

I pitied you in your solitude, and felt sorry that it was not in my power to enliven it. Have you not been too hasty in informing your friends of a certain event? Why did you not leave them to guess a little longer? I shrink from the idea of its being known to everybody. I do, indeed, *sometimes* think of you, but I will not say how often, lest I raise your vanity; and we sometimes talk of you and the doctor. But I believe I should seldom mention your name myself were it not now and then introduced by my cousin. I have never mentioned a word of what is past to anybody. Had I thought this necessary I should have requested you to do it. But I think there is no need, as by some means or other they seem to have a pretty correct notion how matters stand betwixt us; and as their hints, etc., meet with no contradiction from me, my silence passes for confirmation. Mr Fennell has not neglected to give me some serious and encouraging advice, and my aunt takes frequent opportunities of dropping little sentences which I may turn to some advantage. I have long had reason to know that the present state of things would give pleasure to all parties. Your ludicrous account of the scene at the Hermitage was highly diverting, we laughed heartily at it; but I fear it will not produce all that compassion in Miss Fennell's breast which you seem to wish. I will now tell you what I was thinking about and doing at the time you mention. I was then toiling up the hill with Jane and Mrs Clapham to take our tea at Mr Tatham's, thinking on the evening when I first took the same walk with you, and on the change which had taken place in my circumstances and views since then—not wholly without a wish that I had your arm to assist me, and your conversation to shorten the walk. Indeed, all our walks have now an insipidity in them which I never thought they would have possessed. When I work, if I wish to get *forward* I may be glad that you are at a distance. Jane begs me to assure you of her kind regards. Mr Morgan is expected to be here this evening. I must assume a bold and steady countenance to meet his attacks!

I have now written a pretty long letter without reserve or caution, and if all the sentiments of my heart are not laid open to you believe me it is not because I wish them to be concealed, for, I hope there is nothing there that would give you pain or displeasure. My most sincere and earnest wishes are for your happiness and welfare, for this includes my own. Pray much for me that I may be made a blessing and not a hindrance to you. Let me not interrupt your studies nor intrude on that time which ought to be dedicated to better purposes. Forgive my freedom, my dearest friend, and rest assured that you are and ever will be dear to Write very soon. Maria Branwell.

To
the Rev. Patrick Brontë, A.B., *Hartshead.*
Wood House Grove, September 11th, 1812.

My dearest Friend,—Having spent the day yesterday at Miry Shay, a place near Bradford, I had not got your letter till my return in the evening, and consequently have only a short time this morning to write if I send it by this post. You surely do not think you *trouble* me by writing? No, I think I may venture to say if such were your opinion you would *trouble* me no more. Be assured, your letters are and I hope always will be received with extreme pleasure and read with delight. May our Gracious Father mercifully grant the fulfilment of your prayers! Whilst we depend entirely on Him for happiness, and receive each other and all our blessings as from His hands, what can harm us or make us miserable? Nothing temporal or spiritual.

Jane had a note from Mr Morgan last evening, and she desires me to tell you that the Methodists' service in church hours is to commence next Sunday week. You may expect frowns and hard words from her when you make your appearance here again, for, if you recollect, she gave you a note to carry to the Doctor, and he has never received it. What have you done with it? If you can give a good account of it you may come to see us as soon as you please and be sure of a hearty welcome from all parties. Next Wednesday we have some thoughts, if the weather be fine, of going to Kirkstall Abbey once more, and I suppose your presence will not make the walk less agreeable to any of us.

The old man is come and waits for my letter. In expectation of seeing you on Monday or Tuesday next,—I remain, yours faithfully and affectionately,
M. B.

To
the Rev. Patrick Brontë, A.B., *Hartshead.*
Wood House Grove, September 18th, 1812.

How readily do I comply with my dear Mr B.'s request! You see, you have only to express your wishes, and as far as my power extends I hesitate not to fulfil them. My heart tells me that it will always be my pride and pleasure to contribute to your happiness, nor do I fear that this will ever be inconsistent with my duty as a Christian. My esteem for you and my confidence in you is so great, that I firmly believe you will never exact anything from me which I could not conscientiously perform. I shall in future look to you for assistance and instruction whenever I may need them, and hope you will never withhold from me any advice or caution you may see necessary.

For some years I have been perfectly my own mistress, subject to no *control* whatever—so far from it, that my sisters who are many years older than myself, and even my dear mother, used to consult me in every case of importance, and scarcely ever doubted the propriety of my opinions and actions. Perhaps you will be ready to accuse me of vanity in mentioning this, but you must consider that I do not *boast* of it, I have many times felt it a disadvantage; and although, I thank God, it never led me into error, yet, in circumstances of perplexity and doubt, I have deeply felt the want of a guide and instructor.

At such times I have seen and felt the necessity of supernatural aid, and by fervent applications to a throne of grace I have experienced that my heavenly Father is able and willing to supply the place of every earthly friend. I shall now no longer feel this want, this sense of helpless weakness, for I believe a kind Providence has intended that I shall find in you every earthly friend united; nor do I fear to trust myself under your protection, or shrink from your control. It is pleasant to be subject to those we love, especially when they never exert their authority but for the good of the subject. How few would write in this way! But I do not fear that *you* will make a bad use of it. You tell me to write my thoughts, and thus as they occur I freely let my pen run away with them.

Sat. morn.—I do not know whether you dare show your face here again or not after the blunder you have committed. When we got to the house on Thursday evening, even before we were within the doors, we found that Mr and Mrs Bedford had been there, and that they had requested you to mention their intention of coming—a single hint of which you never gave! Poor I too came in for a share in the hard words which were bestowed upon you, for they all agreed that I was the cause of it. Mr Fennell said you were certainly *mazed*, and talked of sending you to York, etc. And even I begin to think that *this*, together with the *note*, bears some marks of *insanity!* However, I shall suspend my judgment until I hear what excuse you can make for yourself. I suppose you will be quite ready to make one of some kind or another.

Yesterday I performed a difficult and yet a pleasing task in writing to my sisters. I thought I never should accomplish the end for which the letter was designed; but after a good deal of perambulation I gave them to understand the nature of my engagement with you, with the motives and inducements which led me to form such an engagement, and that in consequence of it I should not see them again so soon as I had intended. I concluded by expressing a hope that they would not be less pleased with the information than were my friends here. I think they will not suspect me to have made a wrong step, their partiality for me is so great. And their affection for me will lead them to rejoice in my welfare, even though it should diminish somewhat of their own. I shall think the time tedious till I hear from you, and must beg you will write as soon as possible. Pardon me, my dear friend, if I again caution you against giving way to a weakness of which I have heard you complain. When you find your heart oppressed and your thoughts too much engrossed by one subject let prayer be your refuge—this you no doubt know by experience to be a sure remedy, and a relief from every care and error. Oh, that we had more of the spirit of prayer! I feel that I need it much.

Breakfast-time is near, I must bid you farewell for the time, but rest assured you will always share in the prayers and heart of your own

Maria.

Mr Fennell has crossed my letter to my sisters. With his usual goodness he has supplied my *deficiencies*, and spoken of me in terms of commendation of which I wish I were more worthy. Your character he has likewise displayed in the most favourable light; and I am sure they will not fail to love and esteem you though unknown.

All here unite in kind regards.

Adieu.

To
the Rev. Patrick Brontë, A.B., *Hartshead*.
Wood House Grove, September 23rd, 1812.

My dearest Friend, —Accept of my warmest thanks for your kind affectionate letter, in which you have rated mine so highly that I really blush to read my own praises. Pray that God would enable me to deserve all the kindness you manifest towards me, and to act consistently with the good opinion you entertain of me—then I shall indeed be a helpmeet for you, and to be this shall at all times be the care and study of my future life. We have had to-day a large party of the Bradford folks—the Rands, Fawcetts, Dobsons, etc. My thoughts often strayed from the company, and I would have gladly left them to follow my present employment. To write to and receive letters from my friends were always among my chief enjoyments, but none ever gave me so much pleasure as those which I receive from and write to my newly adopted friend. I am by no means sorry you have given up all thought of the house you mentioned. With my cousin's help I have made known your plans to my uncle and aunt. Mr Fennell immediately coincided with that which respects your present abode, and observed that it had occurred to him before, but that he had not had an opportunity of mentioning it to you. My aunt did not fall in with it so readily, but her objections did not appear to me to be very weighty. For my own part, I feel all the force of your arguments in favour of it, and the objections are so trifling that they can scarcely be called objections. My cousin is of the same opinion. Indeed, you have such a method of considering and digesting a plan before you make it known to your friends, that you run very little risk of incurring their disapprobations, or of having your schemes frustrated. I greatly admire your talents this way—may they never be perverted by being used in a bad cause! And whilst they are exerted for good purposes, may they prove irresistible! If I may judge from your letter, this middle scheme is what would please you best, so that if there should arise no new objection to it, perhaps it will prove the best you can adopt. However, there is yet sufficient time to consider it further. I trust in this and every other circumstance you will be guided by the wisdom that cometh from above—a portion of which I doubt not has guided you hitherto. A belief of this, added to the complete satisfaction with which I read your reasonings on the subject, made me a ready convert to your opinions. I hope nothing will occur to induce you to change your intention of spending the next week at Bradford. Depend on it you shall have letter for letter; but may we not hope to see you here during that time, surely you will not think the way more tedious than usual? I have not heard any particulars respecting the church since you were at Bradford. Mr Rawson is now there, but Mr Hardy and his brother are absent, and I understand nothing decisive can be accomplished without them. Jane expects to hear something more to-morrow. Perhaps ere this reaches you, you will have received some intelligence respecting it from Mr Morgan. If you have no other apology to make for your blunders than that which you have given me, you must not expect to be excused, for I have not mentioned it to any one, so that however it may clear your character in my opinion, it is not likely to influence any other person. Little, very little, will induce me to cover your faults with a veil of charity. I already feel a kind of participation in all that concerns you. All praises and censures bestowed on you must equally affect me. Your joys and sorrows must be mine. Thus shall the one be increased and the other diminished. While this is the case we shall, I hope, always find 'life's cares' to be 'comforts.' And may we feel every trial and distress, for such must be our lot at times, bind us nearer to God and to each other! My heart earnestly joins in your comprehensive prayers. I trust they will unitedly ascend to a throne of grace, and through the Redeemer's merits procure for us peace and happiness here and a life of eternal felicity hereafter. Oh, what sacred pleasure there is in the idea of spending an eternity together in perfect and uninterrupted bliss! This should encourage us to the utmost exertion and fortitude. But whilst I write, my own words condemn me—I am ashamed of my own indolence and backwardness to duty. May I be more careful, watchful, and active than I have ever yet been!

My uncle, aunt, and Jane request me to send their kind regards, and they will be happy to see you any time next week whenever you can conveniently come down from Bradford. Let me hear from you soon—I shall expect a letter on Monday. Farewell, my dearest friend. That you may be happy in yourself and very useful to all around you is the daily earnest prayer of yours truly,

Maria Branwell.

To
the Rev. Patrick Brontë, A.B., *Hartshead*.
Wood House Grove, October 3rd, 1812.

How could my dear friend so cruelly disappoint me? Had he known how much I had set my heart on having a letter this afternoon, and how greatly I felt the disappointment when the bag arrived and I found there was nothing for me, I am sure he would not have permitted a little matter to hinder him. But whatever was the reason of your not writing, I cannot believe it to have been neglect or unkindness, therefore I do not in the least blame you, I only beg that in future you will judge of my feelings by your own, and if possible never let me expect a letter without receiving one. You know in my last which I sent you at Bradford I said it would not be in my power to write the next day, but begged I might be favoured with hearing from you on Saturday, and you will not wonder that I hoped you would have complied with this request. It has just occurred to my mind that it is possible this note was not received; if so, you have felt disappointed likewise; but I think this is not very probable, as the old man is particularly careful, and I never heard of his losing anything committed to his care. The note which I allude to was written on Thursday morning, and you should have received it before you left Bradford. I forget what its contents were, but I know it was written in haste and concluded abruptly. Mr Fennell talks of visiting Mr Morgan to-morrow. I cannot lose the opportunity of sending this to the office by him as you will then have it a day sooner, and if you have been daily expecting to hear from me, twenty-four hours are of some importance. I really am concerned to find that this, what many would deem trifling incident, has so much disturbed my mind. I fear I should not have slept in peace to-night if I had been deprived of this opportunity of relieving my mind by scribbling to you, and now I lament that you cannot possibly receive this till Monday. May I hope that there is now some intelligence on the way to me? or must my patience be tried till I see you on Wednesday? But what nonsense am I writing! Surely after this you can have no doubt that you possess all my heart. Two months ago I could not possibly have believed that you would ever engross so much of my thoughts and affections, and far less could I have thought that I should be so forward as to tell you so. I believe I must forbid you to come here again unless you can assure me that you will not steal any more of my regard. Enough of this; I must bring my pen to order, for if I were to suffer myself to revise what I have written I should be tempted to throw it in the fire, but I have determined that you shall see my whole heart. I have not yet informed you that I received your serio-comic note on Thursday afternoon, for which accept my thanks.

My cousin desires me to say that she expects a long poem on her birthday, when she attains the important age of twenty-one. Mr Fennell joins with us in requesting that you will not fail to be here on Wednesday, as it is decided that on Thursday we are to go to the Abbey if the weather, etc., permits.

Sunday morning.—I am not sure if I do right in adding a few lines to-day, but knowing that it will give you pleasure I wish to finish, that you may have it to-morrow. I will just say that if my feeble prayers can aught avail, you will find your labours this day both pleasant and profitable, as they concern your own soul and the souls of those to whom you preach. I trust in your hours of retirement you will not forget to pray for me. I assure you I need every assistance to help me forward; I feel that my heart is more ready to attach itself to earth than heaven. I sometimes think there never was a mind so dull and inactive as mine is with regard to spiritual things.

I must not forget to thank you for the pamphlets and tracts which you sent us from Bradford. I hope we shall make good use of them. I must now take my leave. I believe I need scarcely assure you that I am yours truly and very affectionately,

Maria Branwell.

MOTHER OF THE BRONTËS

With the sincerest pleasure do I retire from company to converse with him whom I love beyond all others. Could my beloved friend see my heart he would then be convinced that the affection I bear him is not at all inferior to that which he feels for me—indeed I sometimes think that in truth and constancy it excels. But do not think from this that I entertain any suspicions of your sincerity—no, I firmly believe you to be sincere and generous, and doubt not in the least that you feel all you express. In return, I entreat that you will do me the justice to believe that you have not only a *very large portion* of my *affection* and *esteem*, but *all* that I am capable of feeling, and from henceforth measure my feelings by your own. Unless my love for you were very great how could I so contentedly give up my home and all my friends—a home I loved so much that I have often thought nothing could bribe me to renounce it for any great length of time together, and friends with whom I have been so long accustomed to share all the vicissitudes of joy and sorrow? Yet these have lost their weight, and though I cannot always think of them without a sigh, yet the anticipation of sharing with you all the pleasures and pains, the cares and anxieties of life, of contributing to your comfort and becoming the companion of your pilgrimage, is more delightful to me than any other prospect which this world can possibly present. I expected to have heard from you on Saturday last, and can scarcely refrain from thinking you unkind to keep me in suspense two whole days longer than was necessary, but it is well that my patience should be sometimes tried, or I might entirely lose it, and this would be a loss indeed! Lately I have experienced a considerable increase of hopes and fears, which tend to destroy the calm uniformity of my life. These are not unwelcome, as they enable me to discover more of the evils and errors of my heart, and discovering them I hope through grace to be enabled to correct and amend them. I am sorry to say that my cousin has had a very serious cold, but to-day I think she is better; her cough seems less, and I hope we shall be able to come to Bradford on Saturday afternoon, where we intend to stop till Tuesday. You may be sure we shall not soon think of taking such another journey as the last. I look forward with pleasure to Monday, when I hope to meet with you, for as we are no *longer twain* separation is painful, and to meet must ever be attended with joy.

Thursday morning.—I intended to have finished this before breakfast, but unfortunately slept an hour too long. I am every moment in expectation of the old man's arrival. I hope my cousin is still better to-day; she requests me to say that she is much obliged to you for your kind inquiries and the concern you express for her recovery. I take all possible care of her, but yesterday she was naughty enough to venture into the yard without her bonnet! As you do not say anything of going to Leeds I conclude you have not been. We shall most probably hear from the Dr this afternoon. I am much pleased to hear of his success at Bierley! O that you may both be zealous and successful in your efforts for the salvation of souls, and may your own lives be holy, and your hearts greatly blessed while you are engaged in administering to the good of others! I should have been very glad to have had it in my power to lessen your fatigue and cheer your spirits by my exertions on Monday last. I will hope that this pleasure is still reserved for me. In general, I feel a calm confidence in the providential care and continued mercy of God, and when I consider His past deliverances and past favours I am led to wonder and adore. A sense of my small returns of love and gratitude to Him often abases me and makes me think I am little better than those who profess no religion. Pray for me, my dear friend, and rest assured that you possess a very, very large portion of the prayers, thoughts, and heart of yours truly,—M. Branwell.

Mr Fennell requests Mr Bedford to call on the man who has had orders to make blankets for the Grove and desire him to send them as soon as possible. Mr Fennell will be greatly obliged to Mr Bedford if he will take this trouble.

To
the Rev. Patrick Brontë, A.B., *Hartshead.*
W[ood] H[ouse] Grove, Novbr 18th, 1812.

My dear saucy Pat,—Now don't you think you deserve this epithet, far more, than I do that which you have given me? I really know not what to make of the beginning of your last; the winds, waves, and rocks almost stunned me. I thought you were giving me the account of some terrible dream, or that you had had a presentiment of the fate of my poor box, having no idea that your lively imagination could make so much of the slight reproof conveyed in my last. What will you say then when you get a *real, downright scolding?* Since you shew such a readiness to atone for your offences, after receiving a mild rebuke, I am inclined to hope, you will seldom deserve a severe one. I accept—with pleasure your atonement, and send you a free and full forgiveness—But I cannot allow that your affection is more deeply rooted than mine. However we will dispute no more about this—but rather embrace every opportunity to prove its sincerity and strength, by acting, in every respect, as friends and fellow-pilgrims, travelling the same road, actuated by the same motives, and having in view the same end. I think, if our lives are spared twenty years hence, I shall then pray for you with the same, if not greater, fervour and delight that I do now.

I am pleased that you are so fully convinced of my candour, for, to know that you suspected me of a deficiency in this virtue, would grieve and mortify me beyond expression. I do not derive any merit from the possession of it, for in me it is constitutional. Yet I think, where it is possessed, it will rarely exist alone, and where it is wanted, there is reason to doubt the existence of almost every other virtue. As to the other qualities which your partiality attributes to me, although I rejoice to know that I stand so high in your good opinion, yet I blush to think in how small a degree I possess them. But it shall be the pleasing study of my future life, to gain such an increase of grace and wisdom as shall enable me to act up to your highest expectations and prove to you a helpmeet. I firmly believe the Almighty has set us apart for each other; may we by earnest, frequent prayer, and every possible exertion, endeavour to fulfil His will in all things! I do not, cannot, doubt your love, and here I freely declare I love you above all the world besides! I feel very, very grateful to the great Author of all our mercies, for His unspeakable love and condescension towards us, and desire 'to shew forth my gratitude not only with my lips, but by my life and conversation.' I indulge a hope that our mutual prayers will be answered, and that our intimacy will tend much to promote our temporal and eternal interest.

I suppose you never expected to be much the richer for me, but I am sorry to inform you that I am still poorer than I thought myself. I mentioned having sent for my books, clothes, etc. On Saturday evening about the time you were writing the description of your imaginary shipwreck, I was reading and feeling the effects of a real one, having then received a letter from my sister giving me an account of the vessel, in which she had sent my box, being stranded on the coast of Devonshire, in consequence of which the box was dashed to pieces with the violence of the sea and all my little property, with the exception of a very few articles, swallowed up in the mighty deep. If this should not prove the prelude to something worse, I shall think little of it, as it is the first disastrous circumstance which has occurred since I left my home, and having been so highly favoured it would be highly ungrateful in me were I to suffer this to dwell much on my mind.

Mr Morgan was here yesterday, indeed he only left this morning. He mentioned having written to invite you to Bierley on Sunday next, and if you complied with his request it is likely that we shall see you both here on Sunday evening.—As we intend going to Leeds next week, we should be happy if you would accompany us on Monday or Tuesday. I mention this by desire of Miss F[ennell], who begs to be remembered affectionately to you—Notwithstanding Mr F[ennell']s complaints and threats, I doubt not but he will give you a cordial reception whenever you think fit to make your appearance at the Grove—Which you may likewise be assured of receiving from your ever truly affectionate

Maria.

Both the Dr and his lady very much wish to know what kind of address we make use of in our letters to each other—I think they would scarcely hit on *this*!!

To
the Rev. Patrick Brontë, A.B., *Hartshead.*
Wood House Grove, December 5th, 1812.

My dearest Friend,—So you *thought* that *perhaps* I *might* expect to hear from you. As the case was so doubtful, and you were in such great haste, you might as well have deferred writing a few days longer, for you seem to suppose it is a matter of perfect indifference to me whether I hear from you or not. I believe I once requested you to judge of my feelings by your own—am I to think that *you* are thus indifferent? I feel very unwilling to entertain such an opinion, and am grieved that you should suspect me of such a cold, heartless, attachment. But I am too serious on the subject; I only meant to rally you a little on the beginning of your last, and to tell you that I fancied there was a coolness in it which none of your former letters had contained. If this fancy was groundless, forgive me for having indulged it, and let it serve to convince you of the sincerity and warmth of my affection. Real love is ever apt to suspect that it meets not with an equal return; you must not wonder then that my fears are sometimes excited. My pride cannot bear the idea of a diminution of your attachment, or to think that it is stronger on my side than on yours. But I must not permit my pen so fully to disclose the feelings of my heart, nor will I tell you whether I am pleased or not at the thought of seeing you on the appointed day.

Miss Fennell desires her kind regards, and, with her father, is extremely obliged to you for the trouble you have taken about the carpet, and has no doubt but it will give full satisfaction. They think there will be no occasion for the green cloth.

We intend to set about making the cakes here next week, but as the fifteen or twenty persons whom you mention live probably somewhere in your neighbourhood, I think it will be most convenient for Mrs B. to make a small one for the purpose of distributing there, which will save us the difficulty of sending so far.

You may depend on my learning my lessons as rapidly as they are given me. I am already tolerably perfect in the ABC, etc. I am much obliged to you for the pretty little hymn which I have already got by heart, but cannot promise to sing it scientifically, though I will endeavour to gain a little more assurance.

Since I began this Jane put into my hands Lord Lyttelton's *Advice to a Lady*. When I read those lines, 'Be never cool reserve with passion joined, with caution choose, but then be fondly kind, etc.,' my heart smote me for having in some cases used too much reserve towards you. Do you think you have any cause to complain of me? If you do, let me know it. For were it in my power to prevent it, I would in no instance occasion you the least pain or uneasiness. I am certain no one ever loved you with an affection more pure, constant, tender, and ardent than that which I feel. Surely this is not saying too much; it is the truth, and I trust you are worthy to know it. I long to improve in every religious and moral quality, that I may be a help, and if possible an ornament to you. Oh let us pray much for wisdom and grace to fill our appointed stations with propriety, that we may enjoy satisfaction in our own souls, edify others, and bring glory to the name of Him who has so wonderfully preserved, blessed, and brought us together.

If there is anything in the commencement of this which looks like pettishness, forgive it; my mind is now completely divested of every feeling of the kind, although I own I am sometimes too apt to be overcome by this disposition.

Let me have the pleasure of hearing from you again as soon as convenient. This writing is uncommonly bad, but I too am in haste.

Adieu, my dearest.—I am your affectionate and sincere

Maria.

Appendix 2

The Advantages of Poverty in Religious Concerns

'The above was written by my dear wife, and sent for insertion in one of the periodical publications. Keep it, as a memorial of her.'
Patrick Brontë

Poverty is generally, if not universally, considered an evil; and not only an evil in itself, but attended with a train of innumerable other evils. But is not this a mistaken notion—one of those prevailing errors which are so frequently to be met with in the world and are received as uncontroverted truths? Let the understanding be enlightened by divine grace, the judgment improved and corrected by an acquaintance with the holy Scriptures, the spirit of the world subdued, and the heart filled with the earnest desires for heavenly attainments and heavenly enjoyments, and then, what is poverty? *Nothing*—or rather *something,* which, with the assistance and blessing of our Gracious Master will greatly promote our spiritual welfare, and tend to increase and strengthen our efforts to gain that Land of pure delight, where neither our souls nor bodies can possibly know pain or want. Perhaps some who are daily and hourly sinking under the distresses and privations which attend extreme poverty, should this paper fall in the way of any such, may be ready to say that the writer never experienced its horrors, and is therefore unqualified to judge of its effects—they may indignantly exclaim, 'Is it not an evil to be deprived of the necessaries of life? Can there be any anguish equal to that occasioned by the sight of objects, dear as your own soul, famishing with cold and hunger? Is it not an evil to hear the heart-rending cries of your children craving for that which you have it not in your power to give them? And, as an aggravation of this distress, to know that some are surfeited by abundance at the same time that you and yours are perishing for want?' Yes, these are evils indeed of peculiar bitterness; and he must be less than man that can behold them without sympathy and an active desire to relieve them. But those sufferers possess not the qualifications described above, which alone can enable any human being to consider poverty in any

173

other light than an evil. They have not had their hearts, understandings, and judgments changed by divine grace; nor are these the characters who can look forward to another life with the pleasing, invigorating hope of finding it to be a life of perfect, unchanging, and everlasting bliss. Such a wretched extremity of poverty is seldom experienced in this land of general benevolence. When a case of this kind occurs, it is to be feared the sufferers bring it on themselves by their own excess and imprudent folly; but even when they reap the fruit of their doings, they are not permitted long to suffer. The penetrating eye of Christian charity soon discovers, and its hand is as soon stretched out for their relief. The poor but honest and industrious Christian, for whose benefit this humble attempt is made, is scarcely ever suffered to languish in extreme want, yet he may be exposed to great distresses, which at times he is tempted to consider evils hard to be endured: at most repines at his lot, and thinks that the God who is declared to be *merciful to all* and whose *tender mercies* are said to be *over all His works,* has forgotten to be gracious to him. Dismiss these unworthy thoughts, my Christian friends; they come from the enemy of your immortal interests and the father of lies. Rather consider that though you have now no visible supply, and know not from whence the wants of to-morrow are to meet with relief, there is One above in Whose hands are all the riches of the earth, Who sees your necessities, and has faithfully promised that all things shall work together for your good. Consider that you are not exposed to the prevailing temptation of laying up treasure on earth. Though your circumstances prevent you from providing fortunes for your children, yet there are many honest callings and respectable trades open ever to the children of poverty whereby they may get their bread in peace and credit, and with the blessing of their Heavenly Father gain a supply for nature's wants. Being prevented from sharing in the luxuries of life, you are less liable to be assailed by the corrupt dispositions and disorderly passions which an enjoyment of these luxuries tends to produce. You think now, perhaps, that you could be temperate in the midst of plenty, but the human heart is not to be trusted, and we are assured from the sacred writings that 'it is deceitful above all things and desperately wicked.' Possessing the means of gratifying every perverse, idle, and inordinate inclination, who dares say he would not be led into those vain and sinful excesses which would infallibly lead to unhappiness in this world and to endless misery in the world to come? That poverty which is sanctified by true religion is perhaps the state most free from care and discontent, the farthest removed from pride and ambition, and the most calculated to promote scriptural views and feelings, and the universal welfare of the soul. The man who possesses little of this world has consequently but little to attach him to it; he is not so much tempted to be attracted by its riches nor its pleasures; he cannot experimentally love that which he does not possess; he cannot delight in that which he has no opportunity of enjoying. Having nothing to lose, he fears not the approach of the spoiler. Neither oppression nor violence can add to his wants or deprive him of his riches. As he has no property to improve or secure, he is free from the anxious inquietude and perplexing care of the man of business. If his days are spent in honest labour, his nights afford the sweet refreshment or peaceful slumbers. His coarse but wholesome meal, eaten with relish and followed by thankfulness and contentment, invigorates the active body, and fits it for the exertions necessary to earn another. Content with his lot, he envies not his more prosperous neighbour; unless, perhaps, in seasons of peculiar distress, when he has himself been relieved by the bounty of another, a wish has been excited in his heart that it were in his power to show his gratitude to his Heavenly Benefactor by contributing to the necessities of others. But this wish is quickly repressed by the conviction that God knows what is best, and has given to each that portion which will tend most to His glory and the lasting good of His children.

Far removed from the ensnaring and tumultuous scenes of a vain, unthinking world, he is not ambitious of its honour nor proud of its fame. He does not even understand its principles nor its language. It might be said that though the poor man is not liable to the temptations which peculiarly assail the rich, yet he is liable to others which commonly prevail among the poor, such as envy, murmuring, ingratitude, and covetousness. But it is necessary to remind the reader that poverty is here considered as united with religion, and that, so united, it is exposed to fewer temptations than is a state of prosperity, and attended with greater religious advantages. The poor need not fear incurring contempt by making a religious profession. A religious and orderly conduct will ensure him commendation rather than censure. And if his habitual practice is found to agree with his profession, he will meet with that confidence, respect, and attention which he could never have experienced on any other ground. Free from the pride and prejudice of learning and philosophy, his mind is prepared to receive the truths that the Bible inculcates. He yields to the inward workings of the spirit of truth; with simplicity receives the various and unspeakable blessings purchased for him by the Saviour's blood; nor once thinks of opposing the weakness of human reason to the divine Revelation. He may have less leisure for reading, but he has little to call his thoughts from divine meditation and mental prayer, the practice of which tends more to keep up the life of God in the soul than the closest study and most enlarged acquaintance with human learning independent of these. Having no worldly ties, he contemplates with holy joy the inheritance laid up for the saints, and, with a hope full of assurance through the alone merits of his Redeemer, expects ere long to be made a partaker of that inheritance, and to join the heavenly throng in eternal bliss.

Taking this view of Poverty, where are the evils attending it? Do they not appear to be imaginary? But O, what words can express the great misery of those who suffer all the evils of poverty here, and that, too, by their own bad conduct, and have no hope of happiness hereafter, but rather have cause to fear that the end of this miserable life will be the beginning of another, infinitely more miserable, never, never to have an end!

It surely is the duty of all Christians to exert themselves in every possible way to promote the instruction and conversion of the poor, and, above all, to pray with all the ardour of Christian faith and love that every poor man may be a religious man.

M.

Bibliography

BARKER, Juliet, *The Brontës,* Abacus, 2010.

BEDFORD, Kristina, *Patrick Brontë's Lost Landlords,* Brontë Studies, 2008.

CHITHAM, Edward, *The Brontës' Irish Background Revisited*, Brontë Studies, 2014.

DINSDALE, Ann, *At Home With The Brontës: The History of Haworth Parsonage and its Occupants,* Amberley, 2013.

DINSDALE, Ann, *Mrs Brontë's Nurse*, Brontë Studies, 2005.

DUCKETT, Bob, *The Library at Ponden Hall*, Brontë Studies, 2015.

FARR, Grahame, *Ships and Harbours of Exmoor*, The Exmoor Press, 1970.

FERRETT, Mabel, *A Short History of Hartshead Church*, Mabel Ferrett and the Revd. Jesse van der Valk, 1993.

FORSAITH, Peter S., '*...too indelicate to mention...': transgressive male sexualities in early Methodism,* Unpublished paper, 2018.

GREEN, Dudley, *Patrick Brontë: Father of Genius*, Nonsuch Publishing, 2008

GREEN, Dudley, (Editor), *The Letters of the Reverend Patrick Brontë,* Nonsuch Publishing, 2005.

HARDIE-BUDDEN, Melissa, *Maternal Forebears of the Brontë Archive: 'Nothing comes from Nothing'; or Stories from another Canon*, Brontë Studies, 2015.

HARDIE-BUDDEN, Melissa, *Methodist links with the Brontës: Places & faces on the Wesleyan Trail,* Academia, 2015

HILL, Esther and Kerrow, *The Penzance Home of Maria Branwell*, 1996.

LENTON, John, 'Men who left the Wesleyan Ministry 1791-1932: A Database in Progress' in *Brands Plucked From the Burning: Essays on Methodist Memorialisation and Remembering* HART, David J. and JEREMY, David J. (Editors) Wesley Historical Society, 2013.

LOCK, John, and **DIXON**, W. T., *A Man of Sorrow: The Life, Letters and Times of the Rev. Patrick Brontë*, Nelson, 1965.

MACKENZIE, Charlotte, *Merchants and smugglers in eighteenth-century Penzance: the brothers John and James Dunkin*, Troze, the Online Journal of the National Maritime Museum Cornwall, 2016.

PALMER, June (Editor), *In and Around Penzance During Napoleonic Times*, Penwith Local History Group, 2000.

PALMER, June (Editor), *Treasures of the Morrab*, Penwith Local History Group, 2005.

PRITCHARD, F.C., *The Story of Woodhouse Grove School*, Woodhouse Grove School, 1978.

PROTZ, Roger, *Historic Coaching Inns of the Great North Road,* CAMRA Books, 2017.

RATCHFORD, Fannie E., *The Loneliness of a Brontë Cousin,* Brontë Studies, 1957.

REES, Edgar A., *Old Penzance*, published by the author, 1956.

SHORTER, Clement King, *Charlotte Brontë and Her Circle,* Hodder and Stoughton, 1896.

SMITH, Michael, *Thornton Thoroughfares: People and Places*, Thornton Antiquarian Society, 2017

SMITH, Margaret (Editor), *The Letters of Charlotte Brontë, Volume One, 1829-1847,* Clarendon Press, 1995.

SMITH, Margaret (Editor), *The Letters of Charlotte Brontë, Volume Two, 1848-1851,* Clarendon Press, 2000.

Spen Valley Civic Society, *Thornbush Farm, Formerly Lousy Farm: An Early Home of the Rev. Patrick Brontë*, Brontë Studies, 2004.

THORMÄHLEN, Marianne (Editor), *The Brontës in Context*, Cambridge University Press, 2012.

WATSON, Nigel, *Xaipete, Woodhouse Grove: The First 200 Years.* Jeremy Mills Publishing Ltd, 2011.

WHITEHEAD, S. R., *The Brontës' Haworth: The Place and the People The Brontës Knew*, The Brontë Society, 2017.

WHITWORTH, Alan, *The Old Bell Chapel Thornton*, Culva House Publications, 1997.

WILKS, Brian, *Patrick Bronte: the Man Who Arrived at Cambridge University,* Brontë Studies, 2014.

WOOD, Victoria, *Up to You, Porky: The Victoria Wood Sketch Book*, Mandarin, 1986.

WOOLLARD, John, *Patrick Brontë, the Burders and the Wethersfield of 1808*, Brontë Studies, 2012.

Online

The Brontë Society www.bronte.org.uk

Methodist Collections, University of Manchester www.library.manchester.ac.uk

West Penwith Resources www.westpenwith.org.uk

University of Sheffield Library Special Collections www.sheffield.ac.uk/library/special

Index

INDEX

Buckworth, Reverend John 52-3, 55, 57, 96, 101, 112, 135, 152
Burder, Mary 49-51, 58-9, 62, 73-5, 100, 157

Causewayhead, Penzance 37, 81
Chapel Street, Penzance 1, 3, 5, 7-8, 14-15, 17, 22-5, 29, 37-8, 81, 101, 106, 118, 124, 132, 143
Charnock, Reverend James 121, 123, 130, 152
Clough House, Yorkshire 101, 104

Dewsbury, Yorkshire 52-8, 96, 100-1, 103, 110, 112, 135, 152-3

Fennell, Jane (nee Branwell) 15, 38, 40-1, 50-2, 63, 65-6, 68-9, 71, 76, 78-9, 82, 84, 97-8, 100, 103, 110, 144, 161-2, 165-6
Fennell, John 15, 22, 38, 40, 50-2, 61, 63-6, 68, 71, 73, 76, 78, 82-4, 86, 88, 90, 97-100, 103, 110, 118, 160-1, 164-7, 169
Firth, Anne (nee Greame) 109-10, 113, 118, 131, 141
Firth, Elizabeth 106-11, 116-17, 130-1, 141, 144-6, 150-1, 157
Firth, John 106-7, 113, 118, 131, 141, 149
Fisher, Margaret (nee Branwell) 1, 6, 20, 22, 142
Fisher, Charles 20, 22
Fletcher, Mary (nee Bosanquet) 9, 15, 36, 51-2, 108, 110, 116

Garrs, Nancy 111, 120, 132, 134, 140, 144
Garrs, Sarah 120, 132, 134, 144

Gaskell, Elizabeth 24, 28, 43, 45, 69, 107, 137, 140, 147
Giddy, Thomas 20, 31
Glebe House, Thornton 104-6, 115, 121
Greenwood, James 122, 130, 137
Greenwood, William 122, 130
Guiseley Church, Yorkshire 88, 96-7, 99

Hartshead, Yorkshire 57-8, 60-1, 82, 96, 99, 103-4, 133, 137, 152-3
Haworth, Yorkshire 121-30, 132, 134, 136-8, 140, 142, 145-6, 151-3, 157
Heape, Rev Henry 121-3, 125, 128-30
Heaton, Robert 122, 130, 134, 138-9

Kingston, Jane (nee Branwell) 1, 20, 22, 24, 36-8, 52
Kingston, John 22, 24, 35, 37, 52, 108

Ladies' Magazine 32-3, 74, 82, 97, 119
Le Grice, Rev Charles Valentine 26, 123-4
Leeds Intelligencer 58, 118, 123, 125, 128, 130
Leeds Mercury 56, 58-9
Lousy Farm, Yorkshire 58, 75, 84, 96, 99, 101, 104
Luddism 59-61, 75, 99, 101, 107

Madeley, Shropshire 51, 55, 98, 108, 110, 116
Madron, Cornwall 4, 15, 20, 31, 37, 58, 96-8, 124